W0006820

# The Church of God
## at Corinth

# The Church of God at Corinth

## A Verse-by-Verse Commentary on I and II Corinthians

by
John R. Rice

SWORD OF THE LORD PUBLISHERS
Murfreesboro, Tennessee 37130

**Printed and bound in the United States of America**

# TABLE OF CONTENTS

# I CORINTHIANS VI

# I CORINTHIANS VII

# I CORINTHIANS VIII

# I CORINTHIANS IX

# I CORINTHIANS X

# I CORINTHIANS XI

## I CORINTHIANS XII

## I CORINTHIANS XIII

## I CORINTHIANS XIV

## I CORINTHIANS XV

## I CORINTHIANS XVI

## II CORINTHIANS I

## II CORINTHIANS II

## II CORINTHIANS III

## II CORINTHIANS IV

## II CORINTHIANS V

## II CORINTHIANS VI

## II CORINTHIANS VII

## II CORINTHIANS VIII

## II CORINTHIANS IX

## II CORINTHIANS X

## II CORINTHIANS XI

## II CORINTHIANS XII

## II CORINTHIANS XIII

# INTRODUCTION

The city of Corinth is some sixty miles west of Athens on the Peloponnesus peninsula. The old city of Corinth was at the foot of Acrocorinth like many ancient cities. This central hill was a place of worship and a place for defense in case of war. The older Corinth had been destroyed by the Romans in 146 B.C. but it was rebuilt by Julius Caesar in the year 44 B.C., peopled with numerous colonists, mostly Roman freemen. Then many Greeks had come and afterward there was a Jewish colony.

Godet says that "at the time when the apostle arrived in it, the city counted from six to seven hundred thousand inhabitants, of whom two hundred thousand were freemen and four hundred thousand slaves." Corinth was one of the three greater cities of the Roman Empire, along with Rome and Ephesus. It was situated on the isthmus connecting the Peloponnesus with the mainland of Greece. It had two great ports—Cenchrea, nine miles away on the southern side, and Lechaeum, a mile and a half distant on the northern side of the isthmus.

Ellicott says, "The two things which in older days had made Corinth famous in Grecian history still rendered her a place of supreme importance. From a military point of view, she might be regarded as the key to the Peloponnesus, and commercially she was the central point of the vast trade which was carried on between Asia and Europe. The storms which so constantly raged on the southern shore of Greece drove the vast tide of commerce through the safer overland route, which lay through Cenchrea and Lechaeum."

Smaller boats were dragged over the isthmus and larger ships were unloaded and the baggage carried across and loaded on other ships to save the long journey around the peninsula and to save going through stormy seas. Now there is the Corinthian canal, cutting across the isthmus, with much traffic, and cars cross it by bridge going out from Athens to Corinth.

Farrar says, "Corinth was the Vanity Fair of the Roman Empire, at once the London and the Paris of the first century after Christianity. In the Gentile world it was famous-infamous for dishonesty, debauchery and drunkenness."

The population had so many elements, so many languages, that it is not surprising that these were used in the tongues heresy discussed in I Corinthians 14. One commenter says, "Culturally, Corinth was the home of Italians, Greeks, Egyptians, Syrians, Jews and Orientals." Again one says, "The most famous religion of Corinth was that of Aphrodite whose temple was located on top of Mount Acrocorinth. According to Strabo, the geographer who lived in the first century A.D., "At an earlier time more than a thousand women, sacred prostitutes, served the temple of Aphrodite who was really the licentious Phoenician Astarte under a Greek name."

In such a heathen and lewd environment, one ought not be surprised then at a very general looseness in morals that would affect the new converts and require a constant reminder to build up Christian character.

Ussher's chronology places the time of Paul's arrival at Corinth at about 54 A.D. Paul was there more than eighteen months. First Corinthians was written, Farrar says, "at the close of Paul's long sojourn in Ephesus. After writing to the Thessalonians, St. Paul had paid a brief visit to Jerusalem, and had then lived for nearly three years at Ephesus. He had thus been nearly four years absent from his Corinthian converts."

Paul sought the big cities and spent most of his time there—in Corinth, Ephesus and Rome—and would have spent more time in the Jewish center of Jerusalem had he been allowed to do so.

In I and II Corinthians there is more practical, detailed and scriptural instruction about the affairs in a New

Testament church and the problems involved than in all the other epistles of the New Testament.

May the dear Lord make these comments a blessing. First, we come to this holy task with the deepest possible devotion to the Word of God as the infallible, verbally inspired Scripture. We intend to take the Scripture literally in every case except when the context proves some spiritual or figurative meaning. And second, we come to this task after some years in the pastorate, after long years as an evangelist dealing with many, many churches and pastors, and after answering literally thousands of letters from readers of THE SWORD OF THE LORD about church problems.

May God smile upon the Scriptures themselves and open hearts to be blessed by God's message.

**JOHN R. RICE**

1973

# The Church of God at Corinth

## A Verse-by-Verse Commentary on I and II Corinthians

# I CORINTHIANS I

### VERSES 1-3:

PAUL, called to be an apostle of Jesus Christ through the will of God, and Sŏs'-thĕ-nĕs our brother, 2 Unto the church of God which is at Corinth, to them that are sanctified in Christ Jesus, called to be saints, with all that in every place call upon the name of Jesus Christ our Lord, both their's and our's: 3 Grace be unto you, and peace, from God our Father, and from the Lord Jesus Christ.

### The Salutation (vs. 1)

*"Paul, called to be an apostle. . . ."* An apostle is one specially sent from God, not only called to preach but with special revelation from God. Paul insisted concerning the Gospel he preached: "For I neither received it of man, neither was I taught it, but by the revelation of Jesus Christ" (Gal. 1:12). A special requirement of the twelve apostles was that they should have been with Jesus from the baptism of John until the time of His resurrection and ascension (Acts 1:21,22). But Paul had this issue settled otherwise: he had seen Christ personally after His resurrection on the road to Damascus (I Cor. 15:8,9). Paul had the special authority of an apostle (I Cor. 4:18-30). He had the special sufferings assigned to the apostles (I Cor. 9:9-13). As we see from Ephesians 4:11 and I Corinthians 12:28, the apostles were ranked above prophets, evangelists,

pastors and teachers, and they were especially called for
work before the New Testament was completed. After that
time we have no record of other apostles, of men sent with
this special enablement and authority.

Seventeen men are called apostles in the New
Testament. They are the original twelve (Matt. 10:2-4);
then Matthias, elected to take the place of witness in the
apostleship "from which Judas by transgression fell" (Acts
1:23-26); "James the Lord's brother" (Gal. 1:19) who seems
to have presided in the council at Jerusalem in Acts 15;
Barnabas who also is called an apostle (Acts 14:14), with
Paul the apostle; and Jesus Christ is called "the Apostle
and High Priest of our profession" (Heb. 3:1).

"... and Sosthenes our brother" (vs. 1). Sosthenes was
with the Apostle Paul and, we suppose, was writing for
Paul. We see that Paul signed the letter personally (I Cor.
16:21); the inference being that the actual writing was done
by someone following Paul's dictation. Sosthenes was chief
ruler of the synagogue at Corinth (Acts 18:17), probably
converted, as had been Crispus, the high priest before him,
"ruler of the synagogue" at Corinth (Acts 18:8). Now with
Paul, Sosthenes is called in remembrance to his friends and
loved ones at Corinth. Probably Sosthenes simply wrote
Paul's dictation. So Tertius did the epistle to the Romans
(Rom. 16:22). So with Tychicus, who carried Paul's epistle
to the Ephesians; he may have written down at Paul's
dictation (Eph. 6:21). Timothy is named as writing, with
Paul, to the Philippians (Phil. 1:1) and to the Colossians
(Col. 1:1), Silas and Timothy to the Thessalonians (I
Thess. 1:1; II Thess. 1:1).

Dr. Scofield calls attention to Paul's words in Galatians
6:11, "Ye see how large a letter I have written unto you
with mine own hand." But Dr. Scofield says,

> Gr. "with how large letters . . . mine own hand." The
> apostle was, it appears from many considerations,
> afflicted with ophthalmia, a common disease in the East,
> to the point almost of total blindness (e.g. Gal. 4.13-15).
> Ordinarily, therefore, he dictated his letters. But now,

having no amanuensis at hand, but urged by the spiritual
danger of his dear Galatians, he writes, we cannot know
with what pain and difficulty, with his own hand, in the
"large letters" his darkened vision compelled him to use.

We immediately think of Paul's "thorn in the flesh"
mentioned in II Corinthians 12:7-9. Had Paul, ever since
that amazing, blinding seeing of the Lord Jesus on the road
to Damascus, when he was blind for three days, been
troubled with weak eyesight? That is possible. He had said
to his loved converts in Galatia, "And my temptation
which was in my flesh ye despised not, nor rejected; but
received me as an angel of God, even as Christ Jesus.
Where is then the blessedness ye spake of? for I bear you
record, that, if it had been possible, ye would have plucked
out your own eyes, and have given them to me" (Gal.
4:14,15).

*"Unto the church of God which is at Corinth . . ."* (vs.
2). You will note the word *church* is used here of one local
congregation of Christians, just as it is used about ninety
times in the New Testament. The word never refers to a
denomination, never to a group of churches. In the Greek
the word simply means a called-out assembly. In Acts 7:38
it is used about Israel, called out of Egypt around Mount
Sinai, and called "the church in the wilderness." The
Greek word *ecclesia* is translated "assembly" three times in
Acts 19, verses 32, 39 and 41. Everywhere else in the New
Testament it is translated "church."

Other times the word "church" refers to that great
called-out assembly that will meet in Heaven at the
rapture, described in Hebrews 12:23 as "the general
assembly and church of the firstborn, which are written in
heaven." So the word "church" is used several times in the
New Testament referring to that whole body of Christians
who will be called out at the rapture. It is that "general
assembly and church of the firstborn, which are written in
heaven" referred to in Ephesians 5:24, ". . . the church is
subject to Christ," and the one mentioned in verse 25,

"Christ also loved the church, and gave himself for it," and it is also called "the body, the church" (Col. 1:18).

But here in verse 2, as in most of the times in the New Testament, the word "church" refers to a local congregation of Christians. A group of local congregations are always churches, plural, never one church, but "the seven churches which are in Asia" (Rev. 1:4), and "the churches of Galatia" (Gal. 1:2).

". . . to them that are sanctified in Christ Jesus, called to be saints" (vs. 2). Every Christian is a "saint," that is, is set apart and sanctified for God. The word "sanctified" does not mean sinless but simply set apart for God, with varying degrees of perfection. So Hebrews 10:10 says: "By the which will we are sanctified through the offering of the body of Jesus Christ once for all." And verse 14, "For by one offering he hath perfected for ever them that are sanctified." Every person who comes to trust Jesus Christ and is born again is thus set apart for Heaven and eventually to awake in the likeness of Jesus Christ.

The Roman Catholic idea that a few people attain sainthood and perfection, and are so recognized by the church, is not scriptural. All the converts at Corinth were "sanctified in Christ Jesus, called to be saints, with all that in every place call upon the name of Jesus Christ our Lord, both their's and our's."

You note that this epistle is not only addressed to Corinth but to every Christian everywhere. It is the divine Word of God and its authority is as real today for every born-again Christian in the world as it was for the people of Corinth.

All Christians, thank God, are on one sweet level of sanctification in the sense that all are set apart for Heaven, all are bought with the blood, all have become partakers of the divine nature, all are heirs of God and joint-heirs with Jesus Christ.

It is said that once upon a time a Baptist church in Washington, D. C., had two people apply for membership

the same day. One was the President of the United States
and the other was a little Chinese boy, saved in a mission in
the city. Both were received alike and as both stood to
receive the "right hand of fellowship" the pastor declared,
"The ground is wonderfully level around the cross."

Paul the apostle could say, "Jesus Christ our Lord, both
their's and our's." How wonderful that we enter with the
apostles and with all the saints into the blood brotherhood,
children of the same God, brethren of the dear Lord Jesus
and called saints!

*"Grace be unto you, and peace"* (vs. 3). An inspired form
of greeting. There could be no peace for sinful mankind
except it be based upon the grace of God. So in his epistles
Paul addresses the Christians as "grace be unto you, and
peace" (Rom. 1:7; II Cor. 1:2; Gal. 1:3; Eph. 1:2; Phil. 1:2;
Col. 1:2; I Thess. 1:1; II Thess. 1:2; Philemon 1:3).
However, in I and II Timothy and Titus, Paul enlarges the
salutation formula to "grace, *mercy,* and peace" (I Tim.
1:2; II Tim. 1:2; Titus 1:4). And I Peter 1:2 and II Peter 1:2
also use the salutation "grace and peace." So here at the
very first of these epistles is the great  doctrine of God's
grace, and the only hope for man to have peace. Always
grace is first and peace is second. In the case where it is
"grace, mercy, and peace," that is only an elaboration, for
mercy is grace at work. Grace means salvation for people
who do not deserve to be saved. It means God loves those
who are not in themselves lovable. It means that one who
deserves only enmity and punishment from God can have
peace because of the outflow of God's wonderful grace.

Not only is this the basis for the plan of salvation but it is
the basis for daily peace as a Christian walks with God. Oh,
that we might rely on God's grace! Oh, that we might
expect it and rejoice in it and have wonderful faith to claim
His promises because of His grace.

Hebrews 4:16 says, "Let us therefore come boldly unto
the throne of grace, that we may obtain mercy, and find
grace to help in time of need." What a wonderful ground for

expectant, believing prayer! Spurgeon called attention especially to this, saying that this throne to which a Christian comes is not the throne of judgment but the throne of grace and mercy.

---

## VERSES 4-9:

4 I thank my God always on your behalf, for the grace of God which is given you by Jesus Christ;

5 That in every thing ye are enriched by him, in all utterance, and in all knowledge;

6 Even as the testimony of Christ was confirmed in you:

7 So that ye come behind in no gift; waiting for the coming of our Lord Jesus Christ:

8 Who shall also confirm you unto the end, that ye may be blameless in the day of our Lord Jesus Christ.

9 God is faithful, by whom ye were called unto the fellowship of his Son Jesus Christ our Lord.

### The Greatly Blessed Corinthian Christians

*". . . in every thing ye are enriched"* (vs. 5). Just a short time out of heathen darkness, a church made up principally of young converts, yet Paul says to them, ". . . ye come behind in no gift." What a wonderful time of blessing God had given there! Paul had begun preaching there in the Jewish synagogue about five years before, perhaps about 54 A.D. He stayed there eighteen months. The power of God had won a multitude of souls. Paul had taught them and trained them in the Scriptures. They were "behind in no gift." In everything they were enriched.

With soul winning always goes a great spiritual growth. Where God gives a mighty revival and saves many sinners, Christians get the greatest blessings. Some may think that a church which centers on Bible teaching rather than on soul winning makes better Bible Christians; but that is a mistake. The Moodys and Spurgeons and the great soul-winning churches make more mature, godly, Spirit-filled Christians, more Bible-reading and doctrinally sound Christians, than the churches that do not principally win souls. So at Corinth the Christians 'came behind in no gift.'

Since there was a multitude of young converts there, even among such a group of great Christians there were, of course, the errors of immaturity with some. Homes that have babies have diapers to wash, have crayon marks on the wallpaper, have roller skates in the driveway. So there were childish divisions here. One man was openly immoral (I Cor. 5:1,2). Some would go to law with other Christians (I Cor. 6:6). Some were even drunken at the Lord's Supper (I Cor. 11:20-22). There was a tongues heresy at Corinth that must be rebuked in chapter 14. Yet with many baby Christians, there was a great group of godly and spiritually gifted people there who gained Paul's praise.

". . . waiting for the coming of our Lord Jesus Christ" (vs. 7). It is remarkable that we find New Testament Christians were expecting Jesus to return in their lifetime. Paul himself clearly expected to be living at Christ's coming, as you see in I Thessalonians 4:16,17, and in I Corinthians 15:50,51. It ought not be amazing to us, however, because the Lord Jesus had plainly commanded the apostles to watch for His coming. They were plainly told that no one would know the day nor the hour of His coming (see Matt. 24:36 and the remainder of the chapter; Matt. 25:13; Mark 13:32-37; and elsewhere). The apostles were right in thinking that Jesus might come at any time. His coming was always impending, always imminent, with no time set and no way by which anyone could know when. It was to be as sudden and unexpected as the flood came on the people in Noah's day. It is to be as sudden as a master returning at an unexpected hour from a long journey to his home where he has set people to watch for his coming. And the Scripture teaches here, as it does in Titus 2:12 and 13, that the blessed hope of Christ's coming, which Titus was commanded to teach, should result in "denying ungodliness and worldly lusts" so that "we should live soberly, righteously, and godly, in this present world."

So I John 2:28 teaches us, "And now, little children,

abide in him; that, when he shall appear, we may have confidence, and not be ashamed before him at his coming." And again I John 3:3 promises, "And every man that hath this hope in him purifieth himself." Doesn't that fit with verses 7 and 8? These Corinthians were waiting for the coming of Christ that they may be "blameless in the day of our Lord Jesus Christ."

---

## VERSES 10-17:

10 Now I beseech you, brethren, by the name of our Lord Jesus Christ, that ye all speak the same thing, and that there be no divisions among you; but that ye be perfectly joined together in the same mind and in the same judgment.

11 For it hath been declared unto me of you, my brethren, by them which are of the house of Chlō-́ē, that there are contentions among you.

12 Now this I say, that every one of you saith, I am of Paul; and I of Ȧ-pŏl-́lŏs; and I of Cē-́phăs; and I of Christ.

13 Is Christ divided? was Paul crucified for you? or were ye baptized in the name of Paul?

14 I thank God that I baptized none of you, but Crispus and Gāi-́ŭs;

15 Lest any should say that I had baptized in mine own name.

16 And I baptized also the household of Stĕph-́ă-năs: besides, I know not whether I baptized any other.

17 For Christ sent me not to baptize, but to preach the gospel: not with wisdom of words, lest the cross of Christ should be made of none effect.

## The Divisions of Those Carnal
## Christians Rebuked

These good Christians at Corinth (vss. 5-7) were yet carnal as Paul tells them in chapter 3, verses 1 to 3, because they had divisions. They had in them the conflict Paul had, as he said in Romans 7:14-17, the conflict between flesh and spirit declared in Galatians 5:17. Their divisions were over what seemed to them real convictions. One group loved Apollos so much they could not enjoy Paul; others were blessed more by Peter (Cephas) or by Paul and defended them stoutly. Some were so proudly for Christ above all that they had no concern for any of God's anointed preachers.

From their mistake let us learn that God chooses and uses many different kinds of people. All of God's people need the varying ministries of more than one preacher. Paul was not so eloquent as Apollos (Acts 18:24), and his bodily presence is weak and his speech contemptible (II Cor. 10:10), they said. But he was more abundant in labors (II Cor. 11:23), and not behind the very chiefest apostles. Peter had spent three and a half years with Jesus, was chief of the apostles originally, had preached at Pentecost, but later won fewer souls than Paul. God used them all. All were part of His plan. Let us thank God for the Spirit-filled, unlearned D. L. Moody and the scholarly R. A. Torrey, for the rough, spectacular Billy Sunday and the gifted, polished, fervent George W. Truett.

How important is unity of heart among Christians! No doubt a great part of Pentecostal blessing, both cause and effect, was the fact that continually the disciples were "of one accord" (Acts 1:14; 2:1; 2:46; 4:24; 5:12). The strong should help and restore the weak (John 13:14; Gal. 6:1).

It is the unity of the Spirit we seek; not a scheduled, enforced sameness in personality and gifts and opinions but the oneness of people who are "endeavouring to keep the unity of the Spirit in the bond of peace." We are told in Ephesians 4:3-16:

*"There is one body, and one Spirit, even as ye are called in one hope of your calling; One Lord, one faith, one baptism, One God and Father of all, who is above all, and through all, and in you all. But unto every one of us is given grace according to the measure of the gift of Christ. Wherefore he saith, When he ascended up on high, he led captivity captive, and gave gifts unto men. (Now that he ascended, what is it but that he also descended first into the lower parts of the earth? He that descended is the same also that ascended up far above all heavens, that he might fill all things.) And he gave some, apostles; and some, prophets; and some, evangelists; and some, pastors and teachers; For*

*the perfecting of the saints, for the work of the ministry, for the edifying of the body of Christ: Till we all come in the unity of the faith, and of the knowledge of the Son of God, unto a perfect man, unto the measure of the stature of the fulness of Christ: That we henceforth be no more children, tossed to and fro, and carried about with every wind of doctrine, by the sleight of men, and cunning craftiness, whereby they lie in wait to deceive; But speaking the truth in love, may grow up into him in all things, which is the head, even Christ: From whom the whole body fitly joined together and compacted by that which every joint supplieth, according to the effectual working in the measure of every part, maketh increase of the body unto the edifying of itself in love."*

God's children have so much in common that the fellowship should always be sweet. At Inchon, Korea, I preached to old bearded men sitting crosslegged on the polished church floor, and to Christian young people seated on pews in the back. I preached standing barefooted on a pillow. But God gave us tears, repentance, salvation and rejoicing together. God's people are my people. I must love them, have fellowship with them wherever I can. We spoke a different language but had a common Saviour and salvation. Our dress was different but our hearts were alike.

Paul had baptized a few converts himself. Others certainly were baptized by other preachers. But the tender tie one might feel toward Paul who had baptized some, if it led to partisanship, was regretted by Paul. Paul came "not to baptize, but to preach the gospel." That does not mean he did not teach all young converts to obey Christ in this matter. He did. But of Jesus, too, it is said that He came "to seek and to save that which was lost" (Luke 19:10). He "came into the world to save sinners" (I Tim. 1:15). Yet Jesus and Paul both taught that baptism of a believer was right and commanded, even though baptism was not their central purpose. Baptism is a lesser and secondary part of the Great Commission. Getting people saved is first and infinitely more important.

---

18 For the preaching of the cross is to them that perish foolishness; but unto us which are saved it is the power of God.

19 For it is written, I will destroy the wisdom of the wise, and will bring to nothing the understanding of the prudent.

20 Where is the wise? where is the scribe? where is the disputer of this world? hath not God made foolish the wisdom of this world?

21 For after that in the wisdom of God the world by wisdom knew not God, it pleased God by the foolishness of preaching to save them that believe.

22 For the Jews require a sign, and the Greeks seek after wisdom:

23 But we preach Christ crucified, unto the Jews a stumblingblock, and unto the Greeks foolishness;

24 But unto them which are called, both Jews and Greeks, Christ the power of God, and the wisdom of God.

25 Because the foolishness of God is wiser than men; and the weakness of God is stronger than men.

## Man's Wisdom Is Foolishness to God

*"For the preaching of the cross . . . foolishness"* (vs. 18). To the unsaved the cross is foolishness and unattractive to the carnal mind, and the doctrine is foolish. Man by nature is so proud, so self-righteous. Infidel Robert Ingersoll said about the cross, "The wrong man died." He tells how from childhood he hated the idea of another earning salvation for him. Dr. George Buttrick, infamous unbeliever, says of the God who required an atoning sacrifice, "Your God is my Devil" *(The Christian Fact and Modern Doubt),* and he walked out when a Bible preacher expounded Romans 5:7,8. The unrepentant natural man claims that man is good, earns Heaven, needs no atonement, no new birth. But God reveals that the cross is glorious, as is God's love which has provided salvation for guilty sinners who repent.

*"The wisdom of the wise . . ."* (vs. 19). The intellectual, the scientist, the worldling says, "Evolution, no creation." He says that man has risen, and all other life,

"from inherent forces." The intellectual sees man rising from beasts and climbing upward of his own evolving and not created in the image of God, not fallen, ruined. The wise of this world stand in judgment on the Bible, God's Word! God's wisdom says that the way up is down, the way to have is to give, the way to greatness is to be a servant. Man's wisdom produces a Hitler, a Tom Paine, a Bishop Pike. God's wisdom produces a Paul or a D. L. Moody or a Sam Jones.

The world says, with John Dewey and Benjamin Spock, and with other rebels, Don't restrain your desires. Do your thing. No discipline, no death penalty for murder, no preaching against sin. Don't offend people.

God's wisdom says, Discipline children, stay with marriage vows whether happy or not, keep the law, respect authority, warn of judgment to come, remember what one sows he reaps.

*". . . the world by wisdom knew not God"* (vs. 21). Spurgeon once said the natural man is Arminian, wants to earn salvation, get credit for his works and merit. So the Pharisee of Luke 18, boasting in the Temple, is the natural man, as is the religionist of Matthew 7:21,22, who wants credit for casting out devils and doing "many wonderful works," but is sent away from Heaven not recognized by Christ. The poor publican in the Temple who asked for mercy, the penitential harlot at the feet of Jesus at the Bethany supper in Luke 7:36-40, are symbols and examples of grace and thus of the wisdom of God.

*". . . to save them that believe"* (vs. 21). The carnal mind says, Save them who hold out faithful. Save those who deserve it. Save those who are baptized or confirmed. Save those who are in the covenant. How sweet and simple is God's wisdom! One simply depends on Christ, trusts in Him, our atoning Saviour, and is saved! That is God's wisdom.

*"The Jews require a sign . . ."* (vs. 22). Did the many prophecies of Scripture, fulfilled in Christ, convince

unbelieving Jews? No. "For had ye believed Moses, ye would have believed me: for he wrote of me," Jesus said (John 5:46). Even in Hell, the unregenerate rich man wanted a miracle for his five brothers who had the Old Testament Scriptures. The Jews said to Jesus, "Master, we would see a sign from thee" (Matt. 12:38), but none would be given except of Christ's resurrection. They said, "Come down from the cross, and we will believe" (Matt. 27:42), blindly ignoring the fact that that would really annul God's redemption plan and not prove His deity.

*"The Greeks seek after wisdom"* (vs. 22). So Bible scholars pattern after Greek philosophers. Modern infidels follow "scholarly" opinion instead of the Word of God.

---

**VERSES 26-31:**

26 For ye see your calling, brethren, how that not many wise men after the flesh, not many mighty, not many noble, are called:

27 But God hath chosen the foolish things of the world to confound the wise; and God hath chosen the weak things of the world to confound the things which are mighty;

28 And base things of the world, and things which are despised, hath God chosen, yea, and things which are not, to bring to nought things that are:

29 That no flesh should glory in his presence.

30 But of him are ye in Christ Jesus, who of God is made unto us wisdom, and righteousness, and sanctification, and redemption:

31 That, according as it is written, He that glorieth, let him glory in the Lord.

## God Chooses the Weak, Then God Gets the Glory

*". . . not many wise . . . not many noble"* (vs. 26). A biographer said, "Billy Sunday is God's laugh at the preachers." The unlettered baseball player preached to millions, while the doctors and bishops and theologians could not get the ear of the people. They sometimes mocked at the million converts of Mr. Sunday but envied him. Moody, with a fifth grade education, and Spurgeon, who never went to college, show that God chooses the weak and

makes them strong in His strength, so God can get the glory. The twelve apostles were "unlearned and ignorant men" we read in Acts 4:13. But the chief priest "took knowledge of them, that they had been with Jesus" (Acts 4:13). The Bible exalts the widow's mite, the rod in Moses' hands, the five loaves and two fishes of the boy's lunch which fed five thousand, the ox goad in the hands of Judge Shamgar (Judg. 3:31).

Not many wise and noble, but a few! A Moses, a Paul, a Torrey, a Robert Dick Wilson, a Machen, a B. H. Carroll! But Moses must come to failure in Egypt and keep sheep in the desert until he is eighty. And Paul must have a thorn in the flesh if he will be most used. Jesus said, "Blessed be ye poor" (Luke 6:20), but He also said, "Blessed are the poor in spirit . . ." (Matt. 5:3). The rich man can go to Heaven if he is enough poor in spirit to despair of merit and possessions and take by faith the riches of Christ.

". . . the weak," the "despised," the "base." The young man, the daughter, or the servant, the handmaid can be Spirit-filled and prophesy in the power of God as well as the father; the servant as well as the master (Acts 2:17,18). The river thief, Jerry McAuley; the drunkard, Mel Trotter, and many another drunkard, thief and criminal, has been raised up to witness for God.

*"That no flesh should glory in his presence"* (vs. 29). God has the wisdom which the ignorant needs. God has the redemption and gives it freely to those who cannot earn it. He has the righteousness imputed and imparted for our sinfulness. He has the sanctification we ought to have, has it for us—"For Christ is the end of the law for righteousness to every one that believeth" (Rom. 10:4). Paul lamented that the Jews "going about to establish their own righteousness, have not submitted themselves unto the righteousness of God" (Rom. 10:3).

# I CORINTHIANS II

## VERSES 1-8:

AND I, brethren, when I came to you, came not with excellency of speech or of wisdom, declaring unto you the testimony of God.

2 For I determined not to know any thing among you, save Jesus Christ, and him crucified.

3 And I was with you in weakness, and in fear, and in much trembling.

4 And my speech and my preaching was not with enticing words of man's wisdom, but in demonstration of the Spirit and of power:

5 That your faith should not stand in the wisdom of men, but in the power of God.

6 Howbeit we speak wisdom among them that are perfect: yet not the wisdom of this world, nor of the princes of this world, that come to nought:

7 But we speak the wisdom of God in a mystery, even the hidden wisdom, which God ordained before the world unto our glory:

8 Which none of the princes of this world knew: for had they known it, they would not have crucified the Lord of glory.

## Paul Did Not Use Enticing Words of Human Wisdom

*"I was with you in weakness, and in fear, and in much trembling"* (vs. 3). The Apostle Paul had been bold and unafraid in Cyprus (Acts 13:6-12), in Antioch in Pisidia (Acts 13:40-46), in Iconium (Acts 14:1-3). He and Barnabas were believed to be gods in Lystra because of their miraculous power. And when Paul planned to go to Rome he wrote triumphantly, "And I am sure that, when I come unto you, I shall come in the fulness of the blessing of the gospel of Christ" (Rom. 15:29). But when he came to Corinth, he came "in weakness, and in fear, and in much trembling." He had made a determined resolution, in his concern about God's blessing, "not to know any thing among you, save Jesus Christ, and him crucified."

Why a special trepidation as he faced Corinth? Perhaps he was influenced by the fact that he had just come from Athens where the spiritual results were small and Paul left with few converts: "And when they heard of the resurrection of the dead, some mocked: and others said, We will hear thee again of this matter. So Paul departed from among them" (Acts 17:32,33). At Athens Paul, impressed

that he was at the intellectual center of the world, and
facing philosophers, Epicureans and Stoics, had been very
elaborate and learned in his address. Would it have been
better to have preached more simply the Gospel of the
crucified Christ? Was that one reason for little results at
Athens? Perhaps he thought so. Oh, at Corinth he will be
more direct and preach the Gospel more insistently.

It seems that at Athens Paul needed special assurance
from God; so in Acts 18:9-11 God gave it. "Then spake the
Lord to Paul in the night by a vision, Be not afraid, but
speak, and hold not thy peace: For I am with thee, and no
man shall set on thee to hurt thee: for I have much people
in this city. And he continued there a year and six months,
teaching the word of God among them." We will all
remember, as the inspired apostle has been emphasizing in
chapter 1, that God loves to use the weak, the simple, the
direct, instead of human wisdom and scholarship.

". . . *in demonstration of the Spirit and of power*" (vs.
4). Oh, do not forget, it must be Holy Spirit power: "He
giveth power to the faint; and to them that have no might
he increaseth strength. Even the youths shall faint and be
weary, and the young men shall utterly fall: But they that
wait upon the Lord shall renew their strength; they shall
mount up with wings as eagles; they shall run, and not be
weary; and they shall walk, and not faint" (Isa. 40:29-31).
And we must remember: "Not by might, nor by power, but
by my spirit, saith the Lord of hosts" (Zech. 4:6).

However, do you have learning, scholarship, human
wisdom? Then be as humble as a little child with it, and
seek the special enduement of Holy Spirit power.

We can well believe that Paul, facing Corinth, was like
the disciples in Jerusalem seeking a new enduement after
Pentecost and he had it, doubtless, as they did: "And when
they had prayed, the place was shaken where they were
assembled together; and they were all filled with the Holy
Ghost, and they spake the word of God with boldness"
(Acts 4:31). God must have the glory, not man. We doubt

not that Paul went through some serious heart-searching when he pleaded for his thorn in the flesh to be removed but was denied. God would rather give grace for weak men, glorying in their infirmities "that the power of Christ may rest upon me" (II Cor. 12:1-10).

---

**VERSES 9-16:**

9 But as it is written, Eye hath not seen, nor ear heard, neither have entered into the heart of man, the things which God hath prepared for them that love him.

10 But God hath revealed them unto us by his Spirit: for the Spirit searcheth all things, yea, the deep things of God.

11 For what man knoweth the things of a man, save the spirit of man which is in him? even so the things of God knoweth no man, but the Spirit of God.

12 Now we have received, not the spirit of the world, but the spirit which is of God; that we might know the things that are freely given to us of God.

13 Which things also we speak, not in the words which man's wisdom teacheth, but which the Holy Ghost teacheth; comparing spiritual things with spiritual.

14 But the natural man receiveth not the things of the Spirit of God: for they are foolishness unto him: neither can he know them, because they are spiritually discerned.

15 But he that is spiritual judgeth all things, yet he himself is judged of no man.

16 For who hath known the mind of the Lord, that he may instruct him? But we have the mind of Christ.

## The Spiritual Truths Are Not Discovered by Human Sources but Are Revealed

Here the apostle begins the most detailed teaching on inspiration in the New Testament, the inspiration God gave the apostles before the New Testament was written, and the inspiration of the Bible. Some preach on the glories of Heaven, which they think are referred to in verse 9. But they are mistaken. The wonderful things "which God hath prepared for them that love him" are in the Bible. The glories of divine revelation are discussed here. Note here are these great principles. Make sure you see this that certain human sources were not the basis of Scripture as we have it. Scriptures are not human but divine.

*"Eye hath not seen . . ."* (vs. 9). On television we see nightly "Eyewitness News." That is not the way we got the Bible. Who saw and could record as eyewitnesses the creation of the universe and all that is in it in six days, as recorded in Genesis? No, God revealed those facts by His Spirit to Moses. How did Moses know the genealogies of those who lived before the flood and other long lists of genealogies not written down before Moses? Did he see old records and copy them? No, they were revealed by the Spirit of God. Human records would almost certainly be faulty, and a human copyist would somewhere make mistakes. No, wonderful things are prepared for us in the Bible. "Eye hath not seen."

The account that the Gospels give of Jesus feeding the multitudes, or walking on water, or stilling the wind with a word, or raising the dead—are these things written down just as Matthew, Mark, Luke and John saw them? No, human witness is not enough. They were revealed by the Word of God.

Dr. Harry Rimmer told about a boy who reported that he saw a man making a horse. He was just finishing nailing on the horse's feet, the boy declared. But a blacksmith had simply been nailing on horseshoes. Human witness is unreliable. Once after a fatal automobile accident this writer was asked to identify a car. Under oath I reported that the car was black. Under oath the deputy sheriff who pulled in the car declared it was green. We both went to see it—it was dark blue! That is how unreliable is even intelligent, careful human witness. That is not an adequate source for divine revelation. The Bible is not the result of men's eyewitness reports.

It is true that we have the divine record that many people saw Jesus alive after His resurrection. It is the Spirit of God who says so, not these witnesses (I Cor. 15:1-8). The Beloved John reported in I John 1:1 and 2, "That which was from the beginning, which we have heard, which we have seen with our eyes, which we have looked upon, and our hands have handled, of the Word of life; (For the life was manifested, and we have seen it, and bear witness, and shew unto you that eternal life, which was with the Father, and was manifested unto us . . .)." That is perfectly reliable, not because John saw Jesus or touched Him but because the Spirit of God said that John saw Him and handled Him. And what we have are the words of the Spirit of God, not simply John's words. John is true because the Spirit of God revealed the testimony and then reported it truly.

". . . *nor ear heard*" (vs. 9). The Scriptures are not based on the testimony of what people heard. Someone supposes as a church father suggested, that Mark was with Peter, and Peter told Mark of the things that happened in the Gospel, so Mark wrote them down for Peter. No, no! Mark was inspired of God directly. The words were God's words. Someone thinks that Luke must have received the matter about which he wrote from the Apostle Paul, and so the book of Acts would have "apostolic authority" back of it. No, the wonderful things God prepared for us who love Him in God's revelation are not the things which the ear heard.

Some suppose that Luke talked to Mary and thus she told him about the virgin birth. But Mary's word would be human, frail and fallible. We could not trust it in such a divine and eternal matter as the deity of Christ and how God became man. No, Luke himself said that he, "having had perfect understanding of all things *from above*"—not "from the very first" as the King James Version has it, but *anothen*, "from above" (Luke 1:3). Do not make the prologue to Luke's Gospel contradict this plain statement about sources of the Scripture. They did not come from eyewitness, nor from what men heard others say, nor from handed-down "oral tradition," as the liberals say.

Paul, who wonderfully preached the Gospel in its purity, tells us plainly in Galatians 1 and 2 that he did not get the Gospel from others "but when it pleased God, who separated me from my mother's womb, and called me by his grace, To reveal his Son in me, that I might preach him among the heathen; immediately I conferred not with flesh and blood: Neither went I up to Jerusalem to them which were apostles before me; but I went into Arabia, and returned again unto Damascus. Then after three years I went up to Jerusalem to see Peter, and abode with him fifteen days. But other of the apostles saw I none, save James the Lord's brother. Now the things which I write unto you, behold, before God, I lie not. Afterwards I came into the regions of Syria and Cilicia; And was unknown by face unto the churches of Judaea which were in Christ: But they had heard only, That he which persecuted us in times past now preacheth the faith which once he destroyed. And they glorified God in me" (Gal. 1:15-24). Fourteen years later he returned to Jerusalem: "And I went up by revelation, and communicated unto them that gospel which I preach among the Gentiles, but privately to them which were of reputation, lest by any means I should run, or had run, in vain" (Gal. 2:2), but the apostles in Jerusalem ". . . they who seemed to be somewhat in conference added nothing to me" (Gal. 2:6).

No, Paul did not preach what someone told him was the truth about Christ and the Gospel. He preached what was revealed by the Spirit of God to him, and when he wrote it down, he wrote with the authority of God. The wondrous things God has for us in the Scriptures were not received by what the writer saw or heard.

". . . neither have entered into the heart of man, the things which God hath prepared for them that love him" (vs. 9). Did Paul study the Pentateuch, the ceremonial laws, and thus come to wonderfully understand the spiritual import of these things and to write them down perhaps in the book of Hebrews?

In his introduction to Hebrews, Dr. Scofield says, "We undoubtedly have here the method of Paul's synagogue addresses." I do not think so. At least such preparation by

Paul was not the source of the book of Hebrews, if he was the inspired writer. And if Paul followed any such outlines, he learned them from the book of Hebrews which God had inspired. None of the Bible is the result of human reasoning. It seems that the book of Ecclesiastes deliberately sets out to report all that the mind could see and know "under the sun," and we have an inspired record of those human conclusions. But human wisdom is never the same as divine wisdom, and human sight and hearing and reasoning is never the basis for the Scriptures.

Just as Old Testament prophets, who were inspired to prophesy of the coming of Christ and His atoning death, diligently inquired and searched their own Scriptures, trying to understand them (I Pet. 1:10-12), knowing that what they wrote in the Scriptures was for us who would live later and was beyond their complete understanding, so, those who wrote down the New Testament wrote beyond anything they had seen or heard or anything they had reasoned out. God prepared wondrous things in the Scriptures not from human sight and hearing and wisdom, *"But God hath revealed them unto us by his Spirit"* (vs. 10). Revelation, then, reaches into the infinite and is God speaking to man and revealing things man could not know without divine revelation. "For what man knoweth the things of a man, save the spirit of man which is in him? even so the things of God knoweth no man, but the Spirit of God." So the Spirit of God came upon the inspired writer "that we might know the things that are freely given to us of God."

But that kind of perfect revelation involved in the Scriptures, going beyond what man could see or hear or understand so that it is a perfect report, must involve actual verbal word-for-word inspiration. So verse 13 says, "Which things also we speak, not in the words which man's wisdom teacheth, but which the Holy Ghost teacheth; comparing spiritual things with spiritual." And the American Standard Version properly says "comparing spiritual things [or matter] with spiritual words."

Thus we have stated again what the Lord Jesus Christ claimed in Matthew 4:4, quoting from Deuteronomy 8:3, "It is written, Man shall not live by bread alone, but by every word that proceedeth out of the mouth of God." Whence came the Scriptures? "Every word. . .proceedeth out of the mouth of God." By all means read the author's big book, *Our God-Breathed Book—THE BIBLE, the Verbally Inspired, Eternal, Inerrant Word of God.*

Note that God guarantees even the jot and tittle (Matt. 5:18). Notice that God not only gives the very word He means but the singular and plural of it: "He saith not, And to seeds, as of many; but as of one, And to thy seed, which is Christ" (Gal. 3:16). We are not surprised when the Scripture says, "And Moses wrote ALL THE WORDS OF THE LORD" in the Pentateuch (Exod. 24:4). God put the very words in the mouth of Isaiah (Isa. 51:16) and in the mouth of Jeremiah (Jer. 1:9; Jer. 36:28,32), in the mouth of Ezekiel (Ezek. 2:7; 3:10), in the mouth of David (II Sam. 23:1,2). Both the matter and the words of the original autographs were given by God.

And the matter is summed up in verse 14: *"But the natural man receiveth not the things of the Spirit of God: for they are foolishness unto him: neither can he know them, because they are spiritually discerned."* Men may study the Bible reverently, approaching it as the very authority of God, but they dare not sit in judgment on the Word of God.

That means that no scholar, however learned, is fit to teach or expound the Word of God except as he comes in humility, accepting the Bible as the very Word of God and, then, illumined by the Spirit of God to understand what the Spirit had given in the Scriptures. And even so, the enlightened and illumined human mind, enabled by the Holy Spirit, can only bit by bit and partially, less than perfectly, comprehend the wonders of divine inspiration. About the Scriptures, the finite mind, even the mind

enlightened by the Spirit of God, cannot attain the
perfection which divine revelation has in the inspired
Scriptures. And so one must say, "For we know in part, and
we prophesy in part. . . . For now we see through a glass,
darkly; but then face to face: now I know in part; but then
shall I know even as also I am known" (I Cor. 13:9,12).

But it is wonderfully true that one in whom the Spirit of
God dwells in the regenerated heart, and one illumined by
the Spirit, judges all things.

Dr. Bob Jones, Sr., has said that an unlettered woman in
a mountain cabin may better understand the truths of
God's Word than a learned scholar in the university
without the guidance of the Holy Spirit. We have Christ.
His Spirit dwells within us. There is some sweet affinity
between the born-again, Spirit-led Christian and the Word
of God.

*"The natural man  . . ."* (vs. 14). On verse 14 Dr. C. I.
Scofield's notes say:

> "Paul divides men into three classes: *psuchikos,* 'of the
> senses' (Jas. 3. 15; Jude 19), or 'natural,' i.e. the Adamic
> man, unrenewed through the new birth (John 3. 3, 5);
> *pneumatikos,* 'spiritual,' i.e. the renewed man as Spirit-
> filled and walking in the Spirit in full communion with
> God (Eph. 5. 18-20); and *sarkikos,* 'carnal,' 'fleshly,' i.e.
> the renewed man who, walking 'after the flesh,' remains a
> babe in Christ (I Cor. 3. 1-4). The natural man may be
> learned, gentle, eloquent, fascinating, but the spiritual
> content of Scripture is absolutely hidden from him; and
> the fleshly, or carnal, Christian is able to comprehend
> only its simplest truths, 'milk' (I Cor. 3.2)."

# I CORINTHIANS III

AND I, brethren, could not speak unto you as unto spiritual, but as unto carnal, even as unto babes in Christ.

2 I have fed you with milk, and not with meat: for hitherto ye were not able to bear it, neither yet now are ye able.

3 For ye are yet carnal: for whereas there is among you envying, and strife, and divisions, are ye not carnal, and walk as men?

4 For while one saith, I am of Paul; and another, I am of Ă-pŏl´-lŏs; are ye not carnal?

## Fleshly, Immature Baby Christians Have Envy and Strife

*"And I, brethren . . ."* (vs. 1). Paul is writing to brethren, that is, to Christians, saved people, children of God. But they are not mature Christians. It is a mistake to suppose that one who is converted, a true believer, is suddenly mature with all the Christian graces and character. Not so. Some quote II Corinthians 5:17, "Therefore if any man be in Christ, he is a new creature: old things are passed away; behold, all things are become new," to mean that all the old tendencies, old habits, old temptations are automatically gone when one is saved. It is true there is a "new creature" or "new creation"; there is now a "new man." But we still have the "old man," as many Scriptures show.

And now since the Christian has an old nature and a new nature, there is a conflict, a struggle.

*"For that which I do I allow not: for what I would, that do I not; but what I hate, that do I. If then I do that which I would not, I consent unto the law that it is good. Now then it is no more I that do it, but sin that dwelleth in me. For I know that in me (that is, in my flesh,) dwelleth no good thing: for to will is present with me; but how to perform that which is good I find not. For the good that I would I do*

*not: but the evil which I would not, that I do. Now if I do that I would not, it is no more I that do it, but sin that dwelleth in me. I find then a law, that, when I would do good, evil is present with me. For I delight in the law of God after the inward man: But I see another law in my members, warring against the law of my mind, and bringing me into captivity to the law of sin which is in my members. O wretched man that I am! who shall deliver me from the body of this death? I thank God through Jesus Christ our Lord. So then with the mind I myself serve the law of God; but with the flesh the law of sin."*—Rom. 7:15-25.

And do not suppose that the inspired apostle spoke of some time far gone when this was written. Do not urge people to "get out of the 7th chapter of Romans into the 8th chapter." Both belong to every Christian.

There is an inward man who delights in the law of God. But the law in our members, our flesh, wars against the law of the mind, the Scripture says. "So then with the mind I myself serve the law of God; but with the flesh the law of sin." Galatians 5:17 says, "For the flesh lusteth against the Spirit, and the Spirit against the flesh: and these are contrary the one to the other: so that ye cannot do the things that ye would." So, a Christian *should* walk in the Spirit and *should* daily crucify the flesh with the affections and lusts, but the only honest Bible interpretation is that every Christian has the old nature and the new nature. They are contrary the one to the other.

Of the new nature, the born-again nature, we are told, "Whosoever is born of God doth not commit sin; for his seed remaineth in him: and he cannot sin, because he is born of God" (I John 3:9). But every Christian has the old nature which has not yet been transformed.

We are commanded then, "Put on the new man, which after God is created in righteousness and true holiness" (Eph. 4:24. See also Col. 3:10). If the saints at Ephesus were

commanded to put on the new man, that means that many
of them still lived too much after the old man, the old
nature. So they were commanded, "Put off concerning the
former conversation the old man, which is corrupt
according to the deceitful lusts; And be renewed in the
spirit of your mind" (Eph. 4:22,23). And Colossians 3:8-14
says we are to put away lying, etc.

You see, no Christian is a good Christian except as he
works at being a good Christian, being led by the Spirit,
mortifying the deeds of the flesh, growing in grace through
the Word of God. Some untaught Christians say, "Ye shall
know them by their fruits," and assume the right and
ability to judge who is saved and who is not by their works.
But they pervert and misuse the statement of Jesus in
Matthew 7:15-20, "Beware of false prophets, which come to
you in sheep's clothing, but inwardly they are ravening
wolves. . . . Wherefore by their fruits ye shall know
them." You can know a false teacher by his teaching. When
a man openly denies the inspiration of the Bible, the deity
of Christ, His virgin birth, His blood atonement, you know
he is a wolf in sheep's clothing. You can judge a false
teacher by his teaching. That does not mean that any man
is wise enough to see the heart and tell who is born again
and who is not. "Man looketh on the outward appearance,
but the Lord looketh on the heart" (I Sam. 16:7).

Would you say that when Peter cursed and denied Christ
and quit the ministry, he was unsaved? Would you judge
that when David committed adultery and murder, he was
unconverted? God does not put men judges of other men's
hearts in this matter of salvation.

It is remarkable and noticeable that in these letters to
the church at Corinth Paul never hints that these
immature Christians are unsaved. They quarrelled and
had among themselves strife and division and enmity. Yet
they are called brethren. Some of them went to law before
unbelievers (I Cor. 6:6). Some did not eat at the Lord's
Supper worthily and were stricken with sickness, and some

died. And some got drunk at the Lord's Supper (I Cor. 11:21, 30). Yet these are Christians. They are baby Christians, carnal Christians and not mature, but they are children of God.

Blessed is the pastor and blessed are the more mature Christians who have charity and love and who help babes grow into mature Christians and help restore those who fall into sin, according to Galatians 6:1.

*"I have fed you with milk"* (vs. 2). We must remember to put the feed down where the lambs can get it. We must remember that many Christians need to learn again and again the great truths of salvation by grace, God's constant watchcare and keeping, the accessibility of Christ to our prayers, and the wonderful assurance of forgiveness and cleansing when we confess our failures and sins. Some Christians are not able to take meat but they must be given milk.

*"I am of Paul. . . I am of Apollos"* (vs. 4). It is the tendency of immature Christians to follow men without much discernment. They do not have a solid base of doctrinal conviction; they are easy prey for false teachers. They are led into cults. They are led astray on minor matters. They tend toward division and strife over human leadership. So young churches often have strife and splits. Great soul-winning churches necessarily will find they have many young, immature Christians to be taught. The family that has babies will have diapers to wash, will have crayon marks on the wallpaper, will have toys on the floor. Oh, but give us the babies still and let us train them!

---

**VERSES 5-9:**

5 Who then is Paul, and who is Ă-pŏl'-lŏs, but ministers by whom ye believed, even as the Lord gave to every man?

6 I have planted, Ă-pŏl'-lŏs watered; but God gave the increase.

7 So then neither is he that planteth any thing, neither he that watereth;

but God that giveth the increase.
8 Now he that planteth and he that watereth are one: and every man shall receive his own reward accord-ing to his own labour.
9 For we are labourers together with God: ye are God's husbandry, ye are God's building.

## God's Ministers Alike Are Simply Instruments of God

Paul, Apollos and Cephas (Simon Peter mentioned in 1:12) were all greatly used men, especially prepared, men of different gifts, yet all were given to God's people alike. Every Christian needs the ministry of others besides his favorite preacher who won him or baptized him.

Apollos had been to Corinth after Paul had spent eighteen months there and had founded and taught the church (Acts 19:1). Apollos was not as thoroughly indoctrinated as was the Apostle Paul, had not taught the people at Ephesus about receiving the Holy Spirit in soul-winning power, as you see in Acts 19:1-7. Many would properly honor Paul as an apostle without a peer and authenticated by God.

But Apollos was evidently more interesting, more flashy, "an eloquent man, and mighty in the scriptures" (Acts 18:24), while of Paul these same people of Corinth had said, "His letters . . . are weighty and powerful; but his bodily presence is weak, and his speech contemptible" (II Cor. 10:10). It is not surprising that some preferred one and some the other. And Peter, while he may never have been to Corinth, yet was widely known as the chief of the apostles, the preacher at Pentecost, and it is probable that throughout the area wherever Christians went, people talked about the Apostle Peter. And the prominence that led Roman brethren later to claim him as a pope and claim for him authority no others had from God, perhaps made him a favorite of many; but they were wrong to place one against another. All were servants and ministers of God with different gifts. They had the same Christ, the same doctrine, the same end, and all alike represented the Lord Jesus.

Paul said, "Be ye followers of me, even as I also am of Christ" (I Cor. 11:1). Yes, but only as he followed Christ. And so with others. All the Gospel, all the blessings were from Christ, and He should have the primary love and praise. Whosoever plowed, whosoever planted—only God gave the increase. The man won to Christ by Peter should praise God for Paul or Apollos, other ministers of Christ equally sent. So John the Baptist would say about Christ, "He must increase, but I must decrease" (John 3:30).

In going in to conquer Canaan, Israel was commanded not to destroy fruit trees. They were commanded:

*"When thou shalt besiege a city a long time, in making war against it to take it, thou shalt not destroy the trees thereof by forcing an axe against them: for thou mayest eat of them, and thou shalt not cut them down (for the tree of the field is man's life) to employ them in the siege: Only the trees which thou knowest that they be not trees for meat, thou shalt destroy and cut them down; and thou shalt build bulwarks against the city that maketh war with thee, until it be subdued."*—Deut. 20:19,20.

Oh, soul winners are God's fruit trees and they ought to be dear to the heart of every Christian, as they are dear to God. God will reward each one. We are not to cause division over godly men who are essentially right and used of God, although with different gifts.

---

### VERSES 10-15:

10 According to the grace of God which is given unto me, as a wise masterbuilder, I have laid the foundation, and another buildeth thereon. But let every man take heed how he buildeth thereupon.

11 For other foundation can no man lay than that is laid, which is Jesus Christ.

12 Now if any man build upon this foundation gold, silver, precious stones, wood, hay, stubble;

13 Every man's work shall be made manifest: for the day shall declare it, because it shall be revealed by fire; and the fire shall try every man's work of what sort it is.

14 If any man's work abide which

he hath built thereupon, he shall he shall suffer loss: but he himself
receive a reward. shall be saved; yet so as by fire.
15 If any man's work shall be burned,

## Rewards at the Judgment Seat of Christ

Paul was "a wise masterbuilder." By divine inspiration
he could say it and it was true. He was an apostle, one
specially sent, one with special revelation from God, and
with authority and power. He magnified his apostleship (I
Cor. 9:1; Rom. 11:13; Gal. 2:7-9). His inspired epistles, the
thousands of converts, the churches he grew, witness to
him as "a wise masterbuilder."

At Corinth he had labored eighteen months (Acts 18:11)
and there he got many, many of these Corinthians saved.
And what if, after he had laid the foundation—salvation
through Christ—some other built thereupon? Oh, but now
every Christian is responsible for what he builds, that is,
his Christian life after he receives Christ as Saviour.

The foundation is Christ.

*"For other foundation can no man lay than that is laid,
which is Jesus Christ"* (vs. 11). The church is built upon
Christ and on that Living Stone we, as living stones, are
built up a spiritual house (I Pet. 2:4,5). When the Lord
Jesus said to Peter, "Thou art Peter, and upon this rock I
will build my church," He was saying literally, "Thou art
Peter, a movable stone; but on this Rock (another word,
bedrock, Christ Himself) Christ built His church."

In Matthew 21:42-44 we read,

*"Jesus saith unto them, Did ye never read in the
scriptures, The stone which the builders rejected, the same
is become the head of the corner: this is the Lord's doing,
and it is marvellous in our eyes? Therefore say I unto you,
The kingdom of God shall be taken from you, and given to a
nation bringing forth the fruits thereof. And whosoever
shall fall on this stone shall be broken: but on whomsoever
it shall fall, it will grind him to powder."*

Dr. Scofield says on this passage, Matthew 21:42-44:

"Christ as the 'Stone' is revealed in a threefold way: (1) To *Israel* Christ, coming not as a splendid monarch but in the form of a servant, is a stumbling-stone and rock of offence (Isa. 8.14,15; Rom. 9.32,33; I Cor. 1.23; I Pet. 2.8); (2) to the *church,* Christ is the foundation-stone and the head of the corner (I Cor. 3.11; Eph. 2.20-22; I Pet. 2.4,5); (3) to the Gentile world-powers (see 'Gentiles,' Lk. 21.24; Rev. 16.19) He is to be the smiting-stone of destruction (Dan. 2.34). Israel stumbled *over* Christ; the church is built *upon* Christ; Gentile world-dominion will be broken by Christ. (See 'Armageddon,' Rev. 16.14; 19.19.)"

Good brethren sometimes say the foundation was Peter's confession that Christ is building the church. But it is on Christ Himself; "other foundation can no man lay."

Note that this is a judgment of the works of a Christian, not the works of a lost man. Good works may be represented as gold, silver, precious stones. They may vary in value, but all are valuable, and thus refer to the works that have eternal results and thus get eternal rewards. Daniel 12:3 tells us that the *soul winner* will "shine as the brightness of the firmament," and Matthew 10:42 tells us that even a cup of cold water given in Jesus' name will not fail of a reward. In Luke 14:12-14 Jesus said that those who make a dinner, not for friends, brothers, kinsmen or rich neighbors but for "the poor, the maimed, the lame, the blind," there will be recompense in Heaven. Second Timothy 2:12 says, "If we suffer, we shall also reign with him." Oh, you may be sure that every deed done for Christ, every really good deed will be noted at that judgment seat of Christ, whether gold, silver, or precious stones.

But some of the works of a Christian are pictured by "wood, hay, stubble." Again, their value varies. Wood may be the finest Honduras mahogany or Birdseye maple or Rosewood; or it may be hay, useful but common, or maybe stubble, worthless. But however good it is rated among men, many of these works will be burned up, discarded, counted as no value at the judgment.

Oh, then, let every Christian "take heed how he

buildeth" upon this foundation! Oh, how important it is for us to have the mind of Christ, to see things in the light of eternity! The man who piles up treasures will find them sift between his cold fingers at death. The man who builds for himself mansions and castles will find himself lying empty-handed in a narrow casket in the earth!

In II Corinthians 5:10 Paul reminded these same people, "For we must all appear before the judgment seat of Christ; that every one may receive the things done in his body, according to that he hath done, whether it be good or bad."

*"If any man's work abide . . . he shall receive a reward"* (vs. 14). Reward? Yes. Not salvation. This judgment is for people who are already saved, already in glorified, resurrection bodies, already caught up to meet Christ in the air at a judgment seat of Christ in Heaven. Do not confuse this with the judgment on earth when Christ returns to reign and judges the Gentile peoples at the end of the tribulation, told in Matthew 25:31-46. Do not confuse this with the judgment of the unsaved dead out in space at the Great White Throne Judgment and after the thousand years' millennial reign on earth, as discussed in Revelation 20. This is a judgment of born-again Christians and those whose works abide will receive a reward, and the question of salvation is not at stake.

What kind of reward? I suppose feasting in Heaven in payment to giving to others on earth (Luke 14:14-16). Certainly it would include helping Christ reign, for "if we suffer, we shall also reign with him" (II Tim. 2:12).

In the parable of the talents in Matthew 25:14-30, one whose five talents gained five others, and one whose two talents had gained two others, were promised, "Thou hast been faithful over a few things, I will make thee ruler over many things." So, then, Christians will help reign with Christ on this earth when He returns for the millennial kingdom here. And the rewards will not be the same for all in Heaven. Some will sit nearer the head of the table at the banquet. In the parable of the pounds in Luke 19:11-27 one who had gained ten pounds was told, "Have thou authority over ten cities," and the one who had gained five pounds was told, "Be thou also over five cities." Some, alas, whose work is burned, shall suffer loss.

Note carefully that the one who suffers loss at this judgment seat of Christ "he himself shall be saved; yet so as by fire." Loss in Heaven? Yes, if he had loved ones he did not win to Christ and they have gone to Hell, they have still gone. If there were opportunities he missed and vows he did not keep, he will have long to regret them. If others who were willing to suffer for Christ reign with Him, he who was fearful and disloyal will not get to reign. Yes, some Christians will suffer loss in Heaven.

This may well be a reason why, after the Christians have had resurrection bodies and reigned with Christ a thousand years and then after the last judgment of the unsaved dead, when they see their unconverted loved ones and other multitudes cast into the lake of fire, we are told that then "God shall wipe away all tears from their eyes" (Rev. 21:4). Evidently during the millennium and after the thousand years, many Christians will weep over their failures and sins on earth. And God will wipe away tears and then, thank God, "There shall be no more death, neither sorrow, nor crying, neither shall there be any more pain: for the former things are passed away" (Rev. 21:4).

---

### VERSES 16, 17:

16 Know ye not that ye are the temple of God, and that the Spirit of God dwelleth in you?
17 If any man defile the temple of God, him shall God destroy; for the temple of God is holy, which temple ye are.

## The Christian's Body the Temple of God

In Old Testament times God dwelt in the most holy place

in that Shekinah Glory over the mercy seat. God appeared, we believe, in that pillar of cloud by day and of fire by night which led Israel in the wilderness. And so the prophet could say, "The Lord is in his holy temple; let all the earth keep silence before him" (Hab. 2:20). But it is not so today!

Lamenting over Jerusalem, which killed the prophets and rejected Christ, Jesus said, "Behold, your house is left unto you desolate" (Matt. 23:38). We believe that when Jesus died on the cross and "the veil of the temple was rent in twain from the top to the bottom; and the earth did quake, and the rocks rent" (Matt. 27:51), Jesus meant surely that now God lived in that house no longer. It might be open to the whole world. That Temple was destroyed in A.D. 70 by Titus in the destruction of Jerusalem.

Sometimes a church has lettered on the proscenium arch the words of the prophet, "The Lord is in his holy temple: let all the earth keep silence before him," but that is a misuse of the Scripture. God does not dwell in church houses. No church auditorium ought to be called "The sanctuary" for it is not. Any humble dwelling where people pray and love and serve God is as sacred to God as a church building. It is true that people ought to respect the preacher and respect the rights of others, and things ought to be done decently and in order, but reverence for a church house, as such, is misplaced. No church houses are even mentioned in the New Testament. The reverence must be for the Word of God and for the man of God who, filled with the Spirit, gives the message and for other Christians who assemble.

The Spirit of God dwells in the body of a Christian. This began the very day Jesus arose from the dead and when He came and breathed on the disciples and said, "Receive ye the Holy Ghost" (John 20:19-23). From that hour every Christian has the Holy Spirit dwelling within him.

Here is the solemn warning: "If any man defile the temple of God, him shall God destroy." Often the health and the welfare of the body of a Christian depends on whether or not he defiles the body and whether or not he sins. James 5:13-16 makes it clear that forgiveness of sin often goes along with the healing of the body, and Christians are exhorted to "confess your faults one to another, and pray one for another, that ye may be healed." Destruction of the body often comes because of sin. That is more true about fornication, drunkenness and other sins that particularly involve the body (I Cor. 6:18).

---

**VERSES 18-23:**

18 Let no man deceive himself. If any man among you seemeth to be wise in this world, let him become a fool, that he may be wise.

19 For the wisdom of this world is foolishness with God. For it is written, He taketh the wise in their own craftiness.

20 And again, The Lord knoweth the thoughts of the wise, that they are vain.

21 Therefore let no man glory in men. For all things are your's;

22 Whether Paul, or A-pŏl-'lŏs, or Çĕ-'phăs, or the world, or life, or death, or things present, or things to come; all are your's;

23 And ye are Christ's; and Christ is God's.

## We Are Not to Glory in Men but Have All Things in Christ

Since God will reward every man for his labor, according as he deserves, we must leave that in the hands of God. And since God will count as gold, silver, precious stones, things that men may think as foolishness, and since God may count that which seems wise and good to us as wood, hay and stubble, let every one very humbly leave to God the judging of the value of men in His work. May God give us simple and childlike hearts, then.

Should we glory in men? "For all things are your's." Wonderful. Paul and Apollos and the whole world, and life and death and all things are mine. Oh, how humbly we should walk, always giving Christ first place. And how rich is the Christian who owns all things in Christ. Let us rejoice in that riches and in that wisdom, not in worldly wisdom or judgments.

# I CORINTHIANS IV

## VERSES 1-8:

LET a man so account of us, as of the ministers of Christ, and stewards of the mysteries of God.

2 Moreover it is required in stewards, that a man be found faithful.

3 But with me it is a very small thing that I should be judged of you, or of man's judgment: yea, I judge not mine own self.

4 For I know nothing by myself; yet am I not hereby justified: but he that judgeth me is the Lord.

5 Therefore judge nothing before the time, until the Lord come, who both will bring to light the hidden things of darkness, and will make manifest the counsels of the hearts: and then shall every man have praise of God.

6 And these things, brethren, I have in a figure transferred to myself and to Ā-pŏl'-lŏs for your sakes; that ye might learn in us not to think of men above that which is written, that no one of you be puffed up for one against another.

7 For who maketh thee to differ from another? and what hast thou that thou didst not receive? now if thou didst receive it, why dost thou glory, as if thou hadst not received it?

8 Now ye are full, now ye are rich, ye have reigned as kings without us: and I would to God ye did reign, that we also might reign with you.

## Paul and Apollos Are Stewards, Accountable Only to God

No one could judge Paul's stewardship but God. He is a steward of divinely revealed mysteries, a ministry God-given. Who would be wise enough to evaluate his ministry? He must be faithful—God's judgment of his ministry. The Gospel Paul preached was given from God—the power from God. Paul could not claim credit for them and he dared not even judge himself.

Men see only outward things; only God sees the heart (vs. 5). We should all guard against rating God's servants. In the parable of the talents Jesus gave the same sweet phrase, "Well done, thou good and faithful servant: thou hast been faithful over a few things, I will make thee ruler over many things" (Matt. 25:21,23), to the man who doubled two talents and he who doubled five. The widow who gave two mites, Jesus said, gave more than the rich gifts of those who gave more.

And David ruled that "as his part is that goeth down to the battle, so shall his part be that tarrieth by the stuff" (I Sam. 30:24). And the reward to him that giveth a cup of cold water to a prophet may be more than that of one who gives a million (Mark 9:41).

What human wisdom would know how to balance the eloquence of Apollos (Acts 18:24,25) against the "weighty" epistles of Paul with his handicaps: "his bodily presence is weak, and his speech contemptible," as these same Corinthians judged (II Cor. 10:10)?

And more important, the preacher dare not make his ministry to please men. So Paul's preaching was "not with enticing words of man's wisdom" (I Cor. 2:4). Paul cannot please men, for often he must rebuke their sins and correct their false doctrines. To the Galatian Christians he said, "For do I now persuade men, or God? or do I seek to please men? for if I yet pleased men, I should not be the servant of Christ."

When the lying prophets of King Ahab prophesied that he would have great victory at Ramoth-gilead, Micaiah, a true prophet, was urged to do likewise. "And the messenger that was gone to call Micaiah spake unto him, saying, Behold now, the words of the prophets declare good unto the king with one mouth: let thy word, I pray thee, be like the word of one of them, and speak that which is good. And Micaiah said, As the Lord liveth, what the Lord saith unto me, that will I speak" (I Kings 22:13,14). And he prophesied, "I saw all Israel scattered upon the hills, as sheep that have not a shepherd: and the Lord said, These have no master: let them return every man to his house in peace." That did not please Ahab but it was a true prophecy.

When Jeremiah prophesied again and again the coming destruction of Jerusalem if the people did not surrender to Nebuchadnezzar, he was beaten, was put in prison more than once, and came near death. He did not please men but he represented God.

When Peter and John were commanded to speak no more in the name of Jesus, they said, "Whether it be right in the sight of God to hearken unto you more than unto God, judge ye. For we cannot but speak the things which we have seen and heard" (Acts 4:19,20). And the bitter complaint of the high priest was, "Did not we straitly command you that ye should not teach in this name? and, behold, ye have filled Jerusalem with your doctrine, and intend to bring this man's blood upon us" (Acts 5:28).

The apostle warned Timothy on this matter of not preaching to please men. In the farewell message of II Timothy 4:1-5 he says:

*"I charge thee therefore before God, and the Lord Jesus Christ, who shall judge the quick and the dead at his appearing and his kingdom; Preach the word; be instant in season, out of season; reprove, rebuke, exhort with all longsuffering and doctrine. For the time will come when they will not endure sound doctrine; but after their own lusts shall they heap to themselves teachers, having itching ears; And they shall turn away their ears from the truth, and shall be turned unto fables. But watch thou in all things, endure afflictions, do the work of an evangelist, make full proof of thy ministry."*

The preacher then must not preach to please men; he must love men, he must have power to move men and win them. But sometimes people will "turn away their ears from the truth" and sometimes they will turn against the preacher as some turned against Paul, as some turned against Jeremiah and Micaiah. Sometimes when a man preaches plainly and represents God faithfully, as Paul did when he rebuked Peter in Galatians 2:4-11, the man of God will be reproached even by good Christians. But a preacher must please God.

We would not excuse a cantankerous or arrogant spirit in the preacher. He must speak the truth, but he must do it in love. He must preach the truth, but he must have upon him the power of the Holy Spirit. He must be willing to be a servant in order to be great. But the preacher is accountable to God Himself and God will surely give each man what he deserves in reward.

---

**VERSES 9-17:**

9 For I think that God hath set forth us the apostles last, as it were appointed to death: for we are made a spectacle unto the world, and to angels, and to men.

10 We are fools for Christ's sake, but ye are wise in Christ; we are weak, but ye are strong; ye are honourable, but we are despised.

11 Even unto this present hour we both hunger, and thirst, and are naked, and are buffeted, and have no certain dwellingplace;

12 And labour, working with our own hands: being reviled, we bless; being persecuted, we suffer it:

13 Being defamed, we intreat: we are made as the filth of the world, and are the offscouring of all things unto this day.

14 I write not these things to shame you, but as my beloved sons I warn you.

15 For though ye have ten thousand instructers in Christ, yet have ye not many fathers: for in Christ Jesus I have begotten you through the gospel.

16 Wherefore I beseech you, be ye followers of me.

17 For this cause have I sent unto you Ti-mŏth´-ĕ-ŭs, who is my beloved son, and faithful in the Lord, who shall bring you into remembrance of my ways which be in Christ, as I teach every where in every church.

## God's Greatest Ministers Earn Leadership Through Suffering, Reproach and Unceasing Labor

*". . . God hath set forth us the apostles last, as it were appointed to death"* (vs. 9). It surely is in line with this passage that the Apostle James was beheaded, that Stephen was stoned to death, that John the apostle was in exile on a lonely island of Patmos, and that some others died as martyrs. We do not credit Roman traditions, and Peter was never at Rome nor was he crucified there. But the apostles did suffer loss of all things and paid a greater price for their leadership than most others.

It is not surprising that when God calls a man to the

ministry or the mission field, He seems nearly always to rub his face in the dirt of poverty and want. If a preacher does not mean business enough to suffer for Jesus, to be poor for Jesus, to have his family not as well clothed and housed as other men of equal training, he cannot be the best for God. If a man is not willing to have some opposition, to suffer some reproach for the truth, then he is not fit for leadership.

What claim has Paul to leadership when he says, "Wherefore I beseech you, be ye followers of me"? It is that he was to be willing to be counted weak. He was despised. He often went hungry and without sufficient clothes. He worked with his own hands making tents for a living for himself and his helpers sometimes. He was defamed but he still entreated. He had begotten these Corinthians through Christ as a father, and so they should follow him.

We must remember that one who would be a leader must be a servant. Jesus said, "But it shall not be so among you: but whosoever will be great among you, let him be your minister; And whosoever will be chief among you, let him be your servant: Even as the Son of man came not to be ministered unto, but to minister, and to give his life a ransom for many" (Matt. 20:26-28).

Sacrifice, reproach and misunderstanding are part of the man who would earn leadership among God's people.

Billy Sunday was slandered as a money-grabber, although he made no requirement about how much money he should get in any particular campaign, and the greatest offering he ever received in a campaign—in New York City—he turned over to the Servicemen's Center. The offering in a big campaign in Chicago he turned over entirely to the Pacific Garden Mission where he was saved.

It was this writer's pleasure to be in Billy Sunday's little cottage of five or six rooms at Winona Lake, valued at $3,800. And when I myself held citywide revival campaigns all over America, it was my custom to turn in an expense account of only $2.00 a day for meals. I must not give credence to the slanderers who hated evangelism and evangelists.

Note the tenderness in verse 15, *"For though ye have ten thousand instructers in Christ, yet have ye not many fathers: for in Christ Jesus I have begotten you through the gospel."* We are reminded of how the loving heart of Paul was broken over the heresies into which his dear converts of Galatia had fallen with false teachers.

And these people at Corinth will still be reminded of Paul's teaching (vs. 17). Timothy will remind them and teach them to live according to the principles Paul had taught them.

---

### VERSES 18-21:

18 Now some are puffed up, as though I would not come to you.

19 But I will come to you shortly, if the Lord will, and will know, not the speech of them which are puffed up, but the power.

20 For the kingdom of God is not in word, but in power.

21 What will ye? shall I come unto you with a rod, or in love, and in the spirit of meekness?

### Paul Will See Them, Coming With Authority

It is not surprising that in a young church there would be some division with many young converts not solidly grounded. Sometimes there comes arrogancy and false teachers and a turning away from the ones who had gotten them saved and led them in their first steps of spiritual truth.

We remember that Paul pleaded with Timothy, "Be not thou therefore ashamed of the testimony of our Lord, nor of me his prisoner" (II Tim. 1:8).

And Paul, though humble and though he writes with entreaty, yet knows the power of God is upon him. He can come in judgment upon them if need be. In the next chapter he will tell them plainly that on his authority they must withdraw fellowship from an adulterous, sinning Christian.

And then the authority of Paul is not that of a church or denomination but the authority of one with the power of God upon him. And he warns them that if need be he will come with a rod, that is, to rebuke and judge them and put down the arrogant and clean up the church.

And we learn in II Corinthians 1:23,24 that Paul delayed his return to Corinth: ". . . that to spare you I came not as yet unto Corinth."

When did Paul go to Corinth again? Perhaps after his three years at Ephesus, and the events there, described in Acts 19. Acts 20:1-3 tells us he went into Macedonia, then into Greece and stayed three months. That probably included Corinth. Acts 19:21,22 tells us he had planned before to go through Macedonia and Achaia but delayed and sent Timothy and Erastus.

Did Paul visit Corinth a third time? In II Corinthians 13:1 he said, "This is the third time I am coming to you." I do not find an account of a third visit before his trial and his journey to Rome and imprisonment there. But perhaps when Paul was released from his first imprisonment, as we think he was, and then later arrested again and imprisoned and put to death—that may leave room for a visit to Corinth.

There are a number of inferences that Paul was released from prison for a season. He thought he would be and that must have been stated by inspiration of God. Verse 22 of Philemon says, "But withal prepare me also a lodging: for I trust that through your prayers I shall be given unto you." And in Romans 15:24 Paul wrote, "Whensoever I take my journey into Spain, I will come to you: for I trust to see you in my journey." Then that inspired statement indicates that Paul was released from Rome, went on to Spain and then back perhaps to see Philemon and others.

In Philippians 1:25 Paul wrote, "And having this

confidence, I know that I shall abide and continue with you all for your furtherance and joy of faith." And that indicates that he probably expected to be released from prison.

In II Timothy 4:20 Paul writes from Rome, when we think was his second imprisonment, "Erastus abode at Corinth: but Trophimus have I left at Miletum sick." But Paul did not come by way of Trophimus on his first journey to Rome, so this must have been a second journey, and in that case he was probably at Corinth and left Erastus there.

# I CORINTHIANS V

## VERSE 1:

IT is reported commonly that there is fornication among you, and such fornication as is not so much as named among the Gentiles, that one should have his father's wife.

## A Christian Guilty of Fornication

Can a Christian fall into such outrageous sin? Yes, David did. The Christian has all the natural bodily desires as before; so we are commanded to "flee also youthful lusts" (II Tim. 2:22). The Christian is warned, "But fornication, and all uncleanness, or covetousness, let it not be once named among you, as becometh saints; Neither filthiness, nor foolish talking, nor jesting, which are not convenient: but rather giving of thanks" (Eph. 5:3,4).

Chapter 6 gives solemn warning about the sin of fornication, and it is obvious that young Christians are in special danger here.

And in chapter 7, verse 2 says, "Nevertheless, to avoid fornication, let every man have his own wife, and let every woman have her own husband." Christians are commanded to "mortify the deeds of the body" (Rom. 8:13). Surely God's minister ought to solemnly warn Christians of the sin of fornication. Yes, and of the other sins that lead to it. The lewd movies, immodest dress, dirty, pornographic literature, promiscuous necking and petting on the part of young people are sins that lead to other sins, and God's people need to be warned of the desperate danger in playing with sex fire, a fire that is in the bosom of every man and woman. Christians are commanded to "abstain from all appearance of evil" (I Thess. 5:22). Women are commanded to "adorn themselves in modest apparel" (I Tim. 2:9). It would be very foolish to suppose that a child of God does not need to be warned and be on guard against such sin.

2 And ye are puffed up, and have not rather mourned, that he that hath done this deed might be taken away from among you.

3 For I verily, as absent in body, but present in spirit, have judged already, as though I were present, concerning him that hath so done this deed,

4 In the name of our Lord Jesus Christ, when ye are gathered together, and my spirit, with the power of our Lord Jesus Christ,

5 To deliver such an one unto Satan for the destruction of the flesh, that the spirit may be saved in the day of the Lord Jesus.

## The Church to Withdraw From Unrepentant Members Continuing in Gross Sin

Corinthian Christians should have been shocked at the sin of this man living with his own stepmother. Not only fornication but incest and sin against his own father. They were not shocked but doubtless some excused or even defended the sinner.

The church's not mourning over this sin made all of them somewhat guilty of the sin, even as it was with Israel over the sin of Achan. When Achan had stolen some of the devoted things captured in the fall of Jericho and no one had carefully attended nor watched to avoid violation of the plain command of God, then God said to Joshua, "Israel hath sinned" (Josh. 7:11).

Now the church is commanded to take drastic action. They are to withdraw fellowship from this man. They are to *"deliver such an one unto Satan for the destruction of the flesh"* (vs. 5). In Matthew 18 Jesus had given commandment that if an individual had been trespassed against, he should go alone to the offender. Then, if need be, he could take two others with him, and then if he was not heard, the matter should be taken to the church and the church would agree that a brother had been wronged and the offender should hear the church. If not, then "let him be unto thee as an heathen man and a publican," said Jesus (Matt. 18:15-17).

But here in Corinth the offense is not against an individual but against God and the whole church. His sin would mar the image and testimony of the whole church and would infect others. It was a deadly thing. So there is no need for other preliminaries. All had known and discussed his sin. He was not only in gross sin but impenitent, and in verse 13 Paul said, "Therefore put away from among yourselves that wicked person."

He was delivered "unto Satan for the destruction of the flesh." Sin has certain inevitable results. Satan's ways are sad ways and end in destruction. All Satan's apples have worms, all Satan's promises are lies, all Satan's good times end in heartbreak.

But aside from an eventual reaping of his sowing, there seems to be here a special judgment on the man. Paul the apostle has authority and he commands the Corinthians, "In the name of our Lord Jesus Christ, when ye are gathered together, and my spirit, with the power of our Lord Jesus Christ," to deliver this man to Satan. Paul, as an apostle sent of God, was especially fitted to act for God in teaching doctrine and reproving sin, particularly until the New Testament was written. Then the congregation "with the power of our Lord Jesus Christ" had a certain authority, as Jesus gave the disciples in John 20:21-23. Spirit-led and Spirit-filled Christians are promised, "Whose soever sins ye remit, they are remitted unto them; and whose soever sins ye retain, they are retained."

*"The destruction of the flesh. . ."* (vs. 5). Dr. Scofield notes here, "Gr. *olethros,* used elsewhere, 1 Thes. 5.3; 2 Thes. 1.9; 1 Tim. 6.9, never means annihilation."

And the object here is not the ruin or the punishment of this man who has gone wrong so much as it is "that the spirit may be saved in the day of the Lord Jesus." So the earnest warning of a Christian or the rebuke of the whole church is meant to restore the man to fellowship with God and with Christians, not just to hurt him.

In Matthew 18:15 the Lord says that if one goes to his brother with an offense and the brother hear him, then "thou hast gained thy brother." That is the motive. And then in Galatians 6:1 the Scripture says, "Brethren, if a man be overtaken in a fault, ye which are spiritual, restore such an one in the spirit of meekness; considering thyself, lest thou also be tempted."

Paul never does question this man's salvation. That seems strange perhaps, but evidently Paul was right in regarding the man as a backslidden and sinning Christian, not as a lost sinner, for in II Corinthians 2:1-11 we find that the man had repented with much sorrow and was to be received back into fellowship.

Christians here, by continuing in sin, may lose the fellowship of Christians. They may have great punishment in the flesh. And since God will not and cannot send a born-again Christian to Hell, He must punish him here in this life and then he may lose rewards at the judgment seat of Christ and "shall be saved; yet so as by fire" (I Cor. 3:10-15).

It is a part of God's blessed doctrine of everlasting life, eternal salvation for His saints, "for whom the Lord loveth he chasteneth, and scourgeth every son whom he receiveth" (Heb. 12:6). God does not let sin get by.

A good illustration of that is the way God dealt with the dynasty of David, to whom He had promised the throne. In Psalm 89:28-34 the Lord explains:

*"My mercy will I keep for him for evermore, and my covenant shall stand fast with him. His seed also will I make to endure for ever, and his throne as the days of heaven. If his children forsake my law, and walk not in my judgments; If they break my statues, and keep not my commandments; Then will I visit their transgression with the rod, and their iniquity with stripes. Nevertheless my lovingkindness will I not utterly take from him, nor suffer my faithfulness to fail. My covenant will I not break, Nor alter the thing that is gone out of my lips."*

Eventually David's throne will be restored forever, with Christ sitting upon it. So God's covenant He would not break, but He would chastise any of the intermediate descendants of David as necessary. So God will not break His covenant with a Christian, but He chastises him when necessary.

-------

**VERSES 6-8:**

6 Your glorying is not good. Know ye not that a little leaven leaveneth the whole lump?
7 Purge out therefore the old leaven, that ye may be a new lump, as ye are unleavened. For even Christ our passover is sacrificed for us:
8 Therefore let us keep the feast, not with old leaven, neither with the leaven of malice and wickedness; but with the unleavened bread of sincerity and truth.

## Sin, Left Unrebuked, Unpunished, Would Work Like Leaven to Defile the Whole Group

Leaven here is mentioned with a bad spiritual meaning as it is throughout the Bible. Abraham had fed God and two angels with quickly-made cakes without leaven (Gen. 18:6). Lot had made a feast for the two angels "and did bake unleavened bread, and they did eat." The passover feast was always to be eaten with "unleavened bread" (Exod. 12:8). For seven days the feast of unleavened bread was to be continued (Exod. 12:15). No leaven was to be found in their houses in that time (Exod. 12:19,20). Leaven, picturing sin, would not do to represent Christ, the Bread of Life. So here they are warned that Christ our Passover is sacrificed for us and that we are His body, and that sin, unreproved and unpunished, would infect the whole mass of Christians, ruin their testimony and their image and lead to outbroken sin.

Leaven pictures "malice and wickedness" in verse 8.

We remember that Jesus warned the disciples to "beware of the leaven of the Pharisees and of the Sadducees" (Matt. 16:6), and there it meant "the doctrine of the Pharisees and of the Sadducees" (Matt. 16:12). Thus we see the meaning of the parable of the leaven in Matthew 13:33 when Jesus said, "The kingdom of heaven is like unto leaven, which a woman took, and hid in three measures of meal, till the whole was leavened." And that pictures the inevitable downgrade tendency in the Christian life. False doctrine and apostasy, when it is not expelled, leavens the whole lump, takes whole congregations and groups into sin and false doctrine. How important, then, that Christians should avoid any tolerance for sin and false doctrine!

---

**VERSES 9-13:**

9 I wrote unto you in an epistle not to company with fornicators:

10 Yet not altogether with the fornicators of this world, or with the covetous, or extortioners, or with idolaters; for then must ye needs go out of the world.

11 But now I have written unto you not to keep company, if any man that is called a brother be a fornicator, or covetous, or an idolater, or a railer, or a drunkard, or an extortioner; with such an one no not to eat.

12 For what have I to do to judge them also that are without? do not ye judge them that are within?

13 But them that are without God judgeth. Therefore put away from among yourselves that wicked person.

## The Bible Doctrine of Separation From Sinning Christians

Here Paul makes an important distinction. They were to withdraw fellowship from this Christian brother who went into gross sin and was impenitent. But Scripture explains that a Christian cannot avoid all contact with unconverted people. We live in this world and that means necessarily we will have contact with the unsaved and we cannot control them nor judge them.

A Christian who rides on a bus or plane or train must necessarily ride with some who are unsaved. One who buys from a store or filling station will buy from the same place where unsaved people buy. A doctor who joins a medical association will find himself with others of the same profession who are unconverted. A lawyer who is admitted to the bar will find other lawyers, some of whom are not saved.

It is not an unequal yoke to have association where necessary with unsaved people where there is no moral and spiritual bond. Lawyers are all interested in the process of the law and the courts. That is not an unequal yoke. Doctors are interested in the profession of healing and medicine and they are alike in that, whether saved or lost. A government that has diplomatic dealings with a foreign nation will sometimes have a Christian diplomat in a foreign and heathen court. David and Solomon had business dealings with Hiram, king of Tyre, a heathen king and their friend. So the command not to company with fornicators is modified to this extent, "Yet not altogether with the fornicators of this world, or with the covetous, or extortioners, or with idolaters; for then must ye needs go out of the world." No, in the realm of Christian brotherhood and fellowship and spiritual bonds, Christians are to be separate. But Paul says, "For what have I to do to judge them also that are without?" And again, "But them that are without God judgeth."

But Christian people must be very strict in their standards as to with whom they associate. If any man that is called a brother be a fornicator, or covetous, or an idolater, or a railer, or a drunkard, or an extortioner; with such an one no not to eat." I would suppose they are not to be admitted to the Lord's Supper and to Christian fellowship which is involved there, and are not to be received in Christian fellowship otherwise.

Note: *"If any man that is called a brother"* (vs. 11)—whether it be a Christian or one only pretending to be a Christian. Then these grosser sins should simply mean they are not to be accepted in full Christian fellowship until they repent.

I judge this is somewhat kin to the instructions of Paul in II Thessalonians 3:6-12 about those idle busybodies walking disorderly in that they wanted to eat without working and impose on others. Paul said of such a man, "Have no company with him, that he may be ashamed. Yet count him not as an enemy, but admonish him as a brother." In Romans 14:1 we are instructed, "Him that is weak in the faith receive ye, but not to doubtful disputations." One who believes in the great essentials of the Christian faith should be welcomed and received as a good Christian, if he is that, and even if he is weak in some minor matters, but not to disputations. If his fellowship means strife and divisions, then we may not work with him.

But here it is clear that Christians should put away from their fellowship a Christian who continues in gross sin. That means not only fornication but covetousness and railing and drunkenness and extortion they were to put away. "Therefore put away from among yourselves that wicked person."

# I CORINTHIANS VI

DARE any of you, having a matter against another, go to law before the unjust, and not before the saints?

2 Do ye not know that the saints shall judge the world? and if the world shall be judged by you, are ye unworthy to judge the smallest matters?

3 Know ye not that we shall judge angels? how much more things that pertain to this life?

4 If then ye have judgments of things pertaining to this life, set them to judge who are least esteemed in the church.

5 I speak to your shame. Is it so, that there is not a wise man among you? no, not one that shall be able to judge between his brethren?

6 But brother goeth to law with brother, and that before the unbelievers.

7 Now therefore there is utterly a fault among you, because ye go to law one with another. Why do ye not rather take wrong? why do ye not rather suffer yourselves to be defrauded?

8 Nay, ye do wrong, and defraud, and that your brethren.

## Christians Are Forbidden to Go to Law With Each Other

Christians are to settle their differences among themselves, and where two people cannot agree they should take it to other Christians for a decision. "Before the saints" here means simply before Christians. All saved people are saints.

Note, ". . .*the saints shall judge the world*" (vs. 2), *"We shall judge angels"* (vs. 3). To His twelve apostles Jesus said, "When the Son of man shall sit in the throne of his glory, ye also shall sit upon twelve thrones judging the twelve tribes of Israel" (Matt. 19:28). To the faithful servants whose invested talents gained in the parable of the talents, the Lord Jesus said, "Thou hast been faithful over a few things, I will make thee ruler over many things" (Matt. 25:21,23). And in the similar parable of the pounds one faithful servant is promised he shall rule over ten cities and the other over five cities (Luke 19:17,19). Revelation 20:6 tells us that all those in the first resurrection, the Christian resurrection, "shall be priests of God and of Christ, and shall reign with him a thousand years." Shall we judge angels? Yes, angels—"are they not all ministering spirits, sent forth to minister for them who shall be heirs of salvation?" (Heb. 1:14). Surely then, Christians, born-again people with the Spirit of God within them, ought to be able to judge between brethren and help people to have justice and peace.

The strife and accusation and bitterness of the law courts is not for a Christian against another Christian.

Will a Christian thus always get justice? No, sometimes a man will not be satisfied that he gets perfect justice. Other men may see the case differently from him. But even so there is no certainty he would be satisfied in the courts of the land. "Why do ye not rather take wrong? why do ye not rather suffer yourselves to be defrauded?" And sometimes in the law courts one would actually defraud his brother (vs. 8). The judgments of an unconverted judge, with unconverted lawyers and sometimes unsaved and biased juries, are not certain to give justice to a Christian. Even if one should lose, he should love his brethren and live peaceably with his brethren and not bring reproach on the cause of Christ by lawsuits.

Evidently God intended that Christians should be very much different from the world and that thus the society of Christians would be a distinctively sweet and pleasant haven from the wicked world about us.

---

**VERSES 9-12:**

9 Know ye not that the unrighteous shall not inherit the kingdom of God? Be not deceived: neither fornicators, nor idolaters, nor adulterers, nor effeminate, nor abusers of themselves with mankind,

10 Nor thieves, nor covetous, nor drunkards, nor revilers, nor extortioners, shall inherit the kingdom of God.

11 And such were some of you: but ye are washed, but ye are sanctified, but ye are justified in the name of the Lord Jesus, and by the Spirit of our God.

12 All things are lawful unto me, but all things are not expedient: all things are lawful for me, but I will not be brought under the power of any.

## The Unrighteous Shall Not Inherit the Kingdom

These young, immature, carnal Christians at Corinth
did not mourn over fornication. They must be impressed,
then, as we must be impressed. Unrighteousness does not
fit in with Heaven. The sins named here must not be
thought of as fitting for Christians.

Note the vast scale of sin which is mentioned here. Not
only the fornicators and idolaters and adulterers but even
the covetous and revilers are mentioned here. Covetousness
is often not regarded as a wicked sin but God so classes it.
The one who uses reviling words, has disrespect for
authority, uses unkind talk to others, may be counted a
very nice man and that is a minor flaw, but actually such
sins are not fitting for a Christian and they cannot go into
Heaven.

But some of these at Corinth had been the worst of
sinners. They have been saved now; they "are
washed. . .sanctified. . .justified." They are no longer to
be called drunkards and fornicators and idolaters.

It is true that God can make the drunkard sober, can
make the whoremonger clean, can make the infidel into a
believing saint. And that in part is meant here, but God
means much more than that. I think He means that every
child of God has a new nature that does not sin, that abhors
sin, a nature that cannot sin (I John 3:9 and I John 5:18).
It cannot mean that no born-again Christian would ever
commit any of these sins. Who is there who never had a
covetous thought, who never spoke a reviling word after
they were saved? But it does mean that the born-again
person within is changed, forgiven, cleansed and justified.
So a Christian ought to put on the new man and mortify
the deeds of the flesh. We are to be constantly watchful for
the tendency to sin, and we should hate sin.

13 Meats for the belly, and the belly for meats: but God shall destroy both it and them. Now the body is not for fornication, but for the Lord; and the Lord for the body.

14 And God hath both raised up the Lord, and will also raise up us by his own power.

15 Know ye not that your bodies are the members of Christ? shall I then take the members of Christ, and make them the members of an harlot? God forbid.

16 What? know ye not that he which is joined to an harlot is one body? for two, saith he, shall be one flesh.

17 But he that is joined unto the Lord is one spirit.

18 Flee fornication. Every sin that a man doeth is without the body; but he that committeth fornication sinneth against his own body.

19 What? know ye not that your body is the temple of the Holy Ghost which is in you, which ye have of God, and ye are not your own?

20 For ye are bought with a price: therefore glorify God in your body, and in your spirit, which are God's.

## The Christian's Body Is the Temple of the Holy Spirit

We suppose that in ancient Corinth, as people do today, the lustful and the undisciplined Christians made excuses of the constant pull of the flesh, the bodily cry for sex, and the temptations that go in a sex-conscious civilization such as they had at Corinth. So Paul must dwell on this matter until they hate fornication and see its wickedness. The body of a Christian is sacred in a particular way since it is the home of the Spirit of God. The body belongs to the Lord.

And so in Romans 12:1 we are told, "I beseech you therefore, brethren, by the mercies of God, that ye present your bodies a living sacrifice, holy, acceptable unto God, which is your reasonable service." The body belongs to God. Your hands, your feet, your eyes, your ears are His and should be kept for Him. The body is to be resurrected, even as the body of Jesus was resurrected, and so there is something specially, eternally sacred about the Christian's body.

And any yoke of Christians with the unsaved is bad, but particularly fornication is bad, making the member of Christ the member of a harlot! The Scripture says with indignation, "God forbid."

The sex relationship is a sacred matter intended when God joins a man and a woman together in marriage and they two become one flesh, and thus the husband and wife are "as being heirs together of the grace of life," bringing new life into being. And that union, which should be for a lifetime and sanctified by God's blessing permanently, ought not be the joining of a Christian to a harlot, a child of God to a child of the Devil, for sinful pleasure outside the law and outside normal duty and privilege.

Fornication is a sin against the body in a way that other sins are not.

But verse 19 tells us that "your body is the temple of the Holy Ghost which is in you, which ye have of God, and ye are not your own." Romans 8:10 says the same thing: "And if Christ be in you, the body is dead because of sin; but the Spirit is life because of righteousness."

The night before he was crucified Jesus promised the future indwelling of the Spirit: "For he dwelleth with you, and shall be in you" (John 14:17). The indwelling of the Spirit in the body of a Christian was also promised in John 7:37-39:

*"In the last day, that great day of the feast, Jesus stood and cried, saying, If any man thirst, let him come unto me, and drink. He that believeth on me, as the scripture hath said, out of his belly shall flow rivers of living water. (But this spake he of the Spirit, which they that believe on him should receive: for the Holy Ghost was not yet given; because that Jesus was not yet glorified.)"*

Jesus was not then glorified. But when He arose from the dead and appeared in His glorified body, we are told in John 20:22 that He "breathed on them, and saith unto them, Receive ye the Holy Ghost." That day the Spirit of God moved into the body of every Christian, as we understand it, and now when one is born of the Spirit, the Spirit remains within the body of the new convert and makes the body His temple.

There are no other temples of God on earth now. Jesus lamented over Jerusalem and said, "Behold, your house is left unto you desolate" (Luke 13:35). We believe that when the veil of the Temple was torn in two from the top to the bottom at the time of the crucifixion of the Lord Jesus, God was saying to the world that now the Temple at Jerusalem was vacant and the ceremonies there picturing the Gospel were now valueless.

The Old Testament prophet rightly said, "The Lord is in his holy temple: let all the earth keep silence before him" (Hab. 2:20). For over the mercy seat in the holy of holies the Shekinah Glory was the living presence of God. I think that was the same as the pillar of cloud by day and the pillar of fire by night which led the children of Israel in the wilderness. But now God Himself through the Holy Spirit has moved into the bodies of Christians and God has no other temple on earth.

It is significant that not a single church building is mentioned in the New Testament. Were there any church buildings? If so God was particularly careful that no one should revere them or honor them. God does not live in church houses. Many a home where Christians pray and read God's Word and delight in His presence is more nearly a house of God than the church house. It is wrong, then, to speak of "reverence for the house of God." We should respect the rights of other people. We should see that services should be decent and in order, without confusion. We should respect the man of God. But God has no temple on earth but a human body; no church auditorium then ought to be called "the sanctuary." It is not.

O Christian, you are bought with a price! At an awful cost, Jesus Christ suffered for us and bought us for God. It would be dishonest then for any Christian to claim that he had rights to live his own life undirected, uncontrolled, unsupervised by the blessed Spirit of God.

# I CORINTHIANS VII

NOW concerning the things whereof ye wrote unto me: It is good for a man not to touch a woman.

2 Nevertheless, to avoid fornication, let every man have his own wife, and let every woman have her own husband.

3 Let the husband render unto the wife due benevolence: and likewise also the wife unto the husband.

4 The wife hath not power of her own body, but the husband: and likewise also the husband hath not power of his own body, but the wife.

5 Defraud ye not one the other, except it be with consent for a time, that ye may give yourselves to fasting and prayer; and come together again, that Satan tempt you not for your incontinency.

6 But I speak this by permission, and not of commandment.

7 For I would that all men were even as I myself. But every man hath his proper gift of God, one after this manner, and another after that.

8 I say therefore to the unmarried and widows, It is good for them if they abide even as I.

9 But if they cannot contain, let them marry: for it is better to marry than to burn.

## Marriage Is Honorable, Blessed of God

*"It is good for a man not to touch a woman"* (vs. 1). Does that seem strange? Remember that the angels of God "neither marry, nor are given in marriage," and in the perfect state of glorified resurrection bodies, we will not marry. So if there be no strong desire or unusual pressure of sex instinct, one might find a blessed, happy life without marriage.

But since the sex instinct is stronger than any but self-preservation, we are told, it would take a consuming devotion, like that of Paul, and the highest form of Christian love and Holy Spirit possession, like that mentioned by Jesus in Luke 14:26, so that for Christ a man would "hate . . . his father, and mother, and wife, and children, and brethren, and sisters, yea, and his own life also," to be a disciple of Christ. Only a consuming, surpassing love for Christ and occupation with His business would usually make normal men and women content to live without the normal happiness and blessing of marriage and home and children. No doubt the sex interest and instinct, so powerful, was made that way by God's plan: first for procreation and second for the happiness and comfort of husband and wife. But Paul and a few others have found all the instinct and sex attraction sublimated, fulfilled, in love for Christ and His work.

Jesus said in Matthew 19:12, "For there are some eunuchs, which were so born from their mother's womb: and there are some eunuchs, which were made eunuchs of men: and there be eunuchs, which have made themselves eunuchs for the kingdom of heaven's sake. He that is able to receive it, let him receive it." It is obvious that no doubt a few people are intended to be happy single. But others are not so intended, and each one should take the place and plan of life given him of God.

Normal sex life in marriage has no restrictions but what love and kindness and mutual happiness require. As we see in verses 4 and 5, the wife does not have authority over her body; it belongs to her husband. The husband does not have authority over his body; it belongs to his wife. They are to satisfy each the other and neither is to defraud the other. Where God has not made any rules, men should not make rules.

And here we are told that the husband and wife may consent to be apart for a time, to give themselves to fasting and prayer. But that is only permitted, it is not commanded. Even so, they should not be apart long enough to make it a matter of temptation or unusual desire and fret to them.

Yes, Paul would rather all were burning with such holy concern for souls and such preoccupation with the Lord and His work that they need not marry. So, if one is single or a widow and has no need, let him be happy to remain unmarried. But it is better to marry than to burn, better than to be troubled with unfulfilled desires, we are told.

10 And unto the married I command, yet not I, but the Lord, Let not the wife depart from her husband:

11 But and if she depart, let her remain unmarried, or be reconciled to her husband: and let not the husband put away his wife.

12 But to the rest speak I, not the Lord: If any brother hath a wife that believeth not, and she be pleased to dwell with him, let him not put her away.

13 And the woman which hath an husband that believeth not, and if he be pleased to dwell with her, let her not leave him.

14 For the unbelieving husband is sanctified by the wife, and the unbelieving wife is sanctified by the husband: else were your children unclean; but now are they holy.

15 But if the unbelieving depart, let him depart. A brother or a sister is not under bondage in such cases: but God hath called us to peace.

16 For what knowest thou, O wife, whether thou shalt save thy husband? or how knowest thou, O man, whether thou shalt save thy wife?

## Marriage Is Not to Be Broken

The wife is not to depart from her husband. If the marriage seems intolerable and she feels she cannot live with him, then "let her remain unmarried, or be reconciled to her husband." And the husband is not to put away the wife.

This is a repetition of the commandment Jesus gave; so Paul says, "I command, yet not I, but the Lord." He refers to the command of the Lord Jesus in the Gospels: in Matthew 5:31,32 and 19:3-12; Mark 10:1-12; Luke 16:18. Mark and Luke report this saying of Jesus, "What therefore God hath joined together, let not man put asunder," and again, "Whosoever shall put away his wife, and marry another, committeth adultery against her. And if a woman shall put away her husband, and be married to another, she committeth adultery" (Mark 10:9,11,12). But in the two references in Matthew, Jesus adds the condition for divorce, "except it be for fornication."

Some would make a distinction that fornication is a sin committed before marriage and that adultery is a sin committed after marriage. That seems not to be a scriptural interpretation, for in this case the man under question in I Corinthians 5:1 and following committed fornication with his stepmother. She certainly was married and very possibly he was. No, fornication is the same sin as adultery and covered in the same one of the Ten Commandments, "Thou shalt not commit adultery." However, fornication seems to indicate a repeated or habitual sin. The Greek word is *porneuo* and the term *whoremonger* in the Scriptures is á form of the same word. So, fornication, that is, continued adultery, is allowed to break the marriage. Divorce is not commanded in such a case but is permitted according to the words of the Saviour in Matthew 5:31,32 and Matthew 19:9.

Yet always divorce is hateful and wrong and always, when possible, it is right to have reconciliation and restoration of the marriage. Sometimes if a continued course of prostitution or adultery on the part of a wife would seem to make proper continuation of marriage impossible, the same might be true about a continual course of whoremongering on the part of the husband.

Does divorce give a right to remarriage? Well, bear in mind verse 11: the wife should "remain unmarried, or be reconciled to her husband."

However, there are times when people precipitately break a marriage and then go on to marry someone else. In such case, the first marriage is broken and seems cannot be restored. And to live with a new husband or wife would surely be the same as continued adultery outside of marriage, which surely makes divorce sometimes permissible, as Jesus seems to teach in Matthew 5:31,32 and in Matthew 19:9.

In the Bible, divorce means what it means in common language today—that the home is broken, that the people involved are no longer married.

In fact, in the Old Testament divorce was allowed on lesser grounds than are required in the New Testament. Deuteronomy 24:1-4 says when a woman has been divorced she has only one husband, and the man to whom she was first married and then divorced is called "her former husband." It is not scriptural language, then, to say that one who has been divorced and remarried "has two living wives."

Divorce is always hateful, is always a handicap and should never be encouraged. But when awful sin has been committed and repented of, sometimes there is nothing to do but to ask forgiveness. If one committed a murder, he could not bring the victim back to life. He could only seek forgiveness for his crime. If one wickedly breaks up a marriage and then marries another, there is no way to undo the sin of divorce, it seems, but it can be forgiven to a repentant heart.

Men sometimes demand that the second marriage be broken. God does not demand that, and we have no authority to do so either.

We do not believe that the requirements that a pastor must be "the husband of one wife" (I Tim. 3:2) definitely refers to one who is divorced. No preacher ought to be divorced, but sometimes a wrecked marriage happened before conversion. And the Bible does not say, and we should not say, that when a sin in the past is forgiven and the person has done all to right it, that he cannot be forgiven and that he cannot be used of God now.

When there has been a divorce, there has been disgrace and a cause of reproach. It must be lived down, because it is a hindrance, but the same thing is true about other gross sins. If one has gotten drunk or has committed a crime, surely that disqualifies him for public service for a time, or until he proves himself by godly living and humility of mind.

But Paul says, *"But to the rest speak I, not the Lord"* (vs. 12). He does not mean at all that his command is not inspired. No, what he is saying is that this is additional revelation from God besides what Jesus the Lord had spoken in the Gospels. Jesus did not take up the matter of a

Christian's living with an unsaved mate as far as the Gospels record.

So Paul says that in such a case the marriage should not be broken just because one is a Christian and the mate is not. No doubt the great gulf that exists between a born-again child of God and an unconverted child of the Devil surely has made questions, has made trouble and turmoil in the heart of many a Christian so placed. But the marriage is a permanent contract. What God has joined together, man shall not put asunder. It is foolish for people to sometimes say the marriage was not made in Heaven, therefore it is all right to break it. Not so. Where human government sanctions a marriage, God holds the marriage binding. The Christian with an unsaved mate should live with that mate patiently and lovingly.

*"For the unbelieving husband is sanctified by the wife"* (vs. 14). That simply means that the marriage is legitimate and the children are legitimate, because the marriage is an honorable marriage.

*"But if the unbelieving depart, let him depart"* (vs. 15). Sometimes a Christian living out and out for God is offensive to his mate, not because the Christian is cantankerous or unkind or rebellious but because the unsaved person hates Christ and Christianity. I think that is rare. If the unbelieving husband depart, let him depart.

*"A brother or a sister is not under bondage in such cases: but God hath called us to peace"* (vs. 15). Dr. Ironside seemed to think that means that if the unconverted mate will not go on with the marriage, then the Christian has a right to a divorce. We do not know since the Scripture is not explicit here, but certainly a Christian is not bound to live with an unsaved mate who will not have him or her.

But far better for the Christian wife to win her unsaved husband. First Peter 3:1,2 encourages that: "Likewise, ye wives, be in subjection to your own husbands; that, if any obey not the word, they also may without the word be won by the conversation of the wives; While they behold your chaste conversation coupled with fear." The godly wife who loves her husband, who obeys him, as the Scripture commands, would surely be a more loving and helpful wife and would surely be a tremendous influence on an ungodly husband; so the Christian mate ought to be able to win the unsaved mate. Because one is now saved and the other unsaved is no real reason for divorce.

---

**VERSES 17-27:**

17 But as God hath distributed to every man, as the Lord hath called every one, so let him walk. And so ordain I in all churches.

18 Is any man called being circumcised? let him not become uncircumcised. Is any called in uncircumcision? let him not be circumcised.

19 Circumcision is nothing, and uncircumcision is nothing, but the keeping of the commandments of God.

20 Let every man abide in the same calling wherein he was called.

21 Art thou called being a servant? care not for it: but if thou mayest be made free, use it rather.

22 For he that is called in the Lord, being a servant, is the Lord's freeman: likewise also he that is called, being free, is Christ's servant.

23 Ye are bought with a price; be not ye the servants of men.

24 Brethren, let every man, wherein he is called, therein abide with God.

25 Now concerning virgins I have no commandment of the Lord: yet I give my judgment, as one that hath obtained mercy of the Lord to be faithful.

26 I suppose therefore that this is good for the present distress, I say, that it is good for a man so to be.

27 Art thou bound unto a wife? seek not to be loosed. Art thou loosed from a wife? seek not a wife.

## The Christian Is to Be Content Wherever God Has Placed Him

It is a part of this old carnal nature of ours to be dissatisfied, to murmur with our circumstances, to wish for a change. So the Christian may even argue to himself that he can be a better Christian if he were somewhere else, if he were pastor of a different church, or if he were a member of a different church, or if he had a different wife.

But this discontent is generally wrong. "God hath not given us the spirit of fear; but of power, and of love, and of a sound [settled] mind." And the psalmist David was inspired to say, "O God, my heart is fixed; I will sing and give praise, even with my glory" (Ps. 108:1). And in Psalm 112:7,8, of "a good man" it is said, "He shall not be afraid of evil tidings: his heart is fixed, trusting in the Lord. His heart is established, he shall not be afraid." So here the divine command is that one is to be content where God has put him.

Is one man circumcised a Jew? Then let him be a Christian Jew but not conceal the fact that he is a Jew and not throw away his contact with loved ones and friends and the blessing God gave to Jews.

Is one a Gentile, uncircumcised? Then, of course, do not try to ape the Jews, do not undertake to follow the ceremonial law. Discontent with your own inheritance is wrong.

Is one called, "being a servant"? that is, a slave (the Greek word is *doulous*). Now it is true that the great impact of the Christian religion where we are commanded to love our neighbors as ourselves, will eventually do away with slavery among Christians. But one who is a slave should not seek a revolution nor seek to avoid the obligations of his state. God permitted slavery under some circumstances in the Old Testament, and doubtless, under certain conditions, some poor, ignorant man might fare better as a slave than running his own life. At any rate, in every individual case, God knows a man's state and permits it and one should feel content in the place God has placed him.

It is a part of our selfish nature that no man wants to take orders, that one feels he must not have a boss. The little child in the highchair, whose mother is carefully feeding him with a spoon, says, "I want to do it myself!" The rebellion of the prodigal son against his father is typical of the carnal nature in all of us. The resentment of the worker against his boss, the resentment of the citizen against the traffic laws and against speed limits, is part of the same thing. Be content where you are. But if God frees the slave, let him rejoice; he is still God's slave. If the laborer gets to be foreman, let him rejoice; but he is still under orders from God.

Is one married, then do not seek to be unmarried. In a great majority of cases, those who break the marriage for "incompatibility" or personality clashes, later find they are unhappy and they lost more than they gained. Somebody says that "love has died," but marriage is a solemn contract not to be broken. People stay married because they have enough character to do right and because they keep their obligations. That is the secret of happiness in marriage.

A letter which has just come tells how a man is not happy with his second wife and longs for his first wife who was divorced. Many divorces come from the weakness of our human nature, longing for a change, imagining other people have better than we have, that the grass on the other side of the fence looks greener, etc.

*"Art thou loosed from a wife? seek not a wife"* (vs. 27). Do not be anxious to marry. Is it so bad to be single, lonely? Worse than being unmarried is to be married to the wrong man or wrong woman. An old proverb says, "Marry in haste, repent at leisure." Often a widower, left desolate by the death of his wife, feels he must have comfort and companionship such as he had before. So he marries hastily and finds the marriage is not blessed, finds he was taken in by a woman seeking security and perhaps his money. A young woman, feeling that her opportunity is slipping away, may hasten to take an offer of marriage because it seems the only one she will have. That does not turn out happily. One who is single should wait for the clear approval of God before marriage. Those who set out to seek marriage overanxiously are likely to have great sorrow.

Many a pastor feels he should move to another field where he will have a greater opportunity. But if God put him where he is, he is to stay until God moves him. More often a man needs a new zeal, a new faith, a new anointing of the Holy Spirit for a greater work where he is. Let Christians, then, learn to be content and thank God for the blessings where they are.

---

### VERSES 28-38:

28 But and if thou marry, thou hast not sinned; and if a virgin marry, she hath not sinned. Nevertheless such shall have trouble in the flesh: but I spare you.

29 But this I say, brethren, the time is short: it remaineth, that both they that have wives be as though they had none;

30 And they that weep, as though they wept not; and they that rejoice, as though they rejoiced not; and they that buy, as though they possessed not;

31 And they that use this world, as not abusing it: for the fashion of this world passeth away.

32 But I would have you without carefulness. He that is unmarried careth for the things that belong to the Lord, how he may please the Lord:

33 But he that is married careth for the things that are of the world, how he may please his wife.

34 There is difference also between a wife and a virgin. The unmarried woman careth for the things of the Lord, that she may be holy both in body and in spirit: but she that is married careth for the things of the world, how she may please her husband.

35 And this I speak for your own profit; not that I may cast a snare upon you, but for that which is comely, and that ye may attend upon the Lord without distraction.

36 But if any man think that he behaveth himself uncomely toward his virgin, if she pass the flower of her age, and need so require, let him do what he will, he sinneth not: let them marry.

37 Nevertheless he that standeth stedfast in his heart, having no necessity, but hath power over his own will, and hath so decreed in his heart that he will keep his virgin, doeth well.

38 So then he that giveth her in marriage doeth well; but he that giveth her not in marriage doeth better.

## To Marry or Not to Marry

Marriage is not wrong. God prepared a wife for Adam and commanded him, "Multiply, and replenish the earth" (Gen. 1:28). Again, after the flood, God said to Noah, "Multiply, and replenish the earth" (Gen. 9:1). And in Hebrews 13:4 we are told, "Marriage is honourable in all, and the bed undefiled."

It is clearly presumed that ordinarily the pastor will be married, and should be, for the instruction is given that he should be "the husband of one wife" (I Tim. 3:2). So marriage is not wrong. The Roman plan to forbid priests to marry was not from God. It is true that some should not marry, but many should, and marriage is properly called among Christians "holy matrimony."

But verses 29 to 31 remind us that time is short, that to be married or not to be married is not a major matter compared to eternal blessedness. One who weeps for loneliness or rejoices in companionship (vs. 30) will soon find that the weeping or the rejoicing over earthly loneliness or fellowship is past and those who own much or own little will find it matters not in the next world.

But there are obligations and dangers in marriage relationship. Paul was inspired to say, *"But I would have you without carefulness"* (vs. 32). There are obligations, there are burdens, with a family. Surely, in the case of Paul, one so wholly dedicated to getting out the Gospel, marriage would have been a hindrance. He had little financial support, he had no settled home, he had no time for the obligations of a wife and family. And so sometimes a missionary or an evangelist, or some other Christian may give himself so wholly day and night to God's work that he can be content and do more for God without marriage and a family. At any rate, one must take it into consideration that there are burdens, there are responsibilities in marriage and these may limit one's service for God. A man may be tempted to please his wife instead of pleasing God. The wife may be tempted to please her husband and not to seek first the kingdom of God.

It is true that the wife must obey her husband, even if he is unsaved (I Pet. 3:1,2) and so an unspiritual husband or an unsaved husband would limit her usefulness. In all this Paul's concern and ours ought to be *"that ye may attend upon the Lord without distraction"* (vs. 35).

But again, he must remind us in verses 36 to 38 that marriage is permissible. It is not wrong, and it is often a part of the best way of happiness and usefulness. It is not a sin to marry and it is not a sin to remain single, provided your heart can be happy and wholly given to the Lord.

However, we have been warned solemnly, in verse 2 above, "Nevertheless, to avoid fornication, let every man have his own wife, and let every woman have her own husband," and in verse 9, "It is better to marry than to burn." God did not mean many men to be apostles, and marriage is normal for the ordinary Christian.

---

### VERSES 39,40:

39 The wife is bound by the law as long as her husband liveth; but if her husband be dead, she is at liberty to be married to whom she will; only in the Lord. 40 But she is happier if she so abide, after my judgment: and I think also that I have the Spirit of God.

## Marriage Is for Life

Marriage is "'til death do us part" as the wedding vows often say. Jesus said, "What therefore God hath joined together, let not man put asunder" (Mark 10:9). A wife is bound "as long as her husband liveth." There is no blameless way to break marriage. Here, as in Mark 10:11,12 and Luke 16:18, no exception is mentioned.

Ordinarily among Christians, for a mate to become a continued adulterer, that is, a fornicator, would be rare. Yet the single exception is mentioned twice by the Lord Jesus in Matthew 5:31,32 and Matthew 19:9. "And I say unto you, Whosoever shall put away his wife, *except it be for fornication,* and shall marry another, committeth adultery: and whoso marrieth her which is put away doth commit adultery." So, the exception is allowed. Probably, in reality, the mate is in continual fornication and has already "put away" the wife, or the husband is already guilty of breaking the marriage spiritually. So divorce is permissible, though not commanded. The wife, "bound to her husband" but for fornication, that is, continued adultery, has already really broken those bonds.

Suppose the home has already been broken, the mates remarried to others; then let us suppose one has become a Christian and is concerned to do right. The wrong cannot be righted, but it can be forgiven. A second divorce or two divorces would not undo the wrong. Even under the law, much less exacting than the New Testament, a woman who has divorced and married another man must not go back to the first husband. He is not now "her husband" but as the Scripture says "her former husband" (Deut. 24:1-4).

Should divorce, even without the cause Jesus allowed—fornication—disqualify one for Christian work? Yes, as any of those sins rated along with fornication does: ". . . a fornicator, or covetous, or an idolater, or a railer, or a drunkard, or an extortioner" (I Cor. 5:11)—any of those sins would mean a Christian is disqualified until he repents and proves it; disqualified until he, in a sense, lives down the sin, never defending it, and proves by his life that he is now a devoted, clean Christian. But the murderer, the covetous, the extortioner, the fornicator can be forgiven; the sin can be washed, the Christian justified, as is plainly stated in I Corinthians 6:11.

Churches should be as anxious for morality as the Lord is, but should be as forgiving as God is also. Where God makes no rule about one who has been divorced and remarried being disqualified to teach or work in a church, then a church should make no such rule. Where God makes no rule that they should break a second marriage, then churches should make none.

# I CORINTHIANS VIII

NOW as touching things offered unto idols, we know that we all have knowledge. Knowledge puffeth up, but charity edifieth.

2 And if any man think that he knoweth any thing, he knoweth nothing yet as he ought to know.

3 But if any man love God, the same is known of him.

4 As concerning therefore the eating of those things that are offered in sacrifice unto idols, we know that an idol is nothing in the world, and that there is none other God but one.

5 For though there be that are called gods, whether in heaven or in earth, (as there be gods many, and lords many,)

6 But to us there is but one God, the Father, of whom are all things, and we in him; and one Lord Jesus Christ, by whom are all things, and we by him.

## The Problem of Meats Offered to Idols

*"We all have knowledge"* (vs. 1). So Christians at Corinth, especially the more mature ones, would know, as we do, that an idol is not God. It is a bit of wood, or stone, or metal, with no life and no power. They could scoff, as does the inspired prophet in Isaiah 44:9,10: "They that make a graven image are all of them vanity; and their delectable things shall not profit; and they are their own witnesses; they see not, nor know; that they may be ashamed. Who hath formed a god, or molten a graven image that is profitable for nothing?" Yes, God's prophet mocks them:

*"He heweth him down cedars, and taketh the cypress and the oak, which he strengtheneth for himself among the trees of the forest: he planteth an ash, and the rain doth nourish it. Then shall it be for a man to burn: for he will take thereof, and warm himself; yea, he kindleth it, and baketh bread; yea, he maketh a god, and worshippeth it; he maketh it a graven image, and falleth down thereto. He burneth part thereof in the fire; with part thereof he eateth flesh; he roasteth roast, and is satisfied: yea, he warmeth himself, and saith, Aha, I am warm, I have seen the fire: And the residue thereof he maketh a god, even his graven*

*image: he falleth down unto it, and worshippeth it, and prayeth unto it, and saith, Deliver me; for thou art my god. They have not known nor understood: for he hath shut their eyes, that they cannot see; and their hearts, that they cannot understand."*—Isa. 44:14-18.

So to an informed Christian, an idol is nothing. So meats offered to idols have no significance to an informed Christian. When offered to an idol ceremoniously and then sold in the market to the general public, they were simply meats. To a Christian buying such food without even asking if or considering if it were offered once ceremoniously to an idol, the meat gave no offence. There is only one God, one Lord Jesus, God's Son. Others are not gods and should not be considered as gods. So, I Corinthians 8:8 says, "But meat commendeth us not to God: for neither, if we eat, are we the better; neither, if we eat not, are we the worse." My standing with God does not depend on whether I eat this kind of meat, or that, or none. Being a good Christian does not mean simply a set of rules. It is far more! It is a heart matter of devoted love and obedience to God and love for others.

---

**VERSES 7-13:**

7 Howbeit there is not in every man that knowledge: for some with conscience of the idol unto this hour eat it as a thing offered unto an idol; and their conscience being weak is defiled.

8 But meat commendeth us not to God: for neither, if we eat, are we the better; neither, if we eat not, are we the worse.

9 But take heed lest by any means this liberty of your's become a stumblingblock to them that are weak.

10 For if any man see thee which hast knowledge sit at meat in the idol's temple, shall not the conscience of him which is weak be emboldened to eat those things which are offered to idols;

11 And through thy knowledge shall the weak brother perish, for whom Christ died?

12 But when ye sin so against the brethren, and wound their weak conscience, ye sin against Christ.

13 Wherefore, if meat make my brother to offend, I will eat no flesh while the world standeth, lest I make my brother to offend.

## Christians Must Be Careful Not to Cause Weak Christians to Stumble

But wait! *"Howbeit there is not in every man that knowledge"* (vs. 7). I may know that there is no other God, but some do not know that. Suppose a heathen who is rebuked for offering meats to an idol answers back, "But this Christian eats the same meat dedicated to the idol, laid out before an idol before it is sold on the market." So the Christian might provide an excuse for an idolater, might comfort him in his idolatry.

Of course, if there were only mature Christians to consider, all would know that that was only an excuse. But a weak Christian would stumble at the matter. If he himself eats, he may still have lingering memories of the time he worshipped the same idol, and in his mind the meat is tainted. If he eats thinking it wrong, it is wrong. For one to choose to do what offends his conscience is a sin. "The spirit of man is the candle of the Lord, searching all the inward parts of the belly" (Prov. 20:27).

His conscience represents God as far He knows at the moment. To decide to do wrong is wrong even if otherwise it would not be wrong. "Whatsoever is not of faith is sin" (Rom. 14:23). But many a weak Christian will drink alcoholic beverages if other Christians do, although he is convinced it is wrong. If a Christian goes to the lewd, violent, godless movies, young Christians who feel and resent the wicked, carnal pull of them will also go.

So, the Christians of Corinth, who knew an idol was nothing and who ate meats offered to idols simply as meat, must think of weaker Christians and not cause them to do what they think is wrong. As verse 13 says, it is better never to eat meat at all than to cause a Christian brother to fall into sin and lose his Christian happiness, joy and usefulness. Christians are to "abstain from all appearance of evil" (I Thess. 5:22). We are commanded not only to be honest but to "provide things honest in the sight of all men" (Rom. 12:17).

Note the example of II Kings 18:4 when King Hezekiah destroyed the brasen serpent which had been preserved because it was used to picture Christ in Numbers 21:5-9. It had become an idol and so could not be kept and valued and treasured.

Early Christians, finding statues of the Greek gods and goddesses, broke off their heads, as at Salamis in Cyprus, for example. And so did the crusaders the statues of Roman gods at Caesarea and Ashkelon, and elsewhere.

We must not think, however, that in matters where there is no serious room for leading others astray, one must be enslaved by the conscience of the weak and untaught Christians. Must all Christians refrain from wearing buttons on their clothes because to some groups of Christians it is a sign of vanity? Must a Christian man never wear a tie because to some people it is worldliness? Must I observe the Jewish Sabbath because many confuse Sunday with the Old Testament Sabbath? No, we are plainly commanded, "Let no man therefore judge you in meat, or in drink, or in respect of an holyday, or of the new moon, or of the sabbath days: Which are a shadow of things to come; but the body is of Christ" (Col. 2:16,17). On such matters, Christians are to have liberty and not to judge others who eat meat or do not. Romans 14:1-6 tells us that one who thinks it wrong to eat meat, then let him eat no meat, but not judge others. One who thinks he must observe a certain day that others do not observe, let him do so but not judge others. But Christians are to take heed not to cause other Christians to stumble in doubtful matters.

# I CORINTHIANS IX

AM I not an apostle? am I not free? have I not seen Jesus Christ our Lord? are not ye my work in the Lord?

2 If I be not an apostle unto others, yet doubtless I am to you: for the seal of mine apostleship are ye in the Lord.

3 Mine answer to them that do examine me is this,

4 Have we not power to eat and to drink?

5 Have we not power to lead about a sister, a wife, as well as other apostles, and as the brethren of the Lord, and Cē'-phăs?

6 Or I only and Barnabas, have not we power to forbear working?

## Paul Defends His Apostleship

An apostle was one especially called with special authority to speak for God. When one was elected to take the apostleship of Judas after he had committed suicide, he must be one associated with Jesus all the time—"from the baptism of John"—and so able to give "witness with us of his resurrection" (Acts 1:21,22). Paul was made an exception by a miraculous appearance of Jesus to him on the way to Damascus. He had "seen Jesus Christ our Lord" as was required of an apostle. He had the Gospel specially revealed to him (Gal. 1:11,12) instead of having the instructions the twelve had had in Jesus' personal ministry.

These Christians at Corinth were witnesses of this apostleship. With power and authority beyond the ordinary, he had won them, had set up the church and had proved his apostleship.

Some no doubt thought that Paul, who was not one of the twelve, should not receive an apostle's respect. Some no doubt thought that since he had no family to support and was a skilled tentmaker, as is shown when he first arrived at Corinth (Acts 18:1,2), that he did not deserve financial support. But since he labored so abundantly, did he not have need to eat? Must only he and Barnabas be always going unmarried, laboring night and day?

---

7 Who goeth a warfare any time at his own charges? who planteth a vineyard, and eateth not of the fruit thereof? or who feedeth a flock, and eateth not of the milk of the flock?

8 Say I these things as a man? or saith not the law the same also?

9 For it is written in the law of Moses, Thou shalt not muzzle the mouth of the ox that treadeth out the corn. Doth God take care for oxen?

10 Or saith he it altogether for our sakes? For our sakes, no doubt, this is written: that he that ploweth should plow in hope; and that he that thresheth in hope should be partaker of his hope.

11 If we have sown unto you spiritual things, is it a great thing if we shall reap your carnal things?

12 If others be partakers of this power over you, are not we rather? Nevertheless we have not used this power; but suffer all things, lest we should hinder the gospel of Christ.

13 Do ye not know that they which minister about holy things live of the things of the temple? and they which wait at the altar are partakers with the altar?

14 Even so hath the Lord ordained that they which preach the gospel should live of the gospel.

## They That Preach the Gospel Are to Live by the Gospel

The Gospel is free. Every saved person ought to take the Gospel to all he can. Then why should we pay preachers who spend all their time in the Gospel ministry? So some thought in Paul's day; so some enemies of the Gospel and some untaught and worldly Christians would say today.

No doubt they had known Jewish priests or the priests at an idol temple who were of no help to the people but were idle and worldly. And even today many know ministers who never win a soul, who do not live sacrificial or holy lives. Some pastors with great salaries and big homes may not deserve all the luxuries they have. Now and then a spectacular religious leader makes great claims, makes merchandise of the Gospel and so gives critics an excuse to slander preachers and say they preach for money. But all are wrong who suppose a preacher who labors earnestly in the Gospel should not have support financially. There is a

Bible principle and command that *"they which preach the gospel should live of the gospel"* (vs. 14). If a man goes to war as a soldier, should not the government and thus the people whom he represents and protects, support him (vs. 7)? When a man keeps a farm or vineyard, should he not live off the fruit of it? If a man keeps cattle, should he not have milk and meat?

God taught this very sweetly in the ceremonial law in Deuteronomy 25:4, "Thou shalt not muzzle the ox when he treadeth out the corn." Paul quotes it here in verse 9, and again in I Timothy 5:17. As the ox went round and round on the grain breaking it out of the husk so it could be winnowed and furnish bread for men for a year—must the hungry ox not enjoy what he can eat as he labors? Now we learn that it was not simply for the oxen's sake but for every preacher, who spends all his life for Christ, to know that God wants him cared for. If a man would have concern for his oxen that labor, so God has concern for His workers, and they should be paid.

We are reminded in verse 13 that priests in the Temple lived off the offerings to God. Should not God's preachers then be supported by those who have been won and blessed and helped spiritually by his ministry? That is the teaching also of Galatians 6:6, "Let him that is taught in the word communicate unto him that teacheth in all good things." The one who is taught is to "communicate," that is, "share" material things with the one who feeds him and teaches him spiritually. So the pastor, the evangelist, the radio preacher who blesses others with spiritual food should be blessed by the carnal and material means of those he helps.

And the support should be more for the more ardent, faithful, sacrificial minister. First Timothy 5:17, 18 says, "Let the elders that rule well be counted worthy of double honour, especially they who labour in the word and doctrine. For the scripture saith, Thou shalt not muzzle the ox that treadeth out the corn. And, The labourer is worthy of his reward."

Once a gifted man planned to lay by enough support so that along with retirement pay he could, upon retirement, become a preacher with no offering or salary but he would give his labor free. Thus he gave the main part of his life to the secular world. He thought he could have more influence and win more souls if he never took an offering. He was wrong. Perhaps it was sinful pride, a determination to pay his own way, but that is not God's way. God's plainly announced way is that "they which preach the gospel should live of the gospel."

Actually, when people are taught to give to support the Word of God, they are taught to be better Christians. They will prosper more materially. They will love God more. They will renounce the world more easily and more readily, will trust God more and have more daily proof of God's care and faithfulness. So Paul was inspired to urge that the Christians must be taught "this grace also," the grace of sacrificial, joyful giving even out of great poverty, as he said about the Macedonian Christians when he urged these Corinthian Christians to learn this grace (II Cor. 8:1-6).

---

**VERSES 15-18:**

15 But I have used none of these things: neither have I written these things, that it should be so done unto me: for it were better for me to die, than that any man should make my glorying void.

16 For though I preach the gospel, I have nothing to glory of: for necessity is laid upon me; yea, woe is unto me, if I preach not the gospel!

17 For if I do this thing willingly, I have a reward: but if against my will, a dispensation of the gospel is committed unto me.

18 What is my reward then? Verily that, when I preach the gospel, I may make the gospel of Christ without charge, that I abuse not my power in the gospel.

## But God's Ministers Must Not Be Too Much Concerned About Money

*"But I have used none of these things,"* says Paul (vs.

15). Paul did not demand what they should have given gladly. He had worked at tentmaking with Aquilla and Priscilla when he first came to Corinth, earning his own way while preaching every Sabbath in a synagogue (Acts 18:1-4). But when Silas and Timothy came from Macedonia bringing some support from the Philippian Christians, as we suppose from Philippians 4:15,16, he was free to give himself more completely to the ministry (Acts 18:5).

Paul reminded the Thessalonians, "For ye remember, brethren, our labour and travail: for labouring night and day, because we would not be chargeable unto any of you, we preached unto you the gospel of God" (I Thess. 2:9). Again he wrote them that while with them he "wrought with labour and travail night and day, that we might not be chargeable to any of you" (II Thess. 3:8). And when Christians where he preached did not care for his needs as they should have done, he later wrote them that he "robbed other churches" to serve them. That is, he was taking missionary support to make up for what his immediate hearers neglected to supply (II Cor. 11:8).

No, Paul was not preaching for pay. He would rather die than that any should make void his glorious, sacrificial life for Christ, or for it to even seem as if the Gospel was not free for all. He should claim no credit for preaching since "a dispensation of the gospel" was committed to him (vs. 17). Like Jeremiah, who had "a burning fire" in his bones, could not quit preaching when he would (Jer. 20:7-9), Paul must preach. He will do it willingly and have reward, but if unwillingly, he must still preach!

So, Paul, deserving support, did not demand it for himself, though he taught them it was right and proper. O preachers, we must not be too much concerned about money. It must not be a factor about where or how we preach. This writer had a covenant with God in 1926 when he left the pastorate to become an evangelist that he would never ask or agree to a regular salary nor bargain about what he should receive. What came for him, he would receive gladly; he would never press for more.

Salaries are not wrong, but in this case it was necessary for this writer to set a nationwide pattern, to grow confidence in evangelists and evangelism by making no requirement. God has wonderfully supplied our need. We think that a salary is not wrong when a minister is not overmuch concerned about it and makes no special demands for his needs. It is proper for God's people to provide for pastors, and pastors should teach people what is right, but the preacher must not have his mind set on money.

---

**VERSES 19-27:**

19 For though I be free from all men, yet have I made myself servant unto all, that I might gain the more.

20 And unto the Jews I became as a Jew, that I might gain the Jews; to them that are under the law, as under the law, that I might gain them that are under the law;

21 To them that are without law, as without law, (being not without law to God, but under the law to Christ,) that I might gain them that are without law.

22 To the weak became I as weak, that I might gain the weak: I am made all things to all men, that I might by all means save some.

23 And this I do for the gospel's sake, that I might be partaker thereof with you.

24 Know ye not that they which run in a race run all, but one receiveth the prize? So run, that ye may obtain.

25 And every man that striveth for the mastery is temperate in all things. Now they do it to obtain a corruptible crown; but we an incorruptible.

26 I therefore so run, not as uncertainly; so fight I, not as one that beateth the air:

27 But I keep under my body, and bring it into subjection: lest that by any means, when I have preached to others, I myself should be a castaway.

## The Unselfish Abandon to the Ministry That Makes All Things Secondary to Winning Souls—All Means At Any Cost to Win a Soul

To what lengths did the apostle go to save men? What a price is paid for his apostleship! As he said in chapter 4, verses 9-13, he is willing to appear a fool, though one of the most learned of Jews. He is despised, weak, reviled, willingly accepting the abuse, the persecution, the misunderstanding to get out the Gospel. Poverty, hunger, labor were not shunned nor counted, if they were part of saving sinners and getting out the Gospel. He was a "servant unto all," although a man of learning, a Roman citizen of an important city (Acts 16:37; 21:39; 22:27-29). Yet he was treated as a lawbreaker, a troublemaker.

Did Paul preach to Jews? He was a well-trained rabbi. Concerning the law, blameless. Circumcised the eighth day, of the tribe of Benjamin (Rom. 11:1; Phil. 3:4-6). How he knew the law! He had been of the strictest sect a Pharisee. He spake to Jews on their own ground.

But Paul had a heart for Gentiles as well as Jews. He loved them and stood on their ground. He knew how to "rejoice with them that do rejoice, and weep with them that weep" (Rom. 12:15). On the island of Malta (Melita in Acts 28) after the shipwreck Paul made a fire, carried wood and felt at home with the ignorant, heathen people there, and he healed their sick. His hands were those of a laboring man, a tentmaker, yet his language could be that of a scholar on Mars' Hill at Athens.

The Lord Jesus is the example of all who win men. To save men, He became a man. He became as poor as any man, grew up in poverty and labor, and He could say, "Blessed be ye poor" (Luke 6:20). Of Him it was foretold in Isaiah 61:1; quoted in Luke 4:18, that "He hath anointed me to preach the gospel to the poor; he hath sent me to heal the brokenhearted, to preach deliverance to the captives, and recovering of sight to the blind, to set at liberty them that are bruised." Although sinless, holy as God the Father, yet He was called "the friend of sinners." It was said of Him, "This man receiveth sinners, and eateth with them" (Luke 15:2). He went to their homes, ate with them, loved them, forgave them.

The fallen woman could kiss His feet as she wept over her sins. A leper or a blind beggar felt free to ask for healing and get it. Little children were not afraid to come into His arms!

*"All things. . .to save some"* (vs. 22). Here is no encouragement to compromise. Jesus could love the Pharisee Nicodemus and talk on his plane, yet demand, "Ye must be born again." He looked so tenderly upon the exposed adulteress woman at His feet and so clearly disavowed her pharisaical accusers that she stayed when all the accusers were gone and she could have gone. And she called Him Lord. Yet he commanded, "Go, and sin no more."

No one need call a Christ-rejecting liberal "brother" (II John 9-11) nor yoke up with unbelievers (II Cor. 6:14-18; Eph. 5:11; Ps. 1:1) to have a loving heart for all men, understand their needs, enter into their problems and burdens.

". . . to all men." Saul would never have given his time with one group, one class of people alone. The "children's worker" should try to win everybody—old and young. I do not believe God calls anyone to be a "youth worker" and to ignore all the older sinners. Someone may say he is called to be a "missionary to the Jews." Then so was Peter, in the midst of thousands of Jews. But he was sent to Cornelius, a Roman, and to many, many Gentiles as well, and he learned, "What God hath cleansed, that call not thou common."

A gifted and anointed evangelist, a Jew, was greatly pressured to leave the field as a general evangelist, where he spoke to great crowds with blessed results, and to work among Jews and promote Jewish missions. He asked my counsel. I said I believed he would win many more Jews while winning thousands of others in evangelistic campaigns than if he were winning Jews alone as a Jewish missionary, and it has proved true.

Every Christian ought to feel Christ's burden for "all the world" and "every creature" (Mark 16:15). He ought to feel sent, like the servants who "went out into the highways, and gathered together all as many as they found, both bad and good" (Matt. 22:10). We are to "bring in hither the poor, and the maimed, and the halt, and the blind" (Luke 14:21).

Paul approached the matter of winning souls as an athlete running a race or competing in the Olympic games. There is a crown for the winner. So he trains, he sacrifices the pleasures, the feasts, leisure that others have, that he may win. Oh, to have seriously the burden to play on every string, to seek every prospect, to love every sinner, and to avoid every hindrance or sidetrack that would keep us from winning the lost, the last one possible to win!

Remember the shepherd who had ninety-nine safe sheep went to any length to find the one lost sheep. We should want every one.

Paul feared being "a castaway." Not cast out of God's family, not missing Heaven, not losing salvation. No, but what if he, so greatly used, should be set aside as a preacher? What if the power should be withdrawn? What if the tool became so cumbersome, so unfitted that the Master Workman should lay it aside to use one more pliable, more fitted? Sad it is when the man who has won many souls becomes merely a "Bible teacher," winning a few; or when one greatly anointed becomes powerless and with little fruit! The fig tree without fruit was cursed (Mark 11:13) and could bear no more fruit forever. We do well to fear, as Paul did, that God may lay aside the indifferent worker, the one who loses holy zeal, the man who does not seek to pay any price for power, does not love with holy concern every lost sinner, the man who allows the fleshly nature too much room in his life!

# I CORINTHIANS X

MOREOVER, brethren, I would not that ye should be ignorant, how that all our fathers were under the cloud, and all passed through the sea;

2 And were all baptized unto Moses in the cloud and in the sea;

3 And did all eat the same spiritual meat;

4 And did all drink the same spiritual drink: for they drank of that spiritual Rock that followed them: and that Rock was Christ.

5 But with many of them God was not well pleased: for they were overthrown in the wilderness.

6 Now these things were our examples, to the intent we should not lust after evil things, as they also lusted.

7 Neither be ye idolaters, as were some of them; as it is written, The people sat down to eat and drink, and rose up to play.

8 Neither let us commit fornication, as some of them committed, and fell in one day three and twenty thousand.

9 Neither let us tempt Christ, as some of them also tempted, and were destroyed of serpents.

10 Neither murmur ye, as some of them also murmured, and were destroyed of the destroyer.

11 Now all these things happened unto them for ensamples: and they are written for our admonition, upon whom the ends of the world are come.

12 Wherefore let him that thinketh he standeth take heed lest he fall.

13 There hath no temptation taken you but such as is common to man: but God is faithful, who will not suffer you to be tempted above that ye are able; but will with the temptation also make a way to escape, that ye may be able to bear it.

14 Wherefore, my dearly beloved, flee from idolatry.

15 I speak as to wise men; judge ye what I say.

## "Let Him That Thinketh He Standeth Take Heed Lest He Fall": The Example of Israel

The tenth chapter carries on the same theme of the last verse in the preceding chapter. Paul feared he should be a castaway; now the inspired apostle tells us how Israel, so greatly blessed of God, fell into sin and disaster. And all of Israel ate the manna from Heaven every day, a picture of a Christian living on Christ, the Bread of Life, feeding on Him and on His Word. They all drank from that flood of water gushing out of the rock in the wilderness. And that

rock pictures Jesus Christ. We remember that Jesus said in
John 7:37-39:

*"In the last day, that great day of the feast, Jesus stood
and cried, saying, If any man thirst, let him come unto me,
and drink. He that believeth on me, as the scripture hath
said, out of his belly shall flow rivers of living water. (But
this spake he of the Spirit, which they that believe on him
should receive: for the Holy Ghost was not yet given;
because that Jesus was not yet glorified.)"*

So, the Christian life is pictured as the children of Israel
leaving Egypt and following Christ in the wilderness. Oh,
that rock pictured Christ, the source of our life, and the
Holy Spirit power which is offered. And the pillar of fire in
the night, leading the children of Israel, and a cloud by day,
is a picture of the Spirit of God going with Christians. And
so we are to learn from the mistakes of the Israelites, who
were on the wilderness journey, as we are. Some of them
truly were saved, all of them ought to have been. But as a
group they picture Christians in the Christian life.

But despite all the marvelous leading, deliverance,
provision, of God who saved them and kept them in the
wilderness, many of these Jews fell into sin and suffered.
*"But with many of them God was not well pleased: for they
were overthrown in the wilderness"* (vs. 5). And we are
plainly told, *"Now these things were our examples, to the
intent we should not lust after evil things, as they also
lusted"* (vs. 6).

What were some of the sins that were a ruin to Israel?

(1). Some fell into idolatry. They made a golden calf and
sat down to eat and drink and rose up to play. And
Christians are in danger of idolatry. We take that matter
far too lightly, surely. Would God give the first and second
of the Ten Commandments that we are to have no other
gods before Him and are to make no idols, if there were no
need for us to consider or to fear? We have the command in
I John 5:21, "Keep yourselves from idols." We are warned

against the works of the flesh, and idolatry is particularly mentioned (Gal. 5:20).

In Colossians 3:5, "covetousness, which is idolatry" is put right along with fornication and other awful sins. So covetousness is idolatry. Many, many a Christian puts his church or his denomination before the Lord. Many put the emphasis upon reverence for the house of God instead of reverence to God. Many who do not believe the Apostles' Creed quote it on Sunday because it is a part of their formal religion. And they do not worship God altogether but worship a church and a form of religion. That someway pacifies their minds and eases their consciences. Many a Christian would find that pastors and denominational leaders would count him a great sinner if he is disloyal to the denomination, if he does not support "the program," if he does not worship the denominational idol. Many denominational leaders say in effect, "Great is Diana of the Ephesians," and their idol and their denominational machinery is as truly an idol as was the shrines and the greater idol of Diana at Ephesus. Oh, covetousness and the love of pleasure, and putting family before God—these are idols. Even as Eli, of whom God said "honourest thy sons above me," was guilty of idolatry. In that, some follow those Jews who worshiped the golden calf.

(2). Fornication was a constant temptation to the Israelites. They were led into sin by the daughters of Midian under the leadership of the false prophet Balaam. Oh, every Christian should face solemnly the fact that he has a natural, fleshly body with the temptations and pressures and desires of the flesh and he must mortify the deeds of the flesh. That is the way to ruin, as it was with the Israelites.

(3). They "tempted Christ," that is, they tried the patience of God and grieved Him with their murmuring in Numbers 21:5-9; so some were destroyed by the fiery serpents. The complainers, the murmurers, those dissatisfied with their lot, those who fret, thus tempt God and are guilty of the same sin of which the Israelites were guilty.

But there is blessed assurance here. No one will be tempted above the limit a loving God sets. Let no one think he is tempted and troubled more than others. And remember that God is faithful; He will not suffer you to be tempted above what you can bear, if you ask and have His help. God will, with the temptation, make a way of escape.

Peter in the Garden of Gethsemane was warned, "Watch and pray, that ye enter not into temptation: the spirit indeed is willing, but the flesh is weak." Peter did not have to curse and swear and deny the Saviour. If he had prayed as he should have, he could have had deliverance. So may you. Now and then, reiterating the solemn warning above and somewhat summing it up, we are warned again, "flee from idolatry!" Beware, do not put anything before God.

That is another way of saying what Jesus said in Luke 14:26,27,

*"If any man come to me, and hate not his father, and mother, and wife, and children, and brethren, and sisters, yea, and his own life also, he cannot be my disciple. And whosoever doth not bear his cross, and come after me, cannot be my disciple."*

And again in verse 33 in the same chapter, Jesus said, "So likewise, whosoever he be of you that forsaketh not all that he hath, he cannot be my disciple." Beware lest some leader be more loved than God. Beware lest the church where you found Christ and have been blessed, be more in your thoughts than the Christ who is back of all good things. Beware lest the good things that God gives—money, jobs, homes, business—become in themselves more important than the God who provides all things, the God who feeds the sparrows and clothes the lilies for all His own.

Everyone would do well to review again those fifteen

verses above and be wise men and judge carefully what God
has said to us here.

16 The cup of blessing which we
bless, is it not the communion of the
blood of Christ? The bread which
we break, is it not the communion of
the body of Christ?

17 For we being many are one
bread, and one body: for we are all
partakers of that one bread.

18 Behold Israel after the flesh: are
not they which eat of the sacrifices
partakers of the altar?

19 What say I then? that the idol
is any thing, or that which is offered
in sacrifice to idols is any thing?

20 But I say, that the things which
the Gentiles sacrifice, they sacrifice
to devils, and not to God: and I
would not that ye should have fellowship with devils.

21 Ye cannot drink the cup of the
Lord, and the cup of devils: ye cannot be partakers of the Lord's table,
and of the table of devils.

22 Do we provoke the Lord to
jealousy? are we stronger than he?

## The Lord's Supper, Communion, Is a Frequent
## Reminder of the Difference Between
## Christ and the World

*"The cup of blessing which we bless, is it not the
communion of the blood of Christ? The bread which we
break, is it not the communion of the body of Christ? Do we
provoke the Lord to jealousy? are we stronger than he?"*
(vss. 16,22). After reminding us of the temptation and
snares of Satan which beset a Christian, as they beset
Israel in the wilderness (vss. 1-12), the Lord's Supper is
shown to be a constant plea for separation and holy living.
Does not the cup at the Supper picture the blood of Christ
shed for us? And the bread, does it not picture that we are
partakers of Christ, the Bread of Life, and are thus
ourselves the same bread? So Israel's priests and Levites,
our patterns, when they partook of the sacrifices offered to
God, identified themselves with God. But God is holy, so
His people are holy and should be separate and different.

But what a contrast between the sacrifice of

heathen people for their idols, and our Communion supper. It is true idols of wood or stone are nothing. But they represent devils. So here again the inspired apostle deals with meats offered to idols, which he discussed in chapter 8. Do not take an idol as a little thing: it represents devils, for false religions are anti-God and enemies of Christianity. Only foolish, perverted unbelievers can urge us to combine the Christian and heathen religions to make one universal religion. That is what the beast and the false prophet will do in the tribulation time, and that false religion, the mother of harlots in Revelation 17, will be drunk with the blood of saints and commit fornication with the kings of the earth. Christ worship and Devil worship are totally incompatible. For one to take the Lord's Supper and then to take meat offered to idols and drink wine offered to idols, being conscious of it as such, is blasphemous. God is a jealous God, and for a Christian to be friendly to the modernist or liberal unbeliever and his wicked rejection of the Gospel and of the Christ of the Gospel, entails the wrath of a jealous God. So warns II John 9-11:

*"Whosoever transgresseth, and abideth not in the doctrine of Christ, hath not God. He that abideth in the doctrine of Christ, he hath both the Father and the Son. If there come any unto you, and bring not this doctrine, receive him not into your house, neither bid him God speed: For he that biddeth him God speed is partaker of his evil deeds."*

And to admire, or to praise, or to smile on heathen worship makes God jealous. No wonder many who ate the supper unworthily at Corinth were taken home prematurely, and many were weak (I Cor. 11:30).

---

**VERSES 23-33:**

23 All things are lawful for me, but all things are not expedient: all things are lawful for me, but all things edify not.

24 Let no man seek his own, but every man another's wealth.

25 Whatsoever is sold in the shambles, that eat, asking no question for conscience sake:

26 For the earth is the Lord's, and the fulness thereof.

27 If any of them that believe not bid you to a feast, and ye be disposed to go; whatsoever is set before you, eat, asking no question for conscience sake.

28 But if any man say unto you, This is offered in sacrifice unto idols, eat not for his sake that shewed it, and for conscience sake: for the earth is the Lord's, and the fulness thereof:

29 Conscience, I say, not thine own, but of the other: for why is my liberty judged of another man's conscience?

30 For if I by grace be a partaker, why am I evil spoken of for that for which I give thanks?

31 Whether therefore ye eat, or drink, or whatsoever ye do, do all to the glory of God.

32 Give none offence, neither to the Jews, nor to the Gentiles, nor to the church of God:

33 Even as I please all men in all things, not seeking mine own profit, but the profit of many, that they may be saved.

## Having Consideration of Others Must Limit Our Liberty

*"All things are lawful . . . but all things are not expedient,"* says verse 23. So, a man may go to the market and buy any meat offered, if no question arises (vs. 25). So, one may eat with others anything set before him, asking no questions for conscience' sake (vs. 27). There are many warnings.

One might easily become a Pharisee, a legalist, by always seeking some point upon which to accuse others or to boast of his own superior righteousness, always campaigning to find any meat he could condemn. But quoting from Psalm 24, we are reminded, "The earth is the LORD'S, and the fulness thereof." All good things come from God. Unless some question arises where a weak brother might be injured or offended or led to sin, we can thank God for all the food he provides and seek no reason to condemn it. And so one may eat in an unbeliever's home (vs. 27) without question. But if someone had doubts and raises the question and says the meat was offered to idols, then for his sake and for his weak conscience, one should, on that occasion, not eat it.

The big issue is, we are not to live for ourselves but for

others and what is not wrong of itself may harm others and so be wrong.

The Bible has no explicit command that one is never to taste alcoholic drink although the inference is strong that he should not. The Rechabites were praised that they would not taste wine (Jer. 35). Priests were never to drink wine when they went into the service of the tabernacle (Ezek. 44:21). John the Baptist was specially counted godly because he "would drink neither wine nor strong drink" (Luke 1:15).

There are many warnings against strong drink (Prov. 20:1; 23:21, 29-35), and an awful condemnation of drunkenness. Wine in the Bible may be simply fresh grape juice, "new wine" (Prov. 3:8,9), or it may have fermented. So the instructions may refer to one or the other, depending on the context.

Some say moderate use of alcohol cheers and is a matter of liberty, but we know that if one drinks, he encourages drinking, and of those who do drink at all, many will drink to excess. One out of nine drinkers become problem drinkers, alcoholics. A trail of poverty, broken homes, fornication, accidents and crime follow drinking. So, the Christian sins who, claiming liberty, sets a bad example and leads others to ruin.

Here again we should "abstain from all appearance of evil" (I Thess. 5:22).

Perhaps to buy a soft drink at a beer parlor or beer bar is not explicitly forbidden in Scripture, but the man who claims that liberty thus endorses the wicked work of the liquor seller and leads others to drink alcoholic drinks. One might go to a carefully selected movie and say he had done no harm. But he has thus made movies respectable to others, has encouraged others to go and becomes a part of all the lewdness, violence and godlessness of the movie house and business.

Not what is allowable but what is expedient. We must

ask not what is lawful but what is good for others.

Verse 31 sums it up well: *"Whether therefore ye eat, or drink, or whatsoever ye do, do all to the glory of God."* We are not to offend needlessly Jew or Gentile or weak Christians. We are to please all we can in order to save all we can.

So a Christian should dress so as not to offend. He should have the pleasant way that love indicates in order to win all that he can for Christ.

# I CORINTHIANS XI

BE ye followers of me, even as I also am of Christ.

2 Now I praise you, brethren, that ye remember me in all things, and keep the ordinances, as I delivered them to you.

3 But I would have you know, that the head of every man is Christ; and the head of the woman is the man; and the head of Christ is God.

## The Divine Order of Authority: God, Christ, Man and Woman

God sent the apostles, so we are to follow them as they follow Christ. You are to "obey them that have the rule over you"—Christian leaders and pastors in churches as they follow Christ—"for they watch for your souls, as they that must give account, that they may do it with joy, and not with grief: for that is unprofitable for you" (Heb. 13:17). Paul says about anyone who brings another Gospel, "let him be accursed" (Gal. 1:8,9). But God has leaders, and as they follow Christ, we should follow them.

Churches should have pastors as schools should have teachers, as nations should have rulers, and so in the home the wife should have a husband to lead and rule.

So here is the order of authority. God over Christ, Christ over man, the man over the woman.

---

4 Every man praying or prophesying, having his head covered, dishonoureth his head.

5 But every woman that prayeth or prophesieth with her head uncovered dishonoureth her head: for that is even all one as if she were shaven.

6 For if the woman be not covered, let her also be shorn: but if it be a shame for a woman to be shorn or shaven, let her be covered.

7 For a man indeed ought not to cover his head, forasmuch as he is the image and glory of God: but the woman is the glory of the man.

8 For the man is not of the woman; but the woman of the man.

9 Neither was the man created for the woman; but the woman for the

man.

10 For this cause ought the woman to have power on her head because of the angels.

11 Nevertheless neither is the man without the woman, neither the woman without the man, in the Lord.

12 For as the woman is of the man, even so is the man also by the woman; but all things of God.

13 Judge in yourselves: is it comely that a woman pray unto God uncovered?

14 Doth not even nature itself teach you, that, if a man have long hair, it is a shame unto him?

15 But if a woman have long hair, it is a glory to her: for her hair is given her for a covering.

16 But if any man seem to be contentious, we have no such custom, neither the churches of God.

## Long Hair, Uncut, Should Mark the Godly Woman As Subject to Father and Husband

God made man and woman to be different and to have differing duties and relations. Man was made first, then woman was made as a helpmeet for man. So the wife is commanded to be subject to her husband "as the church is subject to Christ" and "in every thing." The husband should be obeyed "as unto the Lord" (Eph. 5:22-24; Col. 3:18). The Christian wife is even to be in subjection to the unsaved husband (I Pet. 3:1,2). And in the Lord's work, I Timothy 2:11 tells us, "Let the woman learn in silence with all subjection." The woman is to be modestly quiet in services, not feeling free to interrupt the speaker but she is to ask her husband at home if she "will learn any thing" (I Cor. 14:35).

This subjection was to be marked by difference in dress. Deuteronomy 22:5 instructed, "The woman shall not wear that which pertaineth unto a man, neither shall a man put on a woman's garment: for all that do so are abomination unto the LORD thy God." So here the way the hair is worn is to distinguish between man and woman. A woman's long hair is given as a symbolic veiling or covering. Her hair is a glory to her, a part of her femininity and her beauty.

A man should not have a covering or veiling before Christ, so men take off their hats in church while women may wear them. Verse 16 says, *"But if any man seem to be contentious, we have no such custom, neither the churches of God.* " Thus a man symbolizes "I take my responsibility before God for my family," while the woman, by long hair, symbolizes her submission and loyalty to husband or father. Thus the woman has a symbol of "power on her head," that is, a symbol of authority by long hair. And this is "because of the angels." All around us are angels of God, our messengers from God, our servants, our guardians. "Are they not all ministering spirits, sent forth to minister for them who shall be heirs of salvation" (Heb. 1:14)? As far as we know, angels have never been tempted and fallen except on the matter of rebellion against authority. So, a woman who symbolizes rebellion against authority by short hair grieves angels when she prays; perhaps her example would help to tempt them to rebellion.

Note the three ways mentioned that a woman's hair may be worn: "shaved" or "shorn" or "long."

The Bible does not forbid a woman to have nicely braided hair or to dress it other ways. It does expressly say that putting on of apparel or wearing braided hair and gold are not a woman's real adornment. That adornment is "a meek and quiet spirit" (I Pet. 3:3,4).

Long hair for a man is *"a shame unto him,"* says verse 14. Artists have pictured Jesus as having long hair, but that is based wholly on imagination, not on facts. Men in Bible times cut their hair, but not always every two weeks. Absalom "polled his head" every year. Coins of the New Testament times all pictured kings with short hair. In the Vatican Galleries hundreds of statues of Greek and Roman period showed not a man with long hair as far as I could note. Jesus would not have gone contrary to the Bible. He did not have long, uncut hair.

Does one complain? Verse 16 tells us no New Testament churches had long hair for men or custom of short hair for women.

17 Now in this that I declare unto you I praise you not, that ye come together not for the better, but for the worse.

18 For first of all, when ye come together in the church, I hear that there be divisions among you; and I partly believe it.

19 For there must be also heresies among you, that they which are approved may be made manifest among you.

20 When ye come together therefore into one place, this is not to eat the Lord's supper.

21 For in eating every one taketh before other his own supper: and one is hungry, and another is drunken.

22 What? have ye not houses to eat and to drink in? or despise ye the church of God, and shame them that have not? What shall I say to you? shall I praise you in this? I praise you not.

## Disorders at the Lord's Table Rebuked

With hundreds, possibly thousands, just coming from heathendom into the young church at Corinth there was disorder at the Memorial Supper which needed correction.

The divisions and conflicts rebuked in chapter 3 were particularly shameful when the fellowship was not complete as they took the bread and cup in memory of Christ's death.

Surely in sweet witnessing to Christ's death they should be of one mind. But at Corinth each would bring his own supper, have a feast with a group of his own friends, and the new converts or the poor who brought no food were left out, while others made it a dinner to satisfy the body, not a simple ceremony picturing the blood and body of Christ's sacrifice for us. So *"one is hungry, and another is drunken."* Some brought to the meeting of saints elaborate and expensive meals, shaming others who could not bring as much. Their feasting should be at home, not in *'showing the Lord's death till he come.'*

VERSES 23-26:

23 For I have received of the Lord that which also I delivered unto you, That the Lord Jesus the same night in which he was betrayed took bread:

24 And when he had given thanks, he brake it, and said, Take, eat: this

is my body, which is broken for you: this do in remembrance of me.

25 After the same manner also he took the cup, when he had supped, saying, This cup is the new testament in my blood: this do ye, as oft as ye drink it, in remembrance of me.

26 For as often as ye eat this bread, and drink this cup, ye do shew the Lord's death till he come.

## How the Supper Was Given: Its Meaning

*"I have received of the Lord . . ."* (vs. 23), says Paul about the detailed account of Christ's first giving of the Memorial Supper the night before the crucifixion. Note the miraculous form of inspiration. Paul was not present when Christ gave the Supper, the accounts of the Gospels are not yet written, and none of those present had told Paul what had happened. Rather, the Holy Spirit revealed the exact details. So Paul had gotten his Gospel from God, not from men, as he says in Galatians 2. And that reminds us that all inspiration involves direct revelation, not copying of a record, not quoting what one saw or heard. No, "Eye hath not seen, nor ear heard, neither have entered into the heart of man" the material that is given in inspiring the Bible (I Cor. 2:9).

Compare this account of the Lord's Supper with Matthew 26:26-29; Mark 14:22-25; and Luke 22:19,20.

*"This is my body. . ."* (vs. 24). That is, of course, the bread and the fruit of the vine represented Christ's body and blood. They were not actually eating His physical body. Since Christ was actually present in His own body, the bread was not actually His body, of course. This figurative style of language, Christ often used in the Bible. In John 6:35, 40, 48, Jesus said, "I am the bread of life"—not literal bread, of course. He said, "Except ye eat the flesh of the Son of man, and drink his blood, ye have no life in you" (John 6:53).

But He did not mean that taking communion is the way to be saved, and could not have meant that in the communion the bread and the fruit of the vine actually become the body and blood of Christ, BECAUSE in the same chapter Christ has already said twice very plainly

that one who believes or trusts in Christ already has
everlasting life!

In John 6:40 He says, "And this is the will of him that
sent me, that every one which seeth the Son, and believeth
on him, may have everlasting life: and I will raise him up at
the last day." In John 6:47, the words of Jesus are, "Verily,
verily, I say unto you, He that believeth on me hath
everlasting life."

To make the Supper a way of salvation is a perversion of
the Gospel.

Besides this, Hebrews 10:14 says, "For by one offering he
hath perfected for ever them that are sanctified." That was
enough; that settled it. In the same chapter, look at verse
18: "there is no more offering for sin."

So when Jesus said, "this is my body," He was speaking
just as when He said, "I am the door" (John 10:9), and just
as when John the Baptist said, "Behold the Lamb of God."
So, I Corinthians 10:4 says about Israel drinking water
from the smitten rock in the wilderness, "that Rock was
Christ." Christ is called the Foundation Stone, the Chief
Cornerstone, The Mighty Stone. No, Jesus is not literal
bread, not a plank door, not a literal lamb, and not a stone.
But these all picture Him. What folly Rome has committed
here to pervert the Gospel and try to put salvation
exclusively in the frail, carnal hands of her priests!

The Lord's Supper simply shows *"the Lord's death till
he come"* (vs. 26). As Dr. George W. Truett of Texas well
said the Supper is "the Gospel for the eye." It does not save
but it pictures the Gospel.

---

**VERSES 27-34:**

27 Wherefore whosoever shall eat
this bread, and drink this cup of the
Lord, unworthily, shall be guilty of
the body and blood of the Lord.

28 But let a man examine himself,
and so let him eat of that bread, and
drink of that cup.

29 For he that eateth and drinketh

unworthily, eateth and drinketh damnation to himself, not discerning the Lord's body.

30 For this cause many are weak and sickly among you, and many sleep.

31 For if we would judge ourselves, we should not be judged.

32 But when we are judged, we are chastened of the Lord, that we should not be condemned with the world.

33 Wherefore, my brethren, when ye come together to eat, tarry one for another.

34 And if any man hunger, let him eat at home; that ye come not together unto condemnation. And the rest will I set in order when I come.

## Punishment of Those Who Take the Supper Unworthily

How serious a sin it is to take the Lord's Supper in unbelief, making the holy profession here pictured a lie. Dishonoring the blood of Christ is only to make more just, more certain one's own state of condemnation. God is angry with any who trifle about the atonement. Some critics and liberals scoff that fundamentalists are not as loving and forbearing as they are. But in truth, a fundamentalist believer must feel indignant at Christ-rejecters, mockers at the blood. God Himself warns of His jealous wrath on such when He says of the liberals or cultists with a false gospel, "let him be accursed" (Gal. 1:8,9). Why should not all who love and know Christ as Saviour say the same? While we love the sinner God loves, we are commanded to hate the sins God hates.

But here at Corinth some born-again Christians came under His judgment for carnal, unspiritual approaches to the Lord's Supper. While the unconverted unbeliever who takes the Supper thus witnesses to his lost condition, the careless and worldly Christian so approaching the Supper *"drinketh damnation to himself."* Not condemned to Hell, but condemned to premature death (as many at Corinth died in vs. 29), or condemned to be weak and sickly as punishment. Of those who ate the Supper "unworthily," we are told that "many sleep." The term *sleep* God used for Christians who die and never for the unsaved (I Cor. 16:6, 18, 20; I Thess. 4:13, 15; II Pet. 3:4). So those who died at Corinth and those who were weak and sickly because of light or callous or carnal attitudes toward the Lord's

Supper were Christians! We do not doubt that many a
Christian today is likewise condemned because of sin here.
Sins of Christians cannot damn the soul for "they shall
never perish," said Jesus (John 10:27,28). The penitent
believer "hath everlasting life, and shall not come into
condemnation" (John 5:24). But sin brings chastisement on
God's children, for God "chasteneth every son that he
receiveth." And we cannot say that never a Christian
would commit so gross a sin as those at Corinth did. Moses,
David, Solomon and Peter are reminders that God's
choicest saints may fall into grievous sins.

Many Scriptures show that sin may bring sickness unto
death. Keeping God's commandments brings "length of
days, and long life and peace" (Prov. 3:2). To depart from
evil brings "health to thy navel, and marrow to thy bones"
(Prov. 3:7,8). The "fear of the Lord" and "knowledge of the
holy" mean "thy days shall be multiplied, and the years of
thy life shall be increased" (Prov. 9:11). When we pray for
the sick, we pray that their  sins  may be confessed and
forgiven (James 5:13-16).

*"But let a man examine himself"* (vs. 28). First, one
should really beware of the testimony that he is trusting in
the atoning blood that is pictured here. Then surely one
should most prayerfully consider if his heart attitude is one
of loving obedience and his life not a scandal and reproach.
First Corinthians 5:11 reminds us that Christians should
not take the Supper with those in gross sin. "But now I
have written unto you not to keep company, if any man
that is called a brother be a fornicator, or covetous, or an
idolater, or a railer, or a drunkard, or an extortioner; with
such an one no not to eat."

*"Tarry one for another"* (vs. 33). So we call this
"communion." We are united with those who trust in the
atoning blood, who with loving hearts remember Christ's
death for us, and who do not disgrace the Supper and
testimony and the Lord by unrepented, gross sins. We come

"together" (vss. 33, 34; Acts 20:7). There is no Bible example or teaching that a pastor should take the elements and give the Communion Supper to an individual at home. This is a group testimony.

# I CORINTHIANS XII

NOW concerning spiritual gifts, brethren, I would not have you ignorant.

2 Ye know that ye were Gentiles, carried away unto these dumb idols, even as ye were led.

3 Wherefore I give you to understand, that no man speaking by the Spirit of God calleth Jesus accursed: and that no man can say that Jesus is the Lord, but by the Holy Ghost.

4 Now there are diversities of gifts, but the same Spirit.

5 And there are differences of administrations, but the same Lord.

6 And there are diversities of operations, but it is the same God which worketh all in all.

7 But the manifestation of the Spirit is given to every man to profit withal.

## Spiritual Gifts for Every Christian

Those at Corinth had been Gentiles and were accustomed to dumb idols. What could they know of a God whose Spirit would dwell intimately in the Christian's body, be a Comforter, a Guide, a Prayer Helper, a reminder of Christ's words, providing all the evidence, the power and gifts we need? Now every Christian's body is always a temple of God and has the Spirit dwelling within always. The Holy Spirit does not work independent of Christ. One whose heart curses Jesus is not saved, so he has no spiritual gifts. No man can call Jesus Lord but by the Spirit. That means really, no man can make Jesus the Lord of his life, can seriously and truly pronounce Jesus his Lord, except by the Holy Spirit. The heart attitude cannot be right except as the Holy Spirit has control. Not simply to say the word "Lord" but to say yes in the heart to the Lord is what one must have the Holy Spirit's help to do.

Holy Spirit help and manifestation is for every Christian, says verse 7. The gifts and helps of the Spirit will be varied, differing from Christian to Christian. Note then, God did not give the "gift of miracles" to everyone, nor "the gift of tongues" to everyone, but every Christian has already the indwelling presence of the Holy Spirit (I Cor. 6:19,20; Rom. 8:10).

And every Christian can have the manifestation of the Spirit.

---

8 For to one is given by the Spirit the word of wisdom; to another the word of knowledge by the same Spirit; 9 To another faith by the same Spirit; to another the gifts of healing by the same Spirit; 10 To another the working of mira- cles; to another prophecy; to another discerning of spirits; to another divers kinds of tongues; to another the interpretation of tongues: 11 But all these worketh that one and the selfsame Spirit, dividing to every man severally as he will.

## A Listing of Spiritual Gifts

1. *"The word of wisdom"* (vs. 8). Obviously the pastor should have wise counsel for those who need it. The father should have wisdom to speak for the children, those who are to obey him. The husband is responsible to have wisdom for the wife (I Cor. 14:34; Num. 30:3-15). In every congregation there are those who are spiritually wiser than others.

2. *"The word of knowledge"* (vs. 8). It must be of God's plan that some people can have a clearer understanding of facts of doctrine. While all Christians should seek such blessing as God will give, some have an obvious gift here that others have not.

3. *"Faith"* (vs. 9). You remember that faith is the gift of God. One should "think soberly, according as God hath dealt to every man the measure of faith" (Rom. 12:3). The apostles prayed, "Lord, increase our faith" (Luke 17:5). The father of the demon-possessed boy prayed, "Lord, I believe; help thou mine unbelief" (Mark 9:24). Because of need, circumstances and perhaps a degree of our seeking and our devotion to the Word, faith varies (Rom. 10:13).

4. *"Gifts of healing"* (vs. 9). The sick are to "call for the elders of the church" to anoint and pray for those who are sick (James 5:13-16). In Jerusalem the sick and demon-

possessed were brought and laid by the way where Peter would walk, "that the shadow of Peter passing by might overshadow some of them," and they were healed everyone (Acts 5:14-16). It is clear that there was, and doubtless may be today, as needed and as saints seek the best gifts, gifts of healing. God does often heal the sick in answer to prayer and often when clearly all human means have failed. My father, given up to die within hours, was raised up the same day and wonderfully restored to health. In Fort Worth, Texas, in 1931, a woman after two years at a state tuberculosis sanitarium and sent home to die, was healed instantly and in two weeks was doing all her household duties, and after thirty years had no recurrence of that disease to the praise of God. Some people surely have had special gifts in healing and praying for healing.

But we should remember certain facts about divine healing.

Healing is provided in the atonement, as "with his stripes we are healed" (Isa. 53:5; see also Matt. 8:17). But that complete, permanent healing is provided only at the resurrection, in our resurrection bodies. All healing here and now is limited and temporary in this body.

God does not promise now healing for every person. Paul's thorn in the flesh was not taken away. No one has the right to promise healing in a particular case except as God gives the faith for it. "And the prayer of faith shall save the sick" (James 5:15).

5. *"Working of miracles"* (vs. 10). A rare gift, obviously, but still a gift that the Spirit of God may give. Remember the Spirit-filled John the Baptist worked no miracles (John 10:41). By scriptural record we know of only one person that Peter raised from the dead, Dorcas. Only one was raised up by Paul who was counted dead, the young man at Troas. Bible Christians did not go around nonchalantly working miracles, at any suggestion. It is true, however, that the apostles prayed that God would give boldness and

a hearing for the Gospel "by stretching forth thine hand to heal; and that signs and wonders may be done by the name of thy holy child Jesus" (Acts 4:30). With humble hearts we should leave that door open. Evidently that gift is not for all, although all may pray for any miraculous answer needed.

6. *"To another prophecy"* (vs. 10). It is clear that all Christian men, women and children may have the enduement of power that enables one to witness in the Holy Spirit called prophecy (Acts 2:16-18). These Corinthians are encouraged that "if all prophesy" (I Cor. 14:24) wonderful results will appear and they, and we, are urged to "seek earnestly the best gifts but rather that ye may prophesy." Certainly all are to win souls and all may have anointing and be "endued with power from on high" (Luke 24:49). But still there are "diversities of gifts" and not all are endued alike, or in equal measure.

7. *"To another discerning of spirits"* (vs. 10). All Christians are warned to "try the spirits whether they are of God" (I John 4:1). All are to "beware of false prophets" (Matt. 7:15). All are reminded that Satan goes about like a roaring lion, and that we are to put on the whole armour of God, praying always (Eph. 6:11). But some wise men are obviously endued with the wisdom to discern insincerity, false doctrines and unwise applications. Dr. Bob Jones, Sr., seemed to have that gift. So, in some measure have other greatly used men of God. Paul seemed to have more discernment than Peter, for Peter was led into compromise with the Judaizers in Galatians 2:4-11, and Barnabas likewise was led away with his dissimulation. But Paul, with divine wisdom, saw that was wrong and rebuked it openly.

8. *"Divers kinds of tongues"* (vs. 10). Tongues simply means languages. At Pentecost is the classic example. There some had not a "heavenly language," not an "unknown tongue" that nobody speaks regularly, but

simply the miraculous power to speak to the people in their
own tongue in which they were born (Acts 2:8,11). We do
not know that the gift appeared again in New Testament
times. It is possible that the household of Cornelius,
converted in Acts 10, had a miraculous gift. We are simply
told that they spoke in tongues, that is, in more than one
language. Since the Scripture does not say it was
miraculous, and since certainly some were present who
regularly spoke various languages, like Latin, some
Aramaic, some Greek, we would be going beyond Scripture
to say there was a gift of tongues there. Certainly there was
not any occasion for miraculous tongues as there was at
Pentecost. No promise had been given that such converts
were to have that miraculous gift. The same should be said
about the case described in Acts 19:1-7 where some converts
at Ephesus also "spoke in tongues," that is, they witnessed
in more than one language.

Has the gift of tongues passed away? No, not necessarily.
But it, with "the interpretation of tongues" is the last and
the least of all the gifts of the Spirit. It was rarely needed in
Bible times, and almost never today, in circumstances like
Pentecost, when the language barrier would keep some
from hearing the Gospel "in his own tongue in which he
was born," unless as at Pentecost God worked a miracle. I
can say that such a miracle now would be rarely helpful,
and we do not know of any case where it has occurred. At
any rate, the "gift of tongues" is not some meaningless
manifestation given for enjoyment. It was not that in Bible
times but simply a means to get the Gospel to people who
otherwise could not hear it in their own language.

9. *"Interpretation of tongues"* (vs. 10). Here again
remember "tongues" means simply languages. This gift
would be to *understand* other languages, while the gift of
languages would be to speak them. There is no Bible
warrant that one is to speak in some heavenly language
never used of men and another one is to tell what he said.

We do not know of a single case in the New Testament except at Pentecost when those speaking could have understood the questions and professions of those saved from other language groups.

At any rate, the Holy Spirit divides "to every man severally as he wills." No person has all the gifts, nor should have, nor seek to have.

---

### VERSES 12, 13:

12 For as the body is one, and hath many members, and all the members of that one body, being many, are one body: so also is Christ.

13 For by one Spirit are we all bap- tized into one body, whether we be Jews or Gentiles, whether we be bond or free; and have been all made to drink into one Spirit.

### All Christians Baptized Into One Body

When one is saved, he becomes a part of the body of Christ, including all the saved. Several terms are used for this group here and elsewhere. It is "Christ's body." It is that "general assembly and church of the firstborn, which are written in heaven" (Heb. 12:23). It is "the household of God" (Eph. 2:19). It is a "building fitly framed together" that "groweth unto an holy temple in the Lord" and "an habitation of God through the Spirit" (Eph. 2:21,22). It is "a spiritual house" built up with "lively" or living stones (I Pet. 2:5).

Influenced, we suppose, by Plymouth Brethren scholars, Dr. Scofield thinks the term "baptized into one body" refers to what he thinks was the origin of the church at Pentecost. Commenting on Ephesians 3:6 he says, "The mystery 'hid in God' was the divine purpose to make of Jew and Gentile a wholly new thing—'the church, which is his [Christ's] body,' formed by the baptism of the Holy Spirit (I Cor. 12.12,13) . . . ."

The great Scofield stumbled greatly here in a reference

Bible which is the best in the world, usually right. Note
these mistakes.

1. The Bible never even hints that "the church, which is
his body" began at Pentecost. That body, "the general
assembly and church of the firstborn, which are written in
heaven" (Heb. 12:23), will include, at the rapture when it is
called out and assembled (and therefore an *ecclesia* or
church,) the born-again children of God, these "dead in
Christ" of I Thessalonians 4:16,17. So it must include Old
Testament saints. It could not, then, have begun at
Pentecost.

2. These to whom Paul was writing at Corinth had not
been saved, some of them not even born at the time when
disciples were "baptized with the Holy Ghost" (Acts 1:5) at
Pentecost. It did not, surely, include them then.

3. Dr. Scofield misunderstands the meaning of
"baptized" in I Corinthians 12:13. Simply stated, here is
what the word means in Bible usage.

First, *literal,* physical baptism meant the immersion of
the believer in water.

Second, *figuratively* the term is used, (a) one time, in I
Corinthians 10:1, of Israel closed up in the channel through
the Red Sea, covered above, before, behind with clouds. (b)
It is used figuratively sometimes of Christians submerged,
covered, immersed in Holy Spirit power (Matt. 3:11; Mark
1:8; Luke 3:16; John 1:33 and Acts 1:5). That is, of course, a
figurative use of the term baptism. (c) The term *baptized* is
also used to picture Jesus overwhelmed in suffering (Matt.
20:22,23). (d) Then the term is used as a figure here,
picturing each convert put into the body of Christ, buried
there inextricably when he is saved, so "baptized" or
immersed into the body. First Peter 2:5 has the same
picture of Christians, as living stones built into, buried into
and becoming a part of the building.

Note the distinction showing the figurative use of
"baptized" in I Corinthians 12:13 could not be the same as

at Pentecost. At Pentecost *Christ* was the *agent* covering saints with the Holy Spirit. Here the picture is different. *The Holy Spirit* is the *agent,* and the Christian is buried into the body of Christ.

The tongues heresy has put the term "baptized with the Holy Ghost" in bad repute, but it is a Bible term, one of several terms for the enduement of power at Pentecost.

---

## VERSES 14-27:

14 For the body is not one member, but many.

15 If the foot shall say, Because I am not the hand, I am not of the body; is it therefore not of the body?

16 And if the ear shall say, Because I am not the eye, I am not of the body; is it therefore not of the body?

17 If the whole body were an eye, where were the hearing? If the whole were hearing, where were the smelling?

18 But now hath God set the members every one of them in the body, as it hath pleased him.

19 And if they were all one member, where were the body?

20 But now are they many members, yet but one body.

21 And the eye cannot say unto the hand, I have no need of thee: nor again the head to the feet, I have no need of you.

22 Nay, much more those members of the body, which seem to be more feeble, are necessary:

23 And those members of the body, which we think to be less honourable, upon these we bestow more abundant honour; and our uncomely parts have more abundant comeliness.

24 For our comely parts have no need: but God hath tempered the body together, having given more abundant honour to that part which lacked:

25 That there should be no schism in the body; but that the members should have the same care one for another.

26 And whether one member suffer, all the members suffer with it; or one member be honoured, all the members rejoice with it.

27 Now ye are the body of Christ, and members in particular.

## All Christians Members of Christ's Body, Not All Alike

Christians may be as different as a hand, a foot, an eye or an ear—all different but all needed. We cannot expect literal uniformity of gifts, ways and ideas among Christians. We must all be born again. We must all believe the same great essential gospel truths. All should seek to love and serve Christ fully. All the members of one's physical body have the same blood supply, are serving the same person, but still each member is different, suited to the task it is intended for.

So all Christians have need of all Christians. We should care for one another. We belong to one another. If one member be hurt, the body is hurt. We may be tempted to give much honor to some greatly admired Christian, like "our more comely parts," but often we do well to bestow more honor on the uncomely parts of Christ's body.

---

### VERSES 28-31:

28 And God hath set some in the church, first apostles, secondarily prophets, thirdly teachers, after that miracles, then gifts of healings, helps, governments, diversities of tongues. 29 Are all apostles? are all prophets? are all teachers? are all workers of miracles? 30 Have all the gifts of healing? do all speak with tongues? do all interpret? 31 But covet earnestly the best gifts: and yet shew I unto you a more excellent way.

## Varying Members Set in the Church

Here the Lord illustrates how varied are the members of Christ: "Apostles, prophets, teachers" and those with varying gifts. There were only a few apostles, first of all, and none are alive today. Some are prophets, some are teachers, but not all. Not many have gifts of miracles or healings. Not all speak, as at Pentecost, to foreigners in their own language by a miracle, nor could all interpret a language they had not learned.

Since so much attention is given in chapter 14 to tongues, we may be sure that Paul here is inspired to begin answering their heresy. Note tongues and interpreting tongues are the last mentioned and least important. (The order of importance is intended, for apostles are mentioned as "first"). Then it is clearly taught that as not all are apostles, nor all work miracles, obviously not all are to talk in tongues.

The gifted men given to the church are listed again in Ephesians 4:11, "And he gave some, apostles; and some, prophets; and some, evangelists; and some, pastors and teachers."

These evangelists and pastors are added in their proper places in the list. Note evangelists are named before pastors and teachers. There these are given "for the perfecting of the saints, for the work of the ministry" (Eph. 4:12).

"The church" of I Corinthians 12:28 is not some particular, single, local church, nor all the local churches. What local church has apostles? Are all these others named in any particular local church? No, this is 'the church which is his body' and these are the varying members of the body of Christ.

Verse 31 gets ready for the tongues heresy again. Christian love, "charity," is better than all the gifts, specially better than the last and least gift, foreign languages.

# I CORINTHIANS XIII

THOUGH I speak with the tongues of men and of angels, and have not charity, I am become as sounding brass, or a tinkling cymbal.

2 And though I have the gift of prophecy, and understand all mysteries, and all knowledge; and though I have all faith, so that I could remove mountains, and have not charity, I am nothing.

3 And though I bestow all my goods to feed the poor, and though I give my body to be burned, and have not charity, it profiteth me nothing.

## Brotherly Love, Spirit-Given, Is More Important Than All Gifts

"*Charity*" here is a splendid word not meaning the giving of alms to the poor but far more, even Christian brotherly love. The Corinthian Christians had gone wildly into a heresy of the "tongues," using foreign languages in the meetings so that they must be sharply rebuked and their false doctrine corrected in chapter 14. So here the apostle shows the relatively unimportant place of tongues, even had they had the real, miraculous gift of tongues as at Pentecost.

Suppose one were so learned and so gifted that he could speak in all human languages to the amazement and admiration of all! Suppose one could go beyond the gift at Pentecost, beyond every experience by man before and speak whatever other languages the angels could speak! Without Christian love, charity, their boasted languages would be no better than "sounding brass and tinkling cymbals." There would be no real edification of beloved brethren, no honor to God, no conversion of sinners.

This hit at the very heart of the divisions, the strife, the callous unconcern for others which had beset the Corinthian Christians, when they had no concern for the father betrayed by a lustful son and a faithless wife, nor for the enslaved son and woman; when they could have the

Lord's Supper without noting that some were shamed and hungry while others got drunk; when they were arguing over how much better it was to follow Peter or Apollos than Paul, yet their greatest concern was putting on a show of many languages in public! Today, some have a like anxiety for the "gift of tongues" who do not win souls, who have carnal pride, that they have what they call "the baptism of the Holy Ghost" and have the vaunted "evidence" of tongues. Now they need this teaching. Even the scriptural gift of tongues would be literally of no use without the far greater matter of brotherly love. Only in a rare case could a foreign language be of any special edification, or help in getting people saved or Christians taught the Word, but love is always needed in every contact. Without love, helpful, God-given love, why talk to anyone in Jesus' name?

But the greatest of all gifts is prophecy, as I Corinthians 14:1-4 plainly teaches. But the greatest, most eloquent witness, the most learned or scriptural sermon without the loving, compassionate heart God gives would be "nothing," we are told. All the learning, all faith without love would be a shame. What good is it to see a mountain miraculously moved and all the people look on and wonder, if no souls were saved, no blind eyes were opened, no broken hearts were healed, no captives set free as Jesus was anointed to do? (Isa. 61:1, Luke 4:18).

Suppose one gave all his goods to feed the poor. Men have done that to be seen of men (Matt. 6:1,2). Monks have taken vows of poverty and given up all money and possessions, have dressed in sackcloth, have lived on bread and water to attain a human reputation for piety that knew nothing of salvation by grace and neither saved themselves or others.

A lawyer asked Jesus, "What is the greatest commandment?" Here we are told what Jesus said unto him, "Thou shalt love the Lord thy God, with all thy heart,

and with all thy soul, and with all thy mind. This is the
first and great commandment. And the second is like unto
it, Thou shalt love thy neighbour as thyself. On these two
commandments hang all the law and the prophets" (Matt.
22:37-40). What a sin when we make nonfruitful, incidental
things more important than this overmastering love
toward all God's people and sinners!

Romans 13:8-10 tells us:

*"Owe no man anything, but to love one another: for he
that loveth another hath fulfilled the law. For this, Thou
shalt not commit adultery, Thou shalt not kill, Thou shalt
not steal, Thou shalt not bear false witness, Thou shalt not
covet; and if there be any other commandment, it is briefly
comprehended in this saying, namely, Thou shalt love thy
neighbour as thyself. Love worketh no ill to his neighbour:
therefore love is the fulfilling of the law."*

That sad night when Jesus was to be betrayed, He told
the apostles and us: "A new commandment I give unto you,
That ye love one another; as I have loved you, that ye also
love one another. By this shall all men know that ye are my
disciples, if ye have love one to another" (John 13:34,35).

---

### VERSES 4-7:

4 Charity suffereth long, and is kind; charity envieth not; charity vaunteth not itself, is not puffed up, 5 Doth not behave itself unseemly, seeketh not her own, is not easily provoked, thinketh no evil; 6 Rejoiceth not in iniquity, but rejoiceth in the truth; 7 Beareth all things, believeth all things, hopeth all things, endureth all things.

### What Love Will Do

Brotherly love *"suffereth long, and is kind"* (vs. 4).
Others are frail and human, so, of course, people sin
against love. That does not mean sin must be ignored. Paul
loved these Corinthians and corrected them sharply. They
were to love the adulterous, incestuous man, although

while he was in gross sin, they were not to eat with him. Some wronged others but love was not to go to law with him (I Cor. 6:1-8). Paul could weep over his backslidden Galatian converts while he pleaded with them to come back to the truth of salvation by grace. Paul loved Peter when he rebuked him publicly for compromise with the Judaizers (Gal. 2:4-11).

Love is to suffer long and forgive. Love is to seek to restore the erring one (Gal. 6:1) and each is to help wash other spiritual feet (John 13:14). We should forgive "until seventy times seven" (Matt. 18:22). Oh, and the forgiveness must not be simply legal but kind, loving forgiveness.

*"Charity vaunteth not itself, is not puffed up"* (vs. 4). Love is unselfish, so it makes one a servant to all. Love for others is like mother love, which washes diapers, kisses skinned knees, stays awake at night to care for sick babies, will not believe anything bad about a prodigal boy, gives to her children even when they are ungrateful or wasteful!

*". . .is not easily provoked"* (vs. 5). Christian love can conquer quick temper and hot words. Like God, we were all commanded to remember and bless His holy name that "the Lord is merciful and gracious, slow to anger, and plenteous in mercy. He will not always chide: neither will he keep his anger for ever. He hath not dealt with us after our sins; nor rewarded us according to our iniquities" (Ps. 103:8-10).

Love *"thinketh no evil"* (vs. 5). Love and suspicion do not go well together. Do not be easily convinced that a Christian has done some wrong.

Once there came to this writer a sad report that a famous evangelist had fallen into shocking sex sin. The one who reported it insisted that there was convincing evidence, and he was grieved. But my heart so rebelled at the idea; I insisted, "I do not believe it!"

"And why not?"

"Because I do not want to believe it."

Months later the same man came to say it was a misunderstanding, the brother was not guilty, some had jumped to conclusions and the report was now known to be a mistaken report. I wept as I went alone to thank God and to plead, "Lord, You know I didn't believe it. Now when Satan starts some calumny on me, please have people to say, 'I do not believe it.' "

If we have love that *"rejoiceth not in iniquity"* (vs. 6), we will gossip less, we will forgive more quickly, we will restore the failing Christian. If we *"rejoice in the truth"* (vs. 6) we will think about good things; we will obey the command of Philippians 4:8,9, "Finally, brethren, whatsoever things are true, whatsoever things are honest, whatsoever things are just, whatsoever things are pure, whatsoever things are lovely, whatsoever things are of good report; if there be any virtue, and if there be any praise, think on these things. Those things, which ye have both learned, and received, and heard, and seen in me, do: and the God of peace shall be with you." We will keep on hoping, keep on believing. Oh, for Christian charity, compassion, to bear all things, believe all things, keep on hoping and keep on enduring with loving heart!

---

### VERSES 8-13:

8 Charity never faileth: but whether there be prophecies, they shall fail; whether there be tongues, they shall cease; whether there be knowledge, it shall vanish away.

9 For we know in part, and we prophesy in part.

10 But when that which is perfect is come, then that which is in part shall be done away.

11 When I was a child, I spake as a child, I understood as a child, I thought as a child: but when I became a man, I put away childish things.

12 For now we see through a glass, darkly; but then face to face: now I know in part; but then shall I know even as also I am known.

13 And now abideth faith, hope, charity, these three; but the greatest of these is charity.

### Christian Love Never Fails

There is an eternal quality in love. Prophecies about

Christ's coming, the resurrection, the millennial age will all be fulfilled and have their end, but love lives on after all prophecies have ceased. Now, since the tower of Babel the races have been divided by differences in language. In the millennium, we suppose, but certainly after the millennium, that symbol of human division and strife will end and all will have one language, so *"tongues. . .shall cease."* Not simply the gift of tongues but all foreign languages will cease to be different and to need any special attention. But love will go on as everlasting as everlasting life itself!

Gifts of knowledge? But all human knowledge acquired here so hardly will be nothing, vanishing in the presence of perfect, divine knowledge. Now all prophecy, all knowledge is partial, incomplete. Perfection will supercede imperfection. Now all we know and have is childhood compared to perfection when we are with God. Now we see darkly but one day the dark glasses of our humanity will fall away, to leave perfect vision, perfect knowledge.

Then faith will be sight, hope will be fulfilled, but love will be greater, more perfect than all. *"The greatest of these is charity* [*love*]*."*

What a wonderful introduction this chapter is to the reproofs given their foolish heresy on tongues in the next chapter.

# I CORINTHIANS XIV

FOLLOW after charity, and desire spiritual gifts, but rather that ye may prophesy.

2 For he that speaketh in an unknown tongue speaketh not unto men, but unto God: for no man understandeth him; howbeit in the spirit he speaketh mysteries.

3 But he that prophesieth speaketh unto men to edification, and exhortation, and comfort.

4 He that speaketh in an unknown tongue edifieth himself; but he that prophesieth edifieth the church.

5 I would that ye all spake with tongues, but rather that ye prophesied: for greater is he that prophesieth than he that speaketh with tongues, except he interpret, that the church may receive edifying.

6 Now, brethren, if I come unto you speaking with tongues, what shall I profit you, except I shall speak to you either by revelation, or by knowledge, or by prophesying, or by doctrine?

7 And even things without life giving sound, whether pipe or harp, except they give a distinction in the sounds, how shall it be known what is piped or harped?

8 For if the trumpet give an uncertain sound, who shall prepare himself to the battle?

9 So likewise ye, except ye utter by the tongue words easy to be understood, how shall it be known what is spoken? for ye shall speak into the air.

10 There are, it may be, so many kinds of voices in the world, and none of them is without signification.

11 Therefore if I know not the meaning of the voice, I shall be unto him that speaketh a barbarian, and he that speaketh shall be a barbarian unto me.

## A Tongues Heresy at Corinth

The first letter to the Corinthians is largely given to correcting abuses and errors in the services and work of the church. In great detail, the inspired apostle discusses their divisions and strife, their partisanship; he shames them for going to law with one another, for allowing gross sin, for carnal ways at the Lord's Supper, so bad that many died.

No doubt these carnal, immature Christians tried hard to imitate the miraculous gift, and doubtless thought their learning and using foreign languages in the services was like having a gift. But it was not. At Pentecost there was a miraculous gift of regular languages so that people might speak to those in their own tongue in which they were born. And it was directly connected with carrying out the Great Commission. The fullness of the Holy Spirit, the enduement of power from on High, as promised in Luke 24:46-49, was given that the Gospel should be preached in every nation. And that is clear also from Acts 1:8, "But ye shall receive power, after that the Holy Ghost is come upon you: and ye shall be witnesses unto me . . . ." At Pentecost there was no meaning whatever of some personal enjoyment. Some foolish writer speaks of "the tongues of ecstasy." The Bible says nothing like that and means nothing like that. What they had at Pentecost was simply an enduement of power to preach the Gospel to people who needed it and in the language in which they must hear it.

Consider carefully how this whole chapter is filled with reproof of what they had at Corinth. That itself will prove that it was not the miraculous gift they were using but a carnal imitation. Paul is not against the real gift of the Spirit, and he has led up to that carefully in chapters 12 and 13. He does not forbid that gift of the Spirit if God should find occasion to give it "severally as he will"; but what was going on at Corinth on the tongues business is clearly and emphatically rebuked here.

In verse 1 they are commanded to desire spiritual gifts *"but rather that ye may prophesy"* instead of speaking in tongues and he goes into detail to show that talking in a foreign language does no good—no man understands him. No matter how great his testimony would be, it does no good.

At Corinth a man stands up and says something in a foreign language which many do not understand. There is no blessing. He does not edify others. Note if he were "prophesying" here, whatever the language, that would be speaking in the power of the Holy Spirit, words given to bless others. But the Scripture here contrasts the two. "To prophesy" as in Acts 2:16-18 at Pentecost, and as in this chapter, is not included in "tongues" or foreign languages as used at Corinth, mentioned in this chapter. Words in a foreign language, when *"no man understandeth him"* (vs. 2), do no one any good.

Oh, the man talking in a foreign language enjoys it. He is the only one who understands, and so he might tell of God's blessing and be edified but be no help to anyone else. Rather, verses 4 and 5 say, he should prophesy or speak in the power of God that the church be edified.

Is Paul rebuking what they had at Corinth? Obviously. Does God give power for a miracle and then rebuke the miracle? Never! Then what foreign languages they had at Corinth were not miraculous. They were natural languages, unknown to some, particularly the "unlearned" as verses 23 and 24 tell us.

What use is witnessing that does not give *"revelation . . . knowledge . . . prophesying of . . . doctrine"* (vs. 6)?

What use is banging on a piano or blasting notes on a horn with no tune (vs. 7)? The trumpet in battle, if it gives no planned message, does no good (vs. 8).

To talk in a foreign language that none present knows is to be as a barbarian (vss. 10,11).

---

**VERSES 12-22:**

12 Even so ye, forasmuch as ye are zealous of spiritual gifts, seek that ye may excel to the edifying of the church.

13 Wherefore let him that speaketh in an unknown tongue pray that he may interpret.

14 For if I pray in an unknown tongue, my spirit prayeth, but my understanding is unfruitful.

15 What is it then? I will pray with the spirit, and I will pray with the understanding also: I will sing with the spirit, and I will sing with the understanding also.

16 Else when thou shalt bless with the spirit, how shall he that occupieth the room of the unlearned say Amen at thy giving of thanks, seeing he understandeth not what thou sayest?

17 For thou verily givest thanks well, but the other is not edified.

18 I thank my God, I speak with tongues more than ye all:

19 Yet in the church I had rather speak five words with my understanding, that by my voice I might teach others also, than ten thousand words in an unknown tongue.

20 Brethren, be not children in under-

standing: howbeit in malice be ye children, but in understanding be men. 21 In the law it is written, With men of other tongues and other lips will I speak unto this people; and yet for all that will they not hear me, saith the Lord.

22 Wherefore tongues are for a sign, not to them that believe, but to them that believe not: but prophesying serveth not for them that believe not, but for them which believe.

## Only Words That Are Understood Please God, Do Good

Does one speak better in a native tongue to which he was born, but a language not understood by the mass group in the church? Corinth was a great cosmopolitan center, with many races, many nationalities, many languages. But if one feels he cannot express himself well except in this foreign language, let him pray he can interpret his witness into the language all will understand, or be silent as verses 27 and 28 say.

There are two great essentials to witnessing for God or speaking or praying in public. They are the power of the Holy Spirit and speaking to be understood—*"spirit"* and *"understanding"* (vss. 14,16).

*". . . I speak with tongues more than ye all,"* said Paul. But always so people could understand what he said. What languages? He spoke Hebrew, the ancient Jewish language (Acts 21:4), Greek (Acts 21:37), and Aramaic. All his New Testament books were written in Greek. And he preached in Greek everywhere. He, of course, spoke the common Aramaic language spoken at that time throughout Palestine. Probably he spoke Latin, for he was a Roman citizen (Acts 22:25-28). But never a jabber of some "unknown tongue" that people could not understand.

---

### VERSES 23-40

23 If therefore the whole church be come together into one place, and all speak with tongues, and there come in those that are unlearned, or unbelievers, will they not say that ye are mad?

24 But if all prophesy, and there come in one that believeth not, or one unlearned, he is convinced of all, he is judged of all:

25 And thus are the secrets of his heart made manifest; and so falling down on his face, he will worship God, and report that God is in you of a truth.

26 How is it then, brethren? when ye come together, every one of you hath a psalm, hath a doctrine, hath a tongue, hath a revelation, hath an interpretation. Let all things be done unto edifying.

27 If any man speak in an unknown tongue, let it be by two, or at the most by three, and that by course; and let one interpret.

28 But if there be no interpreter, let him keep silence in the church; and let him speak to himself, and to God.

29 Let the prophets speak two or three, and let the other judge.

30 If any thing be revealed to another that sitteth by, let the first hold his peace.

31 For ye may all prophesy one by one, that all may learn, and all may be comforted.

32 And the spirits of the prophets are subject to the prophets.

33 For God is not the author of confusion, but of peace, as in all churches of the saints.

34 Let your women keep silence in the churches: for it is not permitted unto them to speak; but they are commanded to be under obedience, as also saith the law.

35 And if they will learn any thing, let them ask their husbands at home: for it is a shame for women to speak in the church.

36 What? came the word of God out from you? or came it unto you only?

37 If any man think himself to be a prophet, or spiritual, let him acknowledge that the things that I write unto you are the commandments of the Lord.

38 But if any man be ignorant, let him be ignorant.

39 Wherefore, brethren, covet to prophesy, and forbid not to speak with tongues.

40 Let all things be done decently and in order.

## Rules for the Church Services

Here is a rule: *"Let all things be done unto edifying"* (vs. 26).

Note the tongues or foreign languages discussed here are languages not known by the *"unlearned"* (vss. 23,24). They were not miraculous, not the divine "gift of tongues."

How ridiculous it would appear to unsaved and unlearned strangers to be in a service in which people talked languages that could not be understood. That would be obviously foolish and wrong. They would say, *"ye are mad,"* or crazy! But if all witness in the power of the Holy Spirit, they would be convicted and know God was there.

We are commanded in such a service, *"Let all things be*

*done unto edifying"* (vs. 26). Very clearly Paul has taught that prophesying, that is, witnessing in the power of the Spirit in the language of people present so they can understand it and for the edification and building up of the church, results in "edification, and exhortation, and comfort" (vs. 3). Everything is to be done "that the church may receive edifying" (vs. 5). And again the aim is "that ye may excel to the edifying of the church" (vs. 12).

So the inspired apostle here takes a sample case: Suppose a whole church comes together and all speak with foreign languages (vs. 23). What will be the effect on the unbelievers or unlearned who do not know those languages? *"Will they not say that ye are mad?"* The church is not edified and people are not helped. The Corinthians were wrong to have such a service.

But contrasting foreign language and prophecy, the apostle is inspired to tell us if all witness in the power of the Spirit in a language known to all, then "one that believeth not, or one unlearned . . ." coming in is convinced of all, judged of all and he would be expected to fall down and worship God and report that God is with them. So then whatever one has, "Let all things be done unto edifying."

But if there are those who speak some other language than those present, then let it be by one or two or three at most, and let it be in order, one at a time, and let someone interpret what is said; otherwise, let them keep silence. Let such a man, if he talks no language that the people present can hear, just talk to himself and to God and not take the attention of the people whom he could not help.

But should not people speak as the Spirit of God moves their hearts? Well, the Spirit of God will not lead them to have a service with confusion and disorder. "God is not the author of confusion" (vs. 33). And again, "The spirits of the prophets are subject to the prophets" (vs. 32). God's Spirit would not direct two people or more to speak at the same time or direct people to speak to a crowd that could not understand them nor in a language they did not know. Every whim that might cross the mind of such a person is not then the Spirit's leading. In such a case, liberty becomes license and the end is not the edification of others but the confusion, which could not help.

Now, what rules shall the church observe about the foreign languages?

1. Never more than two or at most three are to speak in a foreign language in a service.

2. It must be by course, one at a time.

3. There must be someone who can tell what the man said, or he must not speak.

4. All may prophesy one by one (vs. 31).

5. Women are to keep silent in the churches. They are more often led astray on tongues heresy than others.

6. Let all covet to prophesy, but do not forbid people to speak in their own foreign languages, meeting the above requirements. Women are to "ask their husbands at home" (vs. 35). The husband should be God's high priest in the home, should have in his heart and "teach diligently" God's Word to his family (Deut. 6:6-9). The husband or father was to approve or nullify every vow a wife or daughter made to God (Num. 30).

*"Let your women keep silence in the churches"* (vs. 34). The Bible says very clearly in I Timothy 2:11-15:

*"Let the woman learn in silence with all subjection. But I suffer not a woman to teach, nor to usurp authority over the man, but to be in silence. For Adam was first formed, then Eve. And Adam was not deceived, but the woman being deceived was in the transgression. Notwithstanding she shall be saved in childbearing, if they continue in faith and charity and holiness with sobriety."*

But here there seems to be a good reason why the restriction on women speaking out in the public service is placed just here, where Paul is rebuking confusion and overmuch freedom in the public services, which results in talking that cannot be understood, with no edifying of the church. At Corinth, it seems that women had added to the general confusion others were causing in the church. And often in the Bible women have a bad spiritual meaning in parables.

For example, the woman who was involved in the mystery of the leaven (Matt. 13:33-35), and the woman Jezebel in Revelation 2:20, ". . . Jezebel, which calleth herself a prophetess, to teach and to seduce my servants to commit fornication, and to eat things sacrificed unto idols."

And often women have been especially used in false cults—all the way from wicked Queen Jezebel in the Bible, to the Fox sisters in spiritism, Mrs. Ellen White in the Seventh-Day Adventist cult,     Mrs. Mary Baker Eddy in Christian Science. Perhaps it is thus better understood why in Pentecostal groups and particularly in those that stress the tongues movement most, women preachers have a very prominent place and women do more of the talking in public even than the men. So when there is no careful restraint to keep things orderly so that what is said can be understood and so the people can be blessed, women are likely to offend and to assume a leadership which God has forbidden them in I Timothy 2:11 and here.

So in speaking out boldly in a service, perhaps interrupting others, a woman would do wrong, and the instruction is, *"And if they will learn any thing, let them ask their husbands at home: for it is a shame for women to speak in the church"* (vs. 35).

Now Paul speaks boldly and in challenge. Are these people with their tongues heresy really following the Word of God? Should Paul and others listen to them? Should they learn from their jabbering and their use of foreign languages in the services or should they, as modest young Christians, listen to the Word of God which had already come to them from the Apostle Paul? If any of them were prophets, if they were really spiritual, then let them openly acknowledge that what Paul commands them is right. But if some are ignorant (as many of them were), let them acknowledge their ignorance and quit pretending to be more spiritual because of the confusion and languages used in the services.

Summing it up, Paul says, in effect, "Oh, that all of us might seek first to witness for Christ in the power of the Spirit," that is, to prophesy.

And things are to be done "decently and in order" in the services.

(We suggest you read the extended detailed chapter on tongues in *The Power of Pentecost* by the same author and publisher. It is also in pamphlet form.)

# I CORINTHIANS XV

MOREOVER, brethren, I declare unto you the gospel which I preached unto you, which also ye have received, and wherein ye stand; 2 By which also ye are saved, if ye keep in memory what I preached unto you, unless ye have believed in vain.

3 For I delivered unto you first of all that which I also received, how that Christ died for our sins according to the scriptures; 4 And that he was buried, and that he rose again the third day according to the scriptures:

## "The Gospel," the Essentials of the Christian Faith

All the Bible is the inspired, inerrant, eternal Word of God, but *the Gospel* is a particular part of revealed truth, the good news essential to salvation. These great doctrines are the most important of all. The Lord Jesus said to the Pharisees, "Ye pay tithe of mint and anise and cummin, and have omitted the weightier matters of the law, judgment, mercy, and faith: these ought ye to have done, and not to leave the other undone" (Matt. 23:23). So tithing is right, but there are "weightier matters," Jesus said. The atoning death of Christ, for example, is more important than the doctrine of baptism.

Note these essentials here labeled *"the gospel."*

1. *"Our sins."* Man is a fallen, sinful being. He cannot save himself. He must be born again. If he ever sees God in peace, he must have someone to pay for his sins.

2. *"Christ died for our sins"*—an atoning death so God can be just and justify those who believe in Christ.

3. *"Was buried."* So Christ was literally dead, officially dead, known to be dead.

4. *"And. . .rose again the third day."* The resurrection of Christ proved His deity. Jesus said, "An evil and adulterous generation seeketh after a sign; and there shall no sign be given to it, but the sign of the prophet Jonas: For as Jonas was three days and three nights in the whale's belly; so shall the Son of man be three days and three

nights in the heart of the earth" (Matt. 12:39,40). Romans 1:4 says, ". . .declared to be the Son of God with power, according to the spirit of holiness, by the resurrection from the dead."

5. All this must be *"according to the scriptures."* It is twice repeated here. That means that the reliability of the Bible is essential to the Gospels. Those who do not believe the Bible will not believe in Christ, will not take Him as Saviour.

The New Testament speaks again and again of "the faith," and when the word is used this way, it means a body of doctrine. First Corinthians 16:13 commands, "Stand fast in the faith." In II Corinthians 13:5 we are commanded, "Examine yourselves, whether ye be in the faith." In Galatians 6:10 people are spoken of as being "of the household of faith." Ephesians 4:5 says, "One Lord, one faith. . . ." That is the saved people have the same essentials of the Christian faith. Colossians 1:23 says, "If ye continue in the faith. . . ." Paul calls Timothy "My own son in the faith." Facing death, the apostle could rejoice, "I have kept the faith" (II Tim. 4:7). Titus 1:1 speaks of "the faith of God's elect." In II Peter 1:1 this body of doctrine is called "like precious faith." In Jude 3 we are commanded to "earnestly contend for the faith."

In Philippians 1:27 Paul pleads with his beloved ones to be "striving together for the faith of the gospel." Note the term "the faith of the gospel." It more specifically defines this essential body of doctrine called "the faith."

In II John 9 to 11 this essential body of doctrine is called "the doctrine of Christ," that is, the Bible teaching about Christ. One might misunderstand or think lightly of other teachings of the Bible, but one cannot be saved who doesn't accept what the Bible has to say about Jesus Christ, His deity, His atoning death, His resurrection and such matters.

There is room for Christians who differ on minor matters

but hold to these great essentials, for Romans 14:1 says, "Him that is weak in the faith receive ye, but not to doubtful disputations." One who is "in the faith" may be weak on some lesser doctrines and matters but is a sincere Christian and with him, Christians may have fellowship, if it does not lead to division and strife.

But these essential truths are so important that in II John, verses 10 and 11, we are plainly commanded that if one comes who does not hold to this doctrine of Christ, he is not to be received in your houses nor bidden Godspeed. Rather, he is to be counted what he is—an unconverted sinner.

And Paul said about any who do not accept this simple outline of the Gospel, "But though we, or an angel from heaven, preach any other gospel unto you than that which we have preached unto you, let him be accursed. As we said before, so say I now again, If any man preach any other gospel unto you than that ye have received, let him be accursed" (Gal. 1:8,9).

---

**VERSES 5-11:**

5 And that he was seen of Çḗ-phăs, then of the twelve:

6 After that, he was seen of above five hundred brethren at once; of whom the greater part remain unto this present, but some are fallen asleep.

7 After that, he was seen of James; then of all the apostles.

8 And last of all he was seen of me also, as of one born out of due time.

9 For I am the least of the apostles, that am not meet to be called an apostle, because I persecuted the church of God.

10 But by the grace of God I am what I am: and his grace which was bestowed upon me was not in vain; but I laboured more abundantly than they all: yet not I, but the grace of God which was with me.

11 Therefore whether it were I or they, so we preach, and so ye believed.

## Infallible Proofs of the Resurrection of Christ

Since the resurrection is to be the one great proof of Christ's deity (as we see from His own statement in

Matthew 12:39,40; and Romans 1:4), it ought to be well attested, well proven. So it is, praise the Lord! No event of history has had more abundant, marvelous evidence for it than the resurrection of Jesus Christ. We do not wonder that Jesus "shewed himself alive after his passion by many infallible proofs, being seen of them forty days, and speaking of the things pertaining to the kingdom of God."

Note all those who saw Him. There was Peter. Then the rest of the twelve saw Him. Then after that, He was seen of above five hundred brethren at one time and the greater part of them were remaining alive when Paul wrote this letter! Then He was seen of James and of all the apostles. And last of all, Paul himself, on the road to Damascus, met Jesus, the living, resurrected Saviour, and talked to Him and gave Him his heart forever!

We remember that the disciples themselves could hardly believe that Jesus was risen, but they had to believe the overwhelming evidence. He had them put their hands on Him and said, "A spirit hath not flesh and bones, as ye see me have" (Luke 24:39). He ate broiled fish and honeycomb before them. Not once, not twice, but again and again, through an extended period of forty days, appearing to hundreds and hundreds of Christian people; so there could be no possible doubt that the real Jesus had a literal, bodily resurrection and appeared to so many people so many times that no court in the world would allow a shadow of doubt to such proof.

Paul seems here to remember the requirements, the expected qualifications of an apostle. When Judas committed suicide and they would elect another to take his ministry as a witness, they said, "Wherefore of these men which have companied with us all the time that the Lord Jesus went in and out among us, Beginning from the baptism of John, unto that same day that he was taken up from us, must one be ordained to be a witness with us of his resurrection" (Acts 1:21,22). And so they elected Matthias as that witness to fill that apostleship.

But Paul says sadly, "For I am the least of the apostles, that am not meet to be called an apostle, because I persecuted the church of God." While these other twelve were with Jesus, Paul was unsaved. When they, after His resurrection, went about witnessing, Paul held the garments of those who killed Stephen and he arrested Christians and took them to jail, having great anger against Christians. I do not wonder that he felt unworthy to be listed as an apostle.

And yet, by God's grace not bestowed in vain, Paul labored more than they all! And God made him a special case "as of one born out of due time" (vs. 8), seeing Jesus alive and talking personally with Him and getting the Gospel directly from Him as in direct revelation! Yes, proof of Christ's resurrection is wonderfully overwhelmingly conclusive.

---

**VERSES 12-19:**

12 Now if Christ be preached that he rose from the dead, how say some among you that there is no resurrection of the dead?

13 But if there be no resurrection of the dead, then is Christ not risen:

14 And if Christ be not risen, then is our preaching vain, and your faith is also vain.

15 Yea, and we are found false witnesses of God; because we have testified of God that he raised up Christ: whom he raised not up, if so be that the dead rise not.

16 For if the dead rise not, then is not Christ raised:

17 And if Christ be not raised, your faith is vain; ye are yet in your sins.

18 Then they also which are fallen asleep in Christ are perished.

19 If in this life only we have hope in Christ, we are of all men most miserable.

### How Important Is Christ's Resurrection?

If Christ died for us, could He not be a Saviour whether He arose from the dead or not? No, for the Scriptures had foretold His resurrection and His eternal life as our High Priest. And the Gospel has to be "according to the scriptures."

Some may say that the resurrection was a spiritual resurrection, that in some sense the Spirit of Christ came forth and the body rotted in the grave, but they are utterly wrong. If there is no resurrection, then Christ is not risen, and if Christ is not risen, then verse 14 says our preaching is vain, "and your faith is also vain." Yes, if there is no resurrection, then everybody who ever preached the Gospel is a false prophet, and if Christ is not risen, then it is vain to trust Him. And everyone who ever claimed Him is still dead in his sins, and all those who died trusting Him have perished forever. Oh, if in this life only we have hope and if there is no resurrection for the rest of us, then we are of all men most miserable.

But, praise the Lord, the fact that Jesus rose from the dead proves we also shall rise! And Romans 8:11 tells us, "But if the Spirit of him that raised up Jesus from the dead dwell in you, he that raised up Christ from the dead shall also quicken your mortal bodies by his Spirit that dwelleth in you." Since Jesus Christ arose, my mother will arise, my father will arise, and this poor, frail body, growing old and weakened and dying day by day, will one day gloriously rise again because Christ is risen as *"the firstfruits of them that slept."*

---

**VERSES 20-28:**

20 But now is Christ risen from the dead, and become the firstfruits of them that slept.

21 For since by man came death, by man came also the resurrection of the dead.

22 For as in Adam all die, even so in Christ shall all be made alive.

23 But every man in his own order: Christ the firstfruits; afterward they that are Christ's at his coming.

24 Then cometh the end, when he shall have delivered up the kingdom to God, even the Father; when he shall have put down all rule and all authority and power.

25 For he must reign, till he hath put all enemies under his feet.

26 The last enemy that shall be destroyed is death.

27 For he hath put all things under his feet. But when he saith all things are put under him, it is manifest that he is excepted, which did put all

things under him.
28 And when all things shall be
subdued unto him, then shall the
Son also himself be subject unto him
that put all things under him, that
God may be all in all.

## The Order of the Resurrection

Here is a wonderful contrast. Adam, the first man, the head of the race, sinned and so "death passed upon all men, for that all have sinned" (Rom. 5:12). Oh, then, if we can only have some second Adam, someone to take the place of the whole race again and settle the sin question! Well, that is what Jesus did. Note the order of the resurrection: Christ is *"the firstfruits of them that slept"* (vs. 20). Was no one ever raised before Jesus arose? No, not in the same sense. Lazarus was raised from the dead, and the widow's son of Nain; and Dorcas, and some others. But they did not rise with glorified bodies. They simply came back into the same bodies, with the same frailties, with the same old carnal nature. And Lazarus one day got sick and died again, as did everybody else who for the moment was raised up from a grave.

But the resurrection, the genuine resurrection in the sense on which our hope is based, means that the body is glorified and perfected, is become a heavenly body in the sense that it is fit for Heaven, both the body as well as the spirit. In that genuine sense, Jesus is the first to rise from the dead.

When Jesus died, we learn: "And, behold, the veil of the temple was rent in twain from the top to the bottom; and the earth did quake, and the rocks rent; And the graves were opened; and many bodies of the saints which slept arose, And came out of the graves after his resurrection, and went into the holy city, and appeared unto many" (Matt. 27:51-53). So many bodies of the saints which slept arose. Did they arise with glorified bodies, and did they then go at once to Heaven in their physical bodies? Perhaps they did. At any rate, will you note it was after His resurrection. Jesus is the firstfruits of them that slept; He had to be first.

What a wonderful truth is in verse 22: *"For as in Adam all die, even so in Christ shall all be made alive."* This verse wonderfully came to my mind with miraculous force some years ago. I dealt with a poor, wicked, lost man of Catholic persuasion. But he was hardened and bitter. I played with his children and then asked him, "How many children have you?" And he told me there were five or six. "That is all now," he said. I inquired whether there had been another. "Yes, a little girl of three. She was the smartest of them all and she fell into the Mississippi and drowned." When I urged him that he could meet the little one again, he said, "No," emphatically, a little angrily. "No, no, you don't understand." When I insisted, he said, "But she was not baptized! They wouldn't even let me bury her in the Catholic cemetery." This verse came to mind and I showed it to him at once.

Whatever that little one lost in the sin of Adam, she regained in the death and resurrection of Jesus Christ. Now no one ever goes to Hell for Adam's sin; people go for their own sins after they are willing and conscious sinners. And I showed him the little one was safe in Jesus. I told him how David's baby died and that David said, "I shall go to him, but he shall not return to me" (II Sam. 12:23).

"And was not David's baby baptized?"

"No. And that had nothing to do with the fact that God takes every little unaccountable child to Himself when that little one dies."

Oh, how glad he was to see that Christ had paid for whatever taint there was in his baby. And he soon accepted the Saviour.

Oh, yes, whatever we lost by Adam's sin was regained by Christ.

Note the order of the resurrection. There are really two resurrections—the first resurrection and the second resurrection.

The first resurrection included: (1). Jesus Christ, (2).

Those who are Christ's at His coming, (3). Those saved in the tribulation time who will be wonderfully changed and meet Christ when He comes back to reign and when He receives those on His right hand called "the sheep" (Matt. 25:31-44).

The second resurrection is that of the unsaved dead at the end of the thousand years' millennial reign, when bodies are brought out of the graves and the sea, when death, Hell and the grave will give up the dead that are in them to come to judgment, told in Revelation 20:11-15.

When is the end, mentioned in verse 24, when Christ shall deliver the kingdom up to the Father? I think at the end of the thousand years' millennial reign ere the last rebellion would have been put down, all lost sinners will be sent forever to Hell, and God the Father will come down with Jesus in the Heavenly City prepared as a bride adorned for her husband, and God will make His dwelling with men.

*"The last enemy that shall be destroyed is death"* (vs. 26). Oh, yes, and so Revelation 21:4 says, "And God shall wipe away all tears from their eyes; and there shall be no more death, neither sorrow, nor crying, neither shall there be any more pain: for the former things are passed away."

We do not know all the wonderful unity of the Trinity. We know that Jesus Christ the Son is a definite person and personality, our Saviour. But when God the Father and the Son is in the temple in the new Heaven and the new earth, —when the Son will have delivered all things over to the Father and be subject to Him, then the triumph of creation and salvation will have come to its mighty climax.

---

### VERSES 29-34:

29 Else what shall they do which are baptized for the dead, if the dead rise not at all? why are they then baptized for the dead?

30 And why stand we in jeopardy every hour?

31 I protest by your rejoicing which I have in Christ Jesus our Lord, I die daily.

32 If after the manner of men I have fought with beasts at Ephesus, what advantageth it me, if the dead rise not? let us eat and drink; for to morrow we die.

33 Be not deceived: evil communications corrupt good manners.

34 Awake to righteousness, and sin not; for some have not the knowledge of God: I speak this to your shame.

## Foolish Speculations About the Resurrection Reproved

What does ". . .*baptized for the dead*" mean?

I think if you understand the clear teaching on baptism it will be obvious. Baptism pictures death of the old sinner and a resurrection. It pictures, of course, the death of Christ and His resurrection. Why should we have a baptizing if Jesus did not rise from the dead? The proper picture then would be to bury the Christian in the water and leave him there, if there is no resurrection. Baptism pictures this: "Therefore we are buried with him by baptism into death: that like as Christ was raised up from the dead by the glory of the Father, even so we also should walk in newness of life. For if we have been planted together in the likeness of his death, we shall be also in the likeness of his resurrection" (Rom. 6:4,5). Why have a baptizing picturing the death and resurrection if there were no resurrection of Christ? Everything in the whole gospel plan would be out of joint if you nullify the resurrection.

And why, Paul asks plaintively, would he and many another apostle and missionary and martyr for Christ stand in jeopardy every hour? Why gladly go on in abuse and suffering and misunderstanding, sometimes torture and maybe death for Christ, if there is no resurrection? Hedonists would do right who always seek for what pleasure is at hand, if there were no resurrection and so no glad tomorrow, no payday for those who love the Lord and serve Him. One might say, "Let us eat and drink for tomorrow we die," that is, if all the good anyone will ever have will be this side the grave. Ah, but all one could have here is so light and trifling and inconsequential compared to the blessings beyond the grave, for there is a resurrection of the dead.

So Paul urges these Corinthians, as he urges all of us, to avoid such foolish conversation and avoid fellowship with those who doubt the resurrection. It is shameful to claim to be a Christian and not understand that Christ arose from the dead and we shall arise also.

---

**VERSES 35-50:**

35 But some man will say, How are the dead raised up? and with what body do they come?

36 Thou fool, that which thou sowest is not quickened, except it die:

37 And that which thou sowest, thou sowest not that body that shall be, but bare grain, it may chance of wheat, or of some other grain:

38 But God giveth it a body as it hath pleased him, and to every seed his own body.

39 All flesh is not the same flesh: but there is one kind of flesh of men, another flesh of beasts, another of fishes, and another of birds.

40 There are also celestial bodies, and bodies terrestrial: but the glory of the celestial is one, and the glory of the terrestrial is another.

41 There is one glory of the sun, and another glory of the moon, and another glory of the stars: for one star differeth from another star in glory.

42 So also is the resurrection of the dead. It is sown in corruption; it is raised in incorruption:

43 It is sown in dishonour; it is raised in glory: it is sown in weakness; it is raised in power:

44 It is sown a natural body; it is raised a spiritual body. There is a natural body, and there is a spiritual body.

45 And so it is written, The first man Adam was made a living soul; the last Adam was made a quickening spirit.

46 Howbeit that was not first which is spiritual, but that which is natural; and afterward that which is spiritual.

47 The first man is of the earth, earthy: the second man is the Lord from heaven.

48 As is the earthy, such are they also that are earthy: and as is the heavenly, such are they also that are heavenly.

49 And as we have borne the image of the earthy, we shall also bear the image of the heavenly.

50 Now this I say, brethren, that flesh and blood cannot inherit the kingdom of God; neither doth corruption inherit incorruption.

## What Will the Resurrection Be Like?

What kind of body will we have in the resurrection? It will be the same kind of body but with a glorious, expanded, multiplied difference. One grain of wheat is cast into the ground to rot and sprout; it brings forth a big stalk. One seed is planted in the earth and a fruit tree comes out with years of fruitage and blessing. So when the body of a Christian is planted, oh, there will be a glorious fruitage one day.

We will have bodies like Jesus, who had physical flesh and bones that they could feel. "And they gave him a piece of a broiled fish, and of an honeycomb. And he took it, and did eat before them" (Luke 24:42,43). Oh, yes, there will be feasting in the kingdom of God, as Jesus often said, and one who gives a meal now to the poor, the maimed and the blind, will be recompensed in Heaven far greater (Luke 14:13-15).

What kind of a body? I think a body like Adam had in the Garden of Eden. His body was made right. There was nothing wrong with it. Adam had not been born again. He was simply a blameless, sinless, good man until he took of the forbidden fruit. But his body was perfect and right. I think that such bodies will be ours in the resurrection, with the added wonder that we are redeemed, soul and body, forever and cannot fall into sin nor lose our place as the children of God.

It is true that verse 50 says, *"Flesh and blood cannot inherit the kingdom of God,"* but that does not mean that our bodies will not have blood. If that means we could not have blood in the heavenly bodies, it would mean we could not have flesh either, and that is obviously wrong. Yes, the bodies will eat and drink and have the wonderful mechanism that God has prepared for the digesting of food and the carrying out of all bodily processes, without any disease or sin or failure.

Notice that every person will retain his individuality: *"God giveth it a body as it hath pleased him, and to every seed his own body"* (vs. 38). What changes will there be in these bodies of flesh and blood and bones? I do not know. Whatever the taint of sin is, and whatever are the marks of sin, will be redeemed and changed and made right. The body laid away in the grave "is sown in corruption." Already decay has begun. In a few hours the body will be stinking and worms will destroy that body. But later, at the resurrection, *"it is raised in incorruption: It is sown in dishonour; it is raised in glory: it is sown in weakness; it is raised in power: It is sown a natural body; it is raised a spiritual body"* (vss. 42-44).

As we inherited these natural bodies from Adam, we will inherit spiritual bodies, real, literal, physical bodies but someway Spirit-dominated and Spirit-perfected, like that of Christ. And as we have the image of our earthly parents and tribes and races, oh, praise God, we will have the image of the Lord Jesus in us forever: *"We shall also bear the image of the heavenly"* (vs. 49).

Oh, but remember, no one enters Heaven because of his bloodline here on earth; not because he is a Jew, not because his father and mother had him sprinkled as a baby, not because he is under some covenant, not because he took communion, not because he learned the catechism, not because he was baptized. *"Flesh and blood cannot inherit the kingdom of God; neither doth corruption inherit incorruption"* (vs. 50). It is not the natural inheritance that gets you to Heaven; it must be a resurrected, glorified being in Heaven, and that does not come naturally. It comes with being born again now and then raised at the resurrection by the Spirit of God.

**VERSES 51-53:**

51 Behold, I shew you a mystery; We shall not all sleep, but we shall all be changed,

52 In a moment, in the twinkling of an eye, at the last trump: for the trumpet shall sound, and the dead shall be raised incorruptible, and we shall be changed.

53 For this corruptible must put on incorruption, and this mortal must put on immortality.

## Many Will Go to Heaven Without Dying

But not all Christians will die. It is a mystery and now wonderfully revealed: *"We shall not all sleep, but we shall all be changed."* It is a sweet word—that word "sleep." A Christian who dies is simply "asleep in Jesus."

**"Asleep in Jesus! blessed sleep,**
**From which none ever wake to weep!"**

I have been so comforted at the death of a loved one by the words of the hymn:

**Sleep on, beloved, sleep, and take thy rest;**
**Lay down thy head upon thy Saviour's breast;**
**We love thee well, but Jesus loves thee best—**
**Good-night! Good-night! Good-night!**

But while we have blessed hope for those who are asleep in Jesus, not all will die. "We shall not all sleep." We will all have to have a resurrection body so there must come a wonderful change. When? That will come when Jesus Christ returns back to this world and calls His own out in the air to meet him. Then living Christians will be changed in a moment, in a twinkling of an eye. When the trumpet sounds and the dead arise, then we will be caught up together with them to meet the Lord in the air.

That is told so sweetly in I Thessalonians 4:13-18:

*"But I would not have you to be ignorant, brethren, concerning them which are asleep, that ye sorrow not, even as others which have no hope. For if we believe that Jesus died and rose again, even so them also which sleep in Jesus will God bring with him. For this we say unto you by the word of the Lord, that we which are alive and remain unto the coming of the Lord shall not prevent them which are asleep. For the Lord himself shall descend from heaven with a shout, with the voice of the archangel, and with the trump of God: and the dead in Christ shall rise first: Then we which are alive and remain shall be caught up together with them in the clouds, to meet the Lord in the air: and so*

*shall we ever be with the Lord. Wherefore comfort one another with these words."*

So the Christians who die and go on to meet the Lord are simply sleeping. Those who are alive and remain to the coming of the Lord, when they hear that trumpet sound, they will be changed in a moment and given resurrected, glorified bodies and will be caught up with the redeemed from the graves, to meet the Lord in the air.

---

**VERSES 54-58:**

54 So when this corruptible shall have put on incorruption, and this mortal shall have put on immortality, then shall be brought to pass the saying that is written, Death is swallowed up in victory.

55 O death, where is thy sting? O grave, where is thy victory?

56 The sting of death is sin; and the strength of sin is the law.

57 But thanks be to God, which giveth us the victory through our Lord Jesus Christ.

58 Therefore, my beloved brethren, be ye stedfast, unmoveable, always abounding in the work of the Lord, forasmuch as ye know that your labour is not in vain in the Lord.

## Victory Over Death for All of God's Saints

So there will be victory ahead for us. Death is a terrible enemy. There has been a curse on the earth so that weeds will grow better than corn. There is disruption by cyclone and flood and bitter cold and burning desert sun. There are the ravages by insects, the diseases brought by germs. There are added to nature all the curses of a fallen, sinful race. Death is terrible. It has pockmarked the earth with graves. Thank God, there is victory ahead for every Christian!

We have tried to comfort the grief of a mother over her lost baby. I remember so well the young bride of only a month weeping on a train over her bridegroom who was taken so suddenly. We have stood by so many open graves. Oh, we have shed our tears with those who weep. But one day we will rejoice more with all those who rejoice, for death has been conquered. Jesus Christ has come out of the grave and has overcome death, Hell and the grave.

*"The sting of death is sin"* (vs. 56). But those of us who have had our sins forgiven and purged away will have the glory of triumph over death. Thank God for the victory we have through our resurrected Saviour!

Therefore, let Christians be content. Let us be stedfast. Let us not be tempted nor drawn away nor enticed from the work of God. Our labor is not in vain. There is victory ahead!

# I CORINTHIANS XVI

NOW concerning the collection for the saints, as I have given order to the churches of Galatia, even so do ye.

2 Upon the first day of the week let every one of you lay by him in store, as God hath prospered him, that there be no gatherings when I come.

3 And when I come, whomsoever ye shall approve by your letters, them will I send to bring your liberality unto Jerusalem.

4 And if it be meet that I go also, they shall go with me.

## Concerning the Collection for the Saints

Paul writing to the Christians at Corinth, tells them now that he is in all the churches taking offerings for the poor saints at Jerusalem.

That began, we are told, in Acts 11:27-30:

*"And in these days came prophets from Jerusalem unto Antioch. And there stood up one of them named Agabus, and signified by the Spirit that there should be great dearth throughout all the world: which came to pass in the days of Claudius Caesar. Then the disciples, every man according to his ability, determined to send relief unto the brethren which dwelt in Judaea: Which also they did, and sent it to the elders by the hands of Barnabas and Saul."*

Paul had a regular plan, as the Lord led him, no doubt. He would write ahead to the churches, get them to push the matter ahead of time and have it in their plans. There would be no scurrying around to collect it. It would be ready to be sent to Jerusalem for the poor saints there. And when he came, when Paul should get there, they would elect someone to send along to bring their offering to Jerusalem and to send a letter from them.

Their giving was to be regular—*"Upon the first day of the week"* (vs. 2). That would mean the end of a week and the collection of a week's wages, the selling of a week's produce, perhaps. And thus they would be able to do what

the Bible so clearly taught—give God the firstfruits.
Proverbs 3:9,10 says, "Honour the Lord with thy
substance, and with the firstfruits of all thine increase: So
shall thy barns be filled with plenty, and thy presses shall
burst out with new wine." The widow at Zarephath gave a
little cake for Elijah first, then day upon day throughout
the whole famine she had unfailing meal and oil for herself
and her son.

It should be proportionate giving *"as God hath
prospered"* (vs. 2). I would suppose that with many this
would mean the tenth; probably with many it would mean
more than the tenth. Surely, since the Lord had taught in
the Old Testament that people should bring tithes and
offerings, He would not expect Christians under grace to do
less. The simple truth is that all we have belongs to God
and He has a right to claim it. An Old Testament Jew who
did not bring the tithes and offerings into the storehouse at
Jerusalem was accused of robbing God (Mal. 3:7-10). So
surely these Christians would give to the Lord's cause a
tenth and then free-will offerings besides. How blessed it is
to prove God in this matter, to trust Him and see Him
provide!

Where was the Lord's gift to be stored? Let every
Christian *"lay by him in store"* (vs. 2). Not in a church
treasury but under the control and supervision of a man
who is saving up God's part to be turned over to the Apostle
Paul and what other messengers the church will send.

Sometimes a tithe ought to be given to the local church,
but always it should be considered as belonging to the Lord,
and one should always find the will of God on where to give.
The tithe does not belong to the church nor to the pastor
nor to the denomination. "The tithe. . .is the Lord's."
The giving is to be, "Every man according as he purposeth
in his heart" (II Cor. 9:7). The Apostle Peter told Ananias
he did not need to sell the land, but if he sold the land, the
money was his own and he must decide where it should be

given. The trouble was not that Ananias gave too little to the Lord but that he lied about it to Peter and others (Acts 5:1-11).

Always in the churches there will be a tendency toward popery, a tendency to let the priest or preacher take the place of Christ. Thus, unconsciously perhaps, people begin to count the church or the preacher or the denomination as an idol, and they are more concerned about their idol than they are about Christ and His work. Remember, every person must give an account and every person must please the Lord Jesus Christ in his giving.

If the local church plans are as large as God's plans, and if giving through the local church is exactly what the Spirit of God leads Christians to do, well and good. But every Christian must reserve the right to seek first the will of God in everything. It is always right to pray about one's giving, as it is about one's serving.

Notice how carefully honest the apostle is in the business arrangements. Then the people would have a right to vote and decide and approve someone to carry the money to Jerusalem. They would send along their letter. If they wished, Paul would go along with their messenger.

---

**VERSES 5-24:**

5 Now I will come unto you, when I shall pass through Macedonia: for I do pass through Macedonia.

6 And it may be that I will abide, yea, and winter with you, that ye may bring me on my journey whithersoever I go.

7 For I will not see you now by the way; but I trust to tarry a while with you, if the Lord permit.

8 But I will tarry at Ephesus until Pentecost.

9 For a great door and effectual is opened unto me, and there are many adversaries.

10 Now if Tī-mŏth′-ĕ-ŭs come, see that he may be with you without fear: for he worketh the work of the Lord, as I also do.

11 Let no man therefore despise him: but conduct him forth in peace, that he may come unto me: for I look for him with the brethren.

12 As touching our brother Ă-pŏl′-lŏs, I greatly desired him to come unto you with the brethren: but his will was not at all to come at this time; but he will come when he shall have convenient time.

13 Watch ye, stand fast in the faith, quit you like men, be strong.

14 Let all your things be done with charity.

15 I beseech you, brethren, (ye know the house of Stĕph-́ă-năs, that it is the firstfruits of Ā-chaī-́ă, and that they have addicted themselves to the ministry of the saints,)

16 That ye submit yourselves unto such, and to every one that helpeth with us, and laboureth.

17 I am glad of the coming of Stĕph-́ă-năs and Fôr-tū-nā-́tŭs and Ā-chā-́ĭ-cŭs : for that which was lacking on your part they have supplied.

18 For they have refreshed my spirit and your's: therefore acknowledge ye them that are such.

19 The churches of Asia salute you. Aquila and Priscilla salute you much in the Lord, with the church that is in their house.

20 All the brethren greet you. Greet ye one another with an holy kiss.

21 The salutation of me Paul with mine own hand.

22 If any man love not the Lord Jesus Christ, let him be Ā-năth-́ĕ-mă Măr-ăn-ä-́thă.

23 The grace of our Lord Jesus Christ be with you.

24 My love be with you all in Christ Jesus. Amen.

### Farewell Instructions and Greetings

Paul is coming again to Corinth. He came before through Macedonia, the upper part of what we now call Greece, then down to Corinth; so it will be again. He hopes to winter with them. How eager they were to see their father in the faith! Then after he should winter with them, they might provide the means for his further missionary journey.

Paul feels he must go back to Ephesus and tarry there until Pentecost because a great open door is there. He had spent three years in Ephesus and a great church resulted to whom he wrote the epistle to the Ephesians. There were many adversaries but that did not limit the opportunity.

What a kind word is said for his beloved Timothy, his "son in the ministry." They must not despise that young Spirit-filled man, coming under the instruction of the apostle. Paul would come later, God willing.

Now, some final words: they are to watch and stand fast. They must maintain charity, brotherly love. And then Paul mentions particular Christians who blessed him: Stephanas, the first one saved in his ministry in Southern Greece, at Achaia. They were to remember the early converts, the faithful ones who were leading.

Churches sent greetings, as Paul had passed through. Aquila and Priscilla, whom they knew, sent greetings. They had been among the first friends of Paul when he came to Corinth and he had abode with them and made tents (Acts 18:1). Now they are with Paul and always eager to serve God. They have a *"church . . . in their house"* (vs. 19).

The epistle may well have been written by Timothy or some other helper writing at the dictation of Paul but *"the salutation of me Paul with mine own hand"* (vs. 21). He signed it.

My heart rejoices in the plain statement, *"If any man love not the Lord Jesus Christ, let him be Anathema Maran-atha"* (vs. 22). Yes, let a curse be on anyone who does not love the Lord Jesus. And so Paul finishes his letter with love.

# II CORINTHIANS I

PAUL, an apostle of Jesus Christ by the will of God, and Timothy our brother, unto the church of God which is at Corinth, with all the saints which are in all Ă-chāi-̆ă:

2 Grace be to you and peace from God our Father, and from the Lord Jesus Christ.

## The Salutation

*"Paul, an apostle."* He insists on that title in every one of his epistles except the one to Philippi, I and II Thessalonians and Philemon. These already fully accepted his apostleship, and it was not in question among these loving and devoted ones. That means doubtless that Paul claimed a certain authority that came from direct revelation from God. He was in a peculiar and even in a miraculous sense sent from God. The word "apostle" means "one sent."

The salutation is, "Paul. . .and Timothy." Timotheus is the Greek spelling of Timothy. Remember that Timothy's father was Greek (Acts 16:1) and doubtless Timothy often spelled his name this way. We suppose that Timothy, taking dictation from Paul, wrote the word-for-word message from God. Yes, God's verbal inspiration still allows Paul to include Timothy. "For ever, O Lord, thy word is settled in heaven" (Ps. 119:89), and, "Known unto God are all his works from the beginning of the world" (Acts 15:18). God evidently prepared the circumstances, prepared Timothy and Paul for the occasion, when He gave Paul the words of the Scripture and Paul had Timothy write them down. God, who controlled inspiration, also controls history, men, circumstances. "The earth is the Lord's, and the fulness thereof; the world, and they that dwell therein" (Ps. 24:1). The Lord who gave the words of Scripture had also arranged Paul's weakened eyesight to need an amanuensis.

Note Timothy is called "brother." Paul also called him "My own son in the faith" (I Tim. 1:2), and, "My dearly beloved son" (II Tim. 1:2).

Paul's closest associate had been Barnabas until their separation in Acts 15:39. Then the next chapter tells how Paul found Timothy, who became his closest and most trusted helper (I Cor. 16:10,11; Phil. 2:19,23).

The usual "grace and peace" salutation—grace is the basic truth and peace follows for the one on whom God bestows His grace.

---

**VERSES 3-10:**

3 Blessed be God, even the Father of our Lord Jesus Christ, the Father of mercies, and the God of all comfort;

4 Who comforteth us in all our tribulation, that we may be able to comfort them which are in any trouble, by the comfort wherewith we ourselves are comforted of God.

5 For as the sufferings of Christ abound in us, so our consolation also aboundeth by Christ.

6 And whether we be afflicted, it is for your consolation and salvation, which is effectual in the enduring of the same sufferings which we also suffer: or whether we be comforted, it is for your consolation and salvation.

7 And our hope of you is stedfast, knowing, that as ye are partakers of the sufferings, so shall ye be also of the consolation.

8 For we would not, brethren, have you ignorant of our trouble which came to us in Asia, that we were pressed out of measure, above strength, insomuch that we despaired even of life:

9 But we had the sentence of death in ourselves, that we should not trust in ourselves, but in God which raiseth the dead:

10 Who delivered us from so great a death, and doth deliver: in whom we trust that he will yet deliver us;

## "The Father of Mercies, the God of All Comfort"

What a wonderful God! Notice the three designations here. First, He is the Father of our Lord Jesus Christ. Then if He is like Jesus, how good, how benevolent! Was Jesus moved to compassion at love? He got that from the Father. Did Jesus love the poor, the lowly, the weak, the fallen woman, the crooked Roman tax collector, the little children, the ignorant, the self-seeking multitude? So does God the Father love us all.

A Hindu was asked, "How do you feel toward God?" He answered, "I do not know what God is like; how could I know what I think about Him?"

The missionary answered the Hindu, "God is like Jesus Christ."

Then the Hindu said earnestly, "Then I must love Him!"

God is "the Father of mercies." There could be no mercy without an atoning sacrifice. The mercy of God could not be revealed without His Son and the death on the cross, and a righteous God making a way to save bad sinners. So God, giving His Son, proves Himself "the Father of mercies." Some would give the impression that God is vengeful, but the Lord Jesus is loving. No! Did Jesus die a willing sacrifice, giving Himself for our sins? Oh, yes, but first "God so loved the world, that he gave his only begotten Son." As brokenhearted Abraham gave his son Isaac for a sacrifice, so a brokenhearted God, with compassion and yearning for every sinner, gave His Son. He is the "Father of mercies." How sweet the name! Since He gave His Son in mercy, "How shall he not with him also freely give us all things?" (Rom. 8:32). His mercy is extolled in Psalm 103:8-17:

*"The Lord is merciful and gracious, slow to anger, and plenteous in mercy. He will not always chide: neither will he keep his anger for ever. He hath not dealt with us after our sins; nor rewarded us according to our iniquities. For as the heaven is high above the earth, so great is his mercy toward them that fear him. As far as the east is from the west, so far hath he removed our transgressions from us. Like as a father pitieth his children, so the Lord pitieth them that fear him. For he knoweth our frame; he remembereth that we are dust. As for man, his days are as grass: as a flower of the field, so he flourisheth. For the wind passeth over it, and it is gone; and the place thereof shall know it no more. But the mercy of the Lord is from*

*everlasting to everlasting upon them that fear him, and his righteousness unto children's children."*

And in the 136th Psalm 26 verses say 26 times "for his mercy endureth for ever." What a thought to move poets and minstrels! "The quality of mercy is not strained, it droppeth as the gentle dew from Heaven," says Shakespeare.

"The Father of mercies!" Then God is the Father with the same pity a mother has for her baby. The Father of mercies put the protective instinct in every animal mother.

Yesterday I saw a mare with a newborn, long-legged colt. Other horses crowded about eager to see—but the mother charged at one too close, wheeled and kicked vigorously, driving him away. Always she stayed between the colt and any horse that came too close to her baby. On wobbly legs the little one, a few hours old, would follow the mamma from the stall. With head turned back the mare whinnied softly and would not get ten feet away unless the baby followed. Mother love? God's love! Instinctive protection? The "Father of mercies" made it. Every tear of pity, every forgiving charity, every providing for the needy, is from "the Father of mercies."

I have gone through the concordance reading verse after verse, dozens of them through the Bible which speak of the everlasting mercy of God, of the mercy that is higher than the heavens and deeper than the sea, the mercy that is from everlasting to everlasting. Oh, blessed "Father of mercies."

He is therefore the "God of all comfort." What man could ever have comfort with unforgiven sins? if he faces death and judgment knowing he is guilty, condemned, inescapably condemned, because he is fallen, sinful, depraved and guilty? Oh, no, there would be no comfort for any man were God not the Father of our Lord Jesus Christ, therefore the Father of mercies. So the mercies of God make Him also the "God of all comfort."

The fallen woman who knelt and wept at the feet of

Jesus in the house of Simon in Bethany can now go home
with sweet comfort that she is forgiven! Now every poor,
trembling sinner who puts his trust in the Saviour's
atoning death can have the peace of God that passeth all
understanding. Oh, the Father of mercies is the "God of all
comfort."

The Holy Spirit Himself is called "the Comforter." Oh,
the sweet Paraclete coming alongside to help, standing in
the place of Jesus, entering into every secret closet with us
in all the thoughts, intents, dreams and troubles of the
heart. He is our Guide in the night. He is our Interpreter of
mysteries. He is our Reminder of the teachings of the Lord
Jesus. He is our Helper in the heartcry of prayer. The Holy
Spirit of God is a Comforter. He thus represents "the God
of all comfort."

Isaiah 66:13 says, "As one whom his mother comforteth,
so will I comfort you." So all the comfort God puts in the
heart and arms in the tender caresses of a mother are from
God. All the comfort this world affords has its root and
sources in the "God of all comfort," who is the "Father of
mercies" and the "Father of our Lord Jesus Christ."

*"Who comforteth us in all our tribulation"* (vs. 4). Is
there then comfort for every sorrow? Is there no grief, no
woe, no tribulation beyond the sweet consolation that God
gives? No, there need be none! He is the "God of *all*
comfort" and He "comforteth us in all our tribulation."
The Lord Jesus said, "In the world ye shall have
tribulation: but be of good cheer; I have overcome the
world" (John 16:33). So David could thankfully say, "This
poor man cried, and the Lord heard him, and saved him out
of ALL HIS TROUBLES" (Ps. 34:6). And the inspired
psalmist says, "The Lord is nigh unto them that are of a
broken heart; and saveth such as be of a contrite spirit.
Many are the afflictions of the righteous: but the Lord
delivereth him out of them ALL" (Ps. 34:18,19).

Oh, yes, and how unlimited is the promise in Psalm

145:14, "The Lord upholdeth ALL that fall, and raiseth up ALL those that be bowed down."

**There is never a day so dreary,**
**There is never a night so long,**
**But the soul that is trusting Jesus**
**Will somewhere find a song.**

And we may happily gloat that "surely goodness and mercy shall follow me all the days of my life" (Ps. 23:6).

*". . .that we may be able to comfort them which are in any trouble"* (vs. 4). Oh, then, there is a reason for whatever trouble comes. This old world needs comfort. "Man that is born of a woman is of few days, and full of trouble" (Job 14:1). "Man is born unto trouble, as the sparks fly upward" (Job 5:7). The ground is cursed for man's sake, the elements have freezing cold and desert heat and boisterous winds and fierce storms. Men face the vicissitudes of fortune, the failure of friends, the betrayal by those we trust, the failure of our own good intentions, the recurring and hounding of sin and temptation and conscience. Oh, men everywhere need comfort. So we are to comfort those about us with the comfort which God has given us.

The Lord Jesus came into this world "to heal the brokenhearted" (Isa. 61:1; Luke 4:18).

And the eternal God, "the Father of mercies," will one day "wipe away all tears from their eyes" (Rev. 21:4); but until that time every Christian should have a sweet ministry of comfort.

The Prophet Isaiah cries out, "Comfort ye, comfort ye my people, saith your God" (Isa. 40:1). And concerning the sweet prospect of resurrection change and regathering and glorious reunion with loved ones and Christ at the rapture, we are commanded, "Wherefore comfort one another with these words" (I Thess. 4:18).

God meant that every preacher and every teacher must

be moved with compassion. God intends the father to have pity on the prodigal.

Years ago I saw an ad in the personal column of the *Chicago Tribune* which said, "Emma, please come home. All is forgiven. Mother is sick and calling for you. Please come." That is the kind of comfort we need, comfort for people who sin, comfort for those who fail, comfort for those who are neglected and poor, comfort for those who face death, comfort for those in the stress of poverty and labor, comfort for those hearts bleeding with loneliness. So let us carry the "God of all comfort" to all those about us.

Is it not blessed that God has comfort for every sorrow and that we Christians have the comfort people need?

Does that not mean that the apostle must be poor when others are rich, for he must comfort many? That the Apostle Paul must sometimes be counted weak when others are strong? That he must be bemeaned, slandered and hounded, and sometimes hungry, sometimes in shipwreck, sometimes fighting the wild beasts of Ephesus, sometimes betrayed by false brethren, sometimes beaten with many stripes, because thus he is to comfort others with the comfort wherewith he is comforted? God has consolation for those who are troubled if we are willing to have the comfort of Christ.

I have stood by many a deathbed, and I have tried to comfort so many sorrowing. I have stood with sorrowing loved ones around the open grave. I can remember the time when I, a boy hardly six years old, stood beside the grave of my mother. My father's arms were around two little orphaned boys and two little orphaned girls. We knelt beside that grave where they lay the beloved body of my mother. Oh, I had comfort for myself, and I can pass that comfort to others.

Paul had tremendous burdens and troubles. He nearly died in the province of Asia. He was *"pressed out of measure, above strength, insomuch that we despaired even of life"* (vs. 8). He felt the sentence of death in himself because long ago he had resolved, "I die daily." And he knew that even in life, day by day, he needed the strength, the deliverance of a God who raiseth the dead. So God delivered Paul and now he can tell others of a delivering God who answers prayer.

Was Paul's sickness brought on by his burden and concern over the work? during his day-and-night praying and working? The holy concern he felt is indicated by his burden over sin unrebuked at Corinth (I Cor. 5) and their divisions, their quarrels over meats offered to idols, their tongues heresy, their lawsuits. He had had the similar burden over the Galatians, misled by Judaizers, and Paul's work largely discounted and partly cancelled by these, as you see in Galatians, chapter 1.

Then, too, the same reason for Paul's thorn in the flesh (II Cor. 12:1-7) may have been a reason God had for this humbling time of weakness, sickness and even discouragement. Paul may have been so pressed mentally that he was on the point of a nervous breakdown. He thought he would die. Or was this part of the same occasion when that great exaltation was followed by the thorn in the flesh?

But Paul lived under a daily sentence of death. He had said, "I die daily" (I Cor. 15:31). He knew he could not trust in himself but in God who raised the dead. And so God delivered Paul and restored him again. And he had confidence that *"he will yet deliver us."*

---

**VERSES 11-14:**

11 Ye also helping together by prayer for us, that for the gift bestowed upon us by the means of many persons thanks may be given by many on our behalf.

12 For our rejoicing is this, the testimony of our conscience, that in simplicity and godly sincerity, not with fleshly wisdom, but by the grace of God, we have had our conversation in the world, and more abundantly to you-ward.

13 For we write none other things unto you, than what ye read or

acknowledge; and I trust ye shall acknowledge even to the end; 14 As also ye have acknowledged us in part, that we are your rejoicing, even as ye also are our's in the day of the Lord Jesus.

## Paul's Tender Attitude Toward the Corinthian Christians

*"Ye also helping. . .by prayer"* (vs. 11). Oh, Paul depended on the prayers of God's people. He depended on Philemon's prayers for his deliverance from prison and his coming again to his friends (Philemon 22). He earnestly sought the prayers of the Christians to whom he wrote in his epistles, as we see in Ephesians 6:18,19; Colossians 4:31; Philippians 1:27; II Thessalonians 3:1. He reminded those who read again and again how he prayed for these converts and others daily (Rom. 15:30; Gal. 4:19; Eph. 1:16; 3:14ff; Phil. 1:3,4; Col. 1:3,9; 2:1; I Thess. 1:3; 3:6; II Thess. 1:11; 2:13; II Tim. 1:3 and Phil. 4).

If many prayed for him, then the blessing of God in restoring him would be a blessing to many, and many people may thus be thankful to God, he says.

Note the simplicity and authority of Paul's preaching (vs. 12), not appealing to human wisdom but speaking only as God's Spirit led clearly, keeping to the main thing. Oh, he is thinking again of the vow he made in fear and trembling when he first came to Corinth (I Cor. 2:1-5). Some may have first doubted, but now accept his preaching as with God's authority (vs. 12); so did they in Thessalonica (I Thess. 2:13) as Paul had preached there in Holy Ghost power (I Thess. 1:5,6).

Paul looked forward to the glorious resurrection and the rewards. Then at the day of Christ his converts would be his joy, verse 14 says. He says also in II Corinthians 11:2, "For I am jealous over you with godly jealousy: for I have espoused you to one husband, that I may present you as a chaste virgin to Christ." In Philippians 2:16 Paul said, "Holding forth the word of life; that I may rejoice in the day of Christ, that I have not run in vain, neither laboured in vain." So, looking forward to the glorious crowning day when Christ shall come, Paul calls the Philippian Christians prospectively "my joy and crown" (Phil. 4:1). Converts at Thessalonica, too, were reminded, "For what is our hope, or joy, or crown of rejoicing? Are not even ye in the presence of our Lord Jesus Christ at his coming?" (I Thess. 2:19).

The Lord Jesus had died comforted in the sweet assurance of the wonderful joy He would have at the gathering of glorified saints. So Hebrews 12:2 says, "Looking unto Jesus the author and finisher of our faith; who for the joy that was set before him endured the cross, despising the shame. . . ." And Isaiah 53:11 promised, "He shall see of the travail of his soul, and shall be satisfied." In John 4:31-34 we find that Jesus was so overjoyed at the conversion of the Samaritan woman that He refused to eat. He said, "My meat is to do the will of him that sent me, and to finish his work."

The parable of the lost sheep takes up this theme also. Of the shepherd, representing Jesus, he said, "And when he hath found it, he layeth it on his shoulders, rejoicing. And when he cometh home, he calleth together his friends and neighbours, saying unto them, Rejoice with me; for I have found my sheep which was lost" (Luke 15:5,6). And who are the friends and neighbors in Heaven? The next verse tells us that they represent all the saints. "Likewise joy shall be in heaven over one sinner that repenteth, more than over ninety and nine just persons, which need no repentance." Oh, yes, now in Heaven, Jesus rejoices with His saints over souls saved. But what joy it will be for Jesus and all the saints when those we have won to Christ and brought to know Him meet us after the resurrection time. Then will be true the promise of Daniel 12:3, "And they that be wise shall shine as the brightness of the firmament; and they that turn many to righteousness as the stars for ever and ever."

## VERSES 15-24:

15 And in this confidence I was minded to come unto you before, that ye might have a second benefit;

16 And to pass by you into Macedonia, and to come again out of Macedonia unto you, and of you to be brought on my way toward Judæa.

17 When I therefore was thus minded, did I use lightness? or the things that I purpose, do I purpose according to the flesh, that with me there should be yea yea, and nay nay?

18 But as God is true, our word toward you was not yea and nay.

19 For the Son of God, Jesus Christ, who was preached among you by us, even by me and Sĭl-vā́-nŭs and Tī-mŏth́-ĕ-ŭs, was not yea and nay, but in him was yea.

20 For all the promises of God in him are yea, and in him Amen, unto the glory of God by us.

21 Now he which stablisheth us with you in Christ, and hath anointed us, is God;

22 Who hath also sealed us, and given the earnest of the Spirit in our hearts.

23 Moreover I call God for a record upon my soul, that to spare you I came not as yet unto Corinth.

24 Not for that we have dominion over your faith, but are helpers of your joy: for by faith ye stand.

## Paul's Next Visit to Corinth Is Discussed

They will receive him, will acknowledge his authority, will take his orders, as he hopes in verses 13 and 14. Paul looks forward to preaching to them again, remembering the more than eighteen months of tremendous blessing, when a great host of Jews and heathen people were turned to the Lord, to make up that church.

He plans to "pass by you into Macedonia, and to come again out of Macedonia unto you" (vs. 16). Macedonia was Northern Greece. The southern part, including Athens and Corinth, was Achaia. He would go back up to Macedonia, and we suppose, as at the first trip there, he would visit Philippi, then Thessalonica, then Berea and then down by the obvious land route through Athens to Corinth.

He does not want them to take his coming lightly. He is not coming to compromise about his clear instructions and the rebukes of the first Corinthian letter. There was a sure, positive authority about all Paul's preaching. God had anointed him (vss. 21 and 22) and they must expect firm, solid commands from Paul. Thus far he had delayed coming, he tells us in verse 23, that he might not have to bring some judgment* of God upon them for their disobedience.

Paul is not a dictator; he speaks not for himself but for God and with the authority of God (vs. 24).

# II CORINTHIANS II

BUT I determined this with myself, that I would not come again to you in heaviness.

2 For if I make you sorry, who is he then that maketh me glad, but the same which is made sorry by me?

3 And I wrote this same unto you, lest, when I came, I should have sorrow from them of whom I ought to rejoice; having confidence in you all, that my joy is the joy of you all.

4 For out of much affliction and anguish of heart I wrote unto you with many tears; not that ye should be grieved, but that ye might know the love which I have more abundantly unto you.

5 But if any have caused grief, he hath not grieved me, but in part: that I may not overcharge you all.

6 Sufficient to such a man is this punishment, which was inflicted of many.

7 So that contrariwise ye ought rather to forgive him, and comfort him, lest perhaps such a one should be swallowed up with overmuch sorrow.

8 Wherefore I beseech you that ye would confirm your love toward him.

9 For to this end also did I write, that I might know the proof of you, whether ye be obedient in all things.

10 To whom ye forgive any thing, I forgive also: for if I forgave any thing, to whom I forgave it, for your sakes forgave I it in the person of Christ;

11 Lest Satan should get an advantage of us: for we are not ignorant of his devices.

## Forgive the Penitent Sinner

Paul had longed for the comfort of these dear ones at Corinth, but had delayed his coming, first hoping they would right the things he had rebuked so he would not bring judgment in his power as an apostle (chap. 1, vs. 23), but especially not to bring them grief. He thinks of the first epistle he had written, and here we learn more clearly of "much affliction and anguish of heart" with which he wrote "with many tears." He did not say that in that first epistle. Oh, he had desired that his rebuke would be taken as a sincere proof of his love and care for them (vs. 4).

Now we learn more about the man who had been living in incest with his stepmother, whose sin and that of those who condoned it were rebuked in I Corinthians 5. Paul had commanded that they publicly condemn his sin and publicly withdraw from fellowship with him. This they had done. And the "punishment, which was inflicted of many" had blessed results (vs. 6).

In chapter 7, verses 11 and 12, Paul writes, "For behold this selfsame thing that ye sorrowed after a godly sort, what carefulness it wrought in you, yea, what clearing of yourselves, yea, what indignation, yea, what fear, yea, what vehement desire, yea, what zeal, yea, what revenge! In all things ye have approved yourselves to be clear in this matter. Wherefore, though I wrote unto you, I did it not for his cause that had done the wrong, nor for his cause that suffered wrong, but that our care for you in the sight of God might appear unto you."

Paul does not want the offending man nor others to think he counted their sin a personal affront. It did not grieve him personally so much as for the other Corinthians and for Christ (vs. 5). Christians must forgive the penitent man. They must "confirm your love toward him" (vs. 8). They and we should remember the words of the Lord Jesus: that the penitent sinner must be forgiven even if seventy times seven (Matt. 18:22). And a gracious God Himself is "slow to anger, and plenteous in mercy. He will not always chide: neither will he keep his anger for ever" (Ps. 103:8,9). Satan might take advantage of the grief-stricken sinner, as he often has in such cases, and feeling unworthy or that nobody trusts him, he might have no courage to start out boldly to live for God again. For some such reason surely, fathers are commanded in Colossians 3:21, "Fathers, provoke not your children to anger, lest they be discouraged."

Remember the purpose of rebuking the Christian who sins is "thou hast gained thy brother" (Matt. 18:15). Sometimes persistent sin justifies breaking fellowship with a sinning child of God, as in I Corinthians 5:11. But the purpose is to win a brother back to godly living. So every Christian should seek to "wash one another's feet" (John 13:14). And we should be quick to restore the one who fell, "considering thyself, lest thou also be tempted" (Gal. 6:1).

## VERSES 12,13:

12 Furthermore, when I came to Trō-ăs to preach Christ's gospel, and a door was opened unto me of the Lord,

13 I had no rest in my spirit, because I found not Titus my brother: but taking my leave of them, I went from thence into Macedonia.

## Paul's Earnest Waiting for Titus

Paul "was minded to come unto you" (I Cor. 1:15), but waited at Troas for Titus. That trip is described briefly, we think, in Acts 20:1-3. Paul went to Macedonia and other parts of Greece and stayed three months but did not, at that time, make the journey to Corinth as he had intended. Perhaps the heaviness of heart he had (vss. 1-3) had held him back from coming to Corinth lest he should cause them grief. He waited anxiously for Titus to come to report on the work at Corinth. Later Titus did come and he brought a glowing report of them, to Paul's great comfort and joy (chap. 7, vss. 6-9).

*"I had no rest in my spirit, because I found not Titus my brother."* Part of Paul's anxiety was to hear from Corinth. Did they still love him? Did they heed his loving rebuke? Did they still honor him and obey him as God's apostle? But besides that, Paul, sick and distraught, needed the comfort and perhaps the ministry and loving care of one he loved and trusted. Paul had no wife, no child. His great heart poured out his love to Timothy and Titus and other dear ones. The Christians at Philippi were "dearly beloved and longed for" (Phil. 4:1).

Note the affection in his mention of many, in Romans 16. The life of an apostle and of an evangelist today must often be a lonely life among critics, enemies and strangers, in poverty and burden. We do not wonder that Paul fervently longed for and waited for Titus.

---

## VERSES 14-17:

14 Now thanks be unto God, which always causeth us to triumph in Christ,

and maketh manifest the savour of his knowledge by us in every place.

15 For we are unto God a sweet savour of Christ, in them that are saved, and in them that perish:

16 To the one we are the savour of death unto death; and to the other the savour of life unto life. And who is sufficient for these things?

17 For we are not as many, which corrupt the word of God: but as of sincerity, but as of God, in the sight of God speak we in Christ.

### Triumphant Ministry

". . .which always causeth us to triumph" (vs. 14). This verse and Romans 15:29 together once brought great victory in this writer's life as an evangelist. We had sometimes a blessed revival, then unfruitful service at the next place. Sometimes the people were not ready or burdened, or circumstances were unfavorable. But Paul, going to Rome, the capital of the world, wrote with boldness, "And I am sure that, when I come unto you, I shall come in the fulness of the blessing of the gospel of Christ." Even in that tremendous opportunity and challenge Paul was certain of the blessing of God. And here he thanks God for triumph always. So we said by faith that we must not any more be content to have less than triumph, we would accept no invitation for services except we could be sure it was the will of God and then we would claim and pray through for blessing and success. Paul could say not only, "I have learned, in whatsoever state I am, therewith to be content," but also, "I can do all things through Christ which strengtheneth me" (Phil. 4:11,13).

For Paul to live was for Christ to live (Phil. 1:21). He should have the authority and the power of Christ. So should we. He was the taste, the flavor, the fragrance, the savor of Christ unto God. He was sent, as Christ was sent (John 17:18; John 19:21). So are we. He was an ambassador for Christ. He stood in Christ's stead (II Cor. 5:20). To those who received Christ, Paul and his Gospel were a "savour of life unto life," while to those who rejected Christ, he could promise death and was a "savour of death unto death." Oh, such a responsibility! Who is sufficient to stand before men and speak with Christ's authority and power! Only a Spirit-filled man of God.

So Paul, with holy compunction, spoke the Word of God sincerely, simply, uncorrupted.

# II CORINTHIANS III

DO we begin again to commend ourselves? or need we, as some others, epistles of commendation to you, or letters of commendation from you?

2 Ye are our epistle written in our hearts, known and read of all men:

3 Forasmuch as ye are manifestly declared to be the epistle of Christ ministered by us, written not with ink, but with the Spirit of the living God; not in tables of stone, but in fleshy tables of the heart.

4 And such trust have we through Christ to God-ward:

5 Not that we are sufficient of ourselves to think any thing as of ourselves; but our sufficiency is of God;

## The Proof of One's Ministry: Souls Saved

Paul needed no letters of recommendation. Not only were the thousands of converts written in Paul's heart (vs. 2; Phil. 1:7), but they were letters "known and read of all men." The proof of God's man is souls saved and lives changed. No matter how wisely one interprets Scripture, how sound he be in doctrine, how charming he is in speech, if souls are not saved, he is not a good minister by the apostle's standard, for souls saved shows the working of the Holy Spirit in power. Paul's sufficiency was "of God."

The natural, carnal tendency is to judge one's ministry by his scholarship. The established Christian centers tended to laugh at Moody who mispronounced words, with only a fifth-grade education; and to laugh at Billy Sunday who went only to high school and spoke with slangy baseball language. They tended to laugh first at young Charles Spurgeon, who was without college training. But the power of God to save souls is the great accreditation. Billy Sunday was, as his biographer says, "God's laugh at the preachers." Moody and Spurgeon moved the world and now must be respected for the evidence of their ministry. Now men build monuments to them, when their fathers mocked them.

We are reminded that Jesus said in Luke 11:47,48: "Woe unto you! for ye build the sepulchres of the prophets, and your fathers killed them. Truly ye bear witness that ye allow the deeds of your fathers: for they indeed killed them, and ye build their sepulchres."

Men may judge on other bases, but Paul knew that the accreditation he had was his own marvelous ministry, with souls saved and with the power of God on him.

---

### VERSE 6:

6 Who also hath made us able ministers of the new testament; not of the letter, but of the spirit: for the letter killeth, but the spirit giveth life.

## Ministry of the Spirit, Not of the Letter

*". . .ministers of the new testament,"* not of the ceremonial law. Now Paul and we must preach Christ our Passover instead of the passover lamb. It is the blood of Christ which saves, not the blood of bulls and goats. They "could never take away sin" (Heb. 10:4,11). Now it is regeneration, the spiritual circumcision, not the circumcision of the flesh.

Throughout the book of Hebrews it is emphasized that the Son of God is better than the prophets, is better than the angels, is better than Moses. The heavenly rest is better than any rest that Joshua could give, Christ is better than the Jewish high priest, the heavenly sanctuary is better than the Jewish sanctuary.

*"Not of the letter, but of the spirit."* The letter killeth. Even of the law, the letter alone kills. Does one think any Jew was ever saved through the Mosaic sacrifices or priesthood? No. "The law was our schoolmaster to bring us unto Christ" (Gal. 3:24).

In Acts 10:43 Peter said correctly, "To him give all the prophets witness, that through his name whosoever believeth in him shall receive remission of sins." There has never been any other plan of salvation but by trusting in Christ's atoning death. Abraham "believed in the Lord; and he counted it to him for righteousness" (Gen. 15:6;

Rom. 4:3). One who did not see through the ceremonies and sacrifices, the coming Saviour, did not see that God would give a sacrifice to save sinners was not saved.

Galatians 3:21 tells us, ". . .for if there had been a law given which could have given life, verily righteousness should have been by the law." But no one could be saved by the law. And in Galatians 3:11 we are told, "But that no man is justified by the law in the sight of God, it is evident: for, The just shall live by faith." The letter of the law could not save anyone.

But one may teach the New Testament without power, and even the letter of the Scriptures without Holy Spirit life in it will be dead and deadening. One can do all the outward forms of Christian duty without being saved. Judas Iscariot did. One can learn doctrine, go to church, tithe, pray, live a moral life, give money, even as the Pharisees did, and never be saved. And one can preach and teach the Word of God, and lull people to complacency, and let them go to Hell without the power of the Holy Spirit.

I have known men who quoted many, many Scriptures, who preached in the pulpit, were fanatical church men, but had never been born again. One may know the letter of Scripture without the meaning. One man I knew was religiously reading the Bible through each month, yet he did not know, he told me when asked, whether one were saved forever, by grace, or whether one might lose his salvation. He did not know whether he should expect Christ to return at any time or not. I feel sure he was saved. He knew many Scriptures. He did not know the meaning of Scriptures. He won no souls. He did not witness with the Spirit but with the letter.

America has many "Bible teachers" who give Bible lectures, good men who believe the Bible and who have small crowds "gather around the Word," as they say, but they have no one saved, they have no anointing from God. They are not by Paul's measurement good ministers of Jesus Christ; they are not ministers of the Spirit but of the letter, and even of the Scriptures the letter killeth if it does not have the Spirit of God to make it alive and powerful.

Liberal, unbelieving men slander the Scriptures when they pretend that this passage means we should not regard the letter of the Bible as reliable, that the Bible is not the verbally inspired Word of God but rather a record of God's dealings with men, what men thought about God, and thus that underneath it all the Spirit of God has some message for us. That is blasphemous repudiation of what Paul himself taught and what the Bible claims for itself.

There is nothing wrong with the letter of the Word of God. Paul himself had been inspired to write: "Now we have received, not the spirit of the world, but the spirit which is of God; that we might know the things that are freely given to us of God. Which things also we speak, not in the words which man's wisdom teacheth, but which the Holy Ghost teacheth; comparing spiritual things with spiritual" (I Cor. 2:12,13). Paul himself was inspired to write Timothy, "All scripture is given by inspiration of God, and is profitable for doctrine, for reproof, for correction, for instruction in righteousness" (II Tim. 3:16). The Scriptures everywhere claim what Jesus Christ said so expressly in Matthew 4:4, quoting Deuteronomy 8:3, "Man shall not live by bread alone, but by every word that proceedeth out of the mouth of God."

The preaching of the Word of God without Holy Spirit power is not futile because the Scriptures themselves are wrong or lacking. But preaching only the letter without the spirit means a powerless preaching without spiritual insight into the precious, wonderful truths of God and without the moving Spirit of God to make them effective.

No one really has a ministry of the Spirit who denies the exactness of the letter. Paul is insisting that the perfect letter of the Scripture must be empowered by the Holy Spirit of God to make it effective.

---

**VERSES 7-18:**

7 But if the ministration of death, written and engraven in stones, was glorious, so that the children of Israel could not stedfastly behold the

face of Moses for the glory of his countenance; which glory was to be done away:

8 How shall not the ministration of the spirit be rather glorious?

9 For if the ministration of condemnation be glory, much more doth the ministration of righteousness exceed in glory.

10 For even that which was made glorious had no glory in this respect, by reason of the glory that excelleth.

11 For if that which is done away was glorious, much more that which remaineth is glorious.

12 Seeing then that we have such hope, we use great plainness of speech:

13 And not as Moses, which put a vail over his face, that the children of Israel could not stedfastly look to the end of that which is abolished:

14 But their minds were blinded: for until this day remaineth the same vail untaken away in the reading of the old testament; which vail is done away in Christ.

15 But even unto this day, when Moses is read, the vail is upon their heart.

16 Nevertheless when it shall turn to the Lord, the vail shall be taken away.

17 Now the Lord is that Spirit: and where the Spirit of the Lord is, there is liberty.

18 But we all, with open face beholding as in a glass the glory of the Lord, are changed into the same image from glory to glory even as by the Spirit of the Lord.

## The Glory of a Spirit-Empowered Ministry

The law itself was given of God and given gloriously at Mount Sinai. The law served "because of transgressions, till the seed should come to whom the promise was made" (Gal. 3:19). The Ten Commandments were given word for word by the mouth of God on Mount Sinai and then they were written down with the finger of God "engraven in stones." The occasion and the giving of the law was so glorious that the face of Moses shone with glory and "the children of Israel could not stedfastly behold the face of Moses." But that glory of the law is now to be superseded in the new covenant, the New Testament, when Christ Himself comes fulfilling the law and the types and shadows which pointed to the glorious Saviour.

But if there was a glory in the giving of the law, then how much more the glorious thing when God has sent His Son and now puts upon His ministers the mighty power of the Holy Spirit to preach the Gospel and minister the Word! The law has many, many commands, "Thou shalt not. . . ." But "if the ministration of condemnation be glory, much more doth the ministration of righteousness exceed in glory" (vs. 9). If the ceremonial law, given for a time and then done away, was glorious, how much more glorious is the eternal Word of God, preached in the power of the Holy Spirit, when Christ Himself has been revealed and His wonderful work has been done on Calvary, when He is raised from the dead and now sits on the right hand of the Father.

We do not wonder that Paul spoke with such a hope and would *"use great plainness of speech"* (vs. 12). Moses put a vail over his face. And that vail still remains, blinding the minds of unconverted Jews when they read the Old Testament. But Christ Himself takes away the vail from the law, and Christ Himself makes clear the meaning of all the types, shadows and sacrifices, the priesthood, the tabernacle and the ceremonies.

Verse 17, *"Now the Lord is that Spirit."* There is an identity between Christ and the Holy Spirit. Not till Christ came could the Holy Spirit be given as a Paraclete, another Comforter, to live in the bodies of Christians and represent Christ so that actually the Christian has "Christ in you, the hope of glory" (Col. 1:27). So where we have Christ there is liberty from the bondage of the law, liberty from the curse of the law. There is liberty from the letter because we have Christ the Spirit.

Now when the blessed Spirit of God makes clear the Word of God, we look, as it were, in the Scriptures and see the glory of the Lord and thus we ourselves are changed from day to day and made more and more like the glorious Saviour Himself, as the Spirit of God has His way.

We remember that Paul counseled the elders of Ephesus at Miletus, in Acts 20:32, "I commend you to God, and to the word of his grace, which is able to build you up, and to give you an inheritance among all them which are sanctified." Oh, there is a blessed and glorious revelation of Christ in the Scriptures, when the Spirit of God makes the Scriptures glorious and reveals Christ there to us in all His truth.

# II CORINTHIANS IV

THEREFORE seeing we have this ministry, as we have received mercy, we faint not;

2 But have renounced the hidden things of dishonesty, not walking in craftiness, nor handling the word of God deceitfully; but by manifestation of the truth commending ourselves to every man's conscience in the sight of God.

## An Amazing Responsibility, and Mercy to Fulfill It

*"We have this ministry."* Paul had not worked out an interpretation of the ceremonial law. It was "once delivered unto the saints" and thus to him (Jude 3). "The gospel which was preached of me is not after man. For I neither received it of man, neither was I taught it, but by the revelation of Jesus Christ" (Gal. 1:11,12). His preaching was a career he had not deliberately chosen, but "though I preach the gospel, I have nothing to glory of: for necessity is laid upon me; yea, woe is unto me, if I preach not the gospel! For if I do this thing willingly, I have a reward: but if against my will, a dispensation of the gospel is committed unto me" (I Cor. 9:16,17). Paul had asked, "Lord, what wilt thou have me to do?" (Acts 9:6), and that total surrender left him no choice as to what he would do, as to what he would preach.

Along with the revelation of the Gospel and the dispensation of the Gospel as apostle to the Gentiles God gave special mercy. With God's Gospel, God's autocratic call, went the Holy Spirit power. It would be a cruel, heartbreaking thing for any man to be expected to present miraculous results for God without God's power. How can a mere man, human wisdom, personality, even genius, make black hearts white, drunkards sober, harlots pure, infidels into believing saints? D. L. Moody said, "It is foolish to try to do God's work without God's power." Paul, who otherwise would have fainted under the calling and responsibility, had merciful help and the power from God.

So, with such a message, and with such divine power,

Paul did not depend upon tricks, upon dishonest argument, nor twisting of Scripture. Kings must act like kings. God's apostle can have God's blessing and power so that he can always triumph (chap. 2, vs. 14). He need not maneuver nor trick, but he manifests the power of God and proves his apostleship by his results. Every honest man's conscience must approve.

---

### VERSES 3-7:

3 But if our gospel be hid, it is hid to them that are lost:

4 In whom the god of this world hath blinded the minds of them which believe not, lest the light of the glorious gospel of Christ, who is the image of God, should shine unto them.

5 For we preach not ourselves, but Christ Jesus the Lord; and ourselves your servants for Jesus' sake.

6 For God, who commanded the light to shine out of darkness, hath shined in our hearts, to give the light of the knowledge of the glory of God in the face of Jesus Christ.

7 But we have this treasure in earthen vessels, that the excellency of the power may be of God, and not of us.

## A Gospel for Blinded Minds

The Gospel is so glorious, God's grace so wonderful that, given such an offer of mercy and eternal blessing, how can any lost sinner reject it? How can anyone reject such love, turn down Heaven, go ahead on a course that leads to Hell and eternal suffering and ruin? It is unreasonable. After one is saved, he always sees that his rebellion, his delay, his unbelief were unreasonable folly! Why then do not all who hear the Gospel turn to Christ at once?

Because of two things—their own depraved nature, with a bias toward evil, and Satan's work in deceiving sinners.

Men are blinded (vs. 4), they "loved darkness rather than light, because their deeds were evil." They "hateth the light, neither cometh to the light" (John 3:19,20). Spiritually the sinner is "dead in trespasses and sins" (Eph. 2:1). First Corinthians 2:14 says, "But the natural man receiveth not the things of the Spirit of God: for they are foolishness unto him: neither can he know them,

because they are spiritually discerned." The Christian,
then, must be forewarned. Human wisdom, and even the
letter of Scripture, is not enough. The Spirit of God must
open blind eyes, must bring conviction of sin. The prodigal,
foolish wastrel, pleasure-mad, without decent respect for
father, without honor and duty, would not return for
forgiveness until "he came to himself" (Luke 15:17). A
preacher may get the ear of a sinner but not until the
blessed Holy Spirit works can one get to his heart and
conscience.

Satan, who blinds sinners, is ever near to deceive, to give
invalid excuses. "We wrestle not against flesh and blood"
when we preach the Gospel, but "against principalities,
against powers, against the rulers of the darkness of this
world, against spiritual wickedness in high places" (Eph.
6:12).

But it is not ourselves we preach but the Lord; then let
Him provide the power. We are thus His servants and the
servants of all. Oh, blessed truth! We have glory in our
hearts.

*"God, who commanded the light to shine out of
darkness, hath shined in our hearts, to give the light of the
knowledge of the glory of God in the face of Jesus Christ"*
(vs. 6). What a treasure we have! We have Christ! We have
His Gospel! We have His commission to take it to "every
creature" (Mark 15:16)! Glory! We can have His anointing,
Holy Spirit power, to do what we are commanded to do!
Our vessels are earthen vessels; we are frail, sinful men!
But now we are commanded to do, and may be empowered
to do, the supernatural work of God.

---

**VERSES 8-11:**

8 We are troubled on every side,
yet not distressed; we are perplexed,
but not in despair;

9 Persecuted, but not forsaken; cast
down, but not destroyed;

10 Always bearing about in the
body the dying of the Lord Jesus,
that the life also of Jesus might be
made manifest in our body.

11 For we which live are alway

delivered unto death for Jesus' sake, | made manifest in our mortal flesh.
that the life also of Jesus might be |

## True Christians Suffer for Christ

*"We are troubled on every side."* We might arrange trouble under three heads.

1. Trouble comes because we are fallen men in a fallen and cursed earth. All men have to grow old and have frail bodies. The self-interest of one clashes with the desires and self-interest of others. It is natural to have discontent with what we have and wish for what the other man has—his physique, his job, his wife, his talent, his property. The frailty of mankind makes trouble certain. "Man that is born of a woman is of few days, and full of trouble" (Job 14:1). Old and young, wicked and moral, saved and lost, live in a troubled world. Trouble is the heritage of fallen mankind.

2. Troubles are the price of sin. The drunkard has woes which the sober one does not have. Dope, gambling, adultery, hate, covetousness bring their own troubles. And since "whom the Lord loveth he chasteneth, and scourgeth every son whom he receiveth," then God allows troubles, chastening by sickness or unhappy circumstances or a guilty conscience because of the Christian's sin or failure.

3. Then good Christians suffer as Christians. A good Christian may suffer by sharing the heartbreak of God over sin and the compassionate tears of God for the world's sorrows. No doubt Paul suffered much over the Corinthian Christians whom he had to rebuke and so longed to help. He suffered over the Galatian Christians who were led astray by Judaizers, forsaking Paul's teachings. He suffered in his burden that Israel might be saved and said, "My heart's desire and prayer to God for Israel is, that they might be saved" (Rom. 10:1), and even the turmoil of his heart on this subject he expressed thus: "I could wish that myself were accursed from Christ for my brethren, my kinsmen according to the flesh" (Rom. 9:3).

Then God in lovingkindness must sometimes allow

suffering to come to one of His own in order to make us our best. How many preachers struggle along in poverty because God wants them to enter into the heart-burden of those to whom they minister. God wants a man to serve Him even in sorrow and poverty, and sometimes God allows one to suffer as did Paul with his thorn in the flesh, "lest I should be exalted above measure" (II Cor. 12:7). Sometimes God allows tragedy, the death of a loved one, some heartbreak to come to a man, that the well of human compassion and pity for those about him may be deepened.

Who can comfort one who lays away a loved one and seems utterly desolate, unless he himself has tasted that cup of sorrow? If Jesus must become a man, with a frailty and weakness and humility and poverty and temptations of a man, in order to be a fit substitute to die for man, then surely in some sense we who so represent Christ must enter into the sufferings of the world. And God sometimes allows it. How many soul winners have had some dark times of broken heart.

Spurgeon did when the great disaster struck in his service at Surrey Music Hall and innocent people died in one of his services because some foolish one stampeded the crowd with the cry, "Fire!" So did George W. Truett suffer in the tragic accident that took the life of his dear friend and hunting companion. So did another great man suffer when his baby upon whom he lavished his love died suddenly. So did another with a drunken father. So did another who as a child had lost a beloved mother and had lonely, desolate years! God allows His own to suffer so as to be more akin to a suffering, lost humanity.

Then a *good* Christian must suffer persecution. Does not the plain Word of God say, "Yea, and all that will live godly in Christ Jesus shall suffer persecution" (II Tim. 3:12)? We must remember what Jesus said:

*"If the world hate you, ye know that it hated me before it hated you. If ye were of the world, the world would love his own: but because ye are not of the world, but I have chosen*

*you out of the world, therefore the world hateth you.*
*Remember the word that I said unto you, The servant is*
*not greater than his lord. If they have persecuted me, they*
*will also persecute you; if they have kept my saying, they*
*will keep your's also. But all these things will they do unto*
*you for my name's sake, because they know not him that*
*sent me.''*

And the servant is no better than his lord. So a world
that hated the dear Saviour and scorned Him and crucified
Him will surely not love us too well if we are enough like
Jesus.

Oh, the world of a good Christian, one who is wholly
given over to Jesus Christ, is a crucifixion world. We are
each one plainly invited, "If any man will come after me,
let him deny himself, and take up his cross, and follow me."
That means the cross of crucifixion, the cross of self-denial
and surrender, as Jesus surrendered Himself to die for
others. Jesus set us the pattern here. First Peter 2:21, 22
tells us, "For even hereunto were ye called: because Christ
also suffered for us, leaving us an example, that ye should
follow his steps: Who did no sin, neither was guile found in
his mouth."

Yes, it costs something to really be a disciple of Jesus.
And Jesus said in Luke 14:26,27, "If any man come to me,
and hate not his father, and mother, and wife, and
children, and brethren, and sisters, yea, and his own life
also, he cannot be my disciple. And whosoever doth not
bear his cross, and come after me, cannot be my disciple."
He said we must count the cost. Do you really mean to be
an out-and-out disciple of Jesus? In verse 33 following, He
said, "so likewise, whosoever he be of you that forsaketh
not all that he hath, he cannot be my disciple."

It was not easy for Abraham to leave all his father's
house in Ur of the Chaldees and go to the land of promise.
Tentatively he took his father, but his father would not go
all the way and died in Haran. And perhaps against the
instruction of God, he took his nephew Lot, who held on to

the things of this world and delayed the blessing of God on Abraham. It is not easy for a man to give up pleasing his wife, his father, his mother, his brethren, not easy to give up all he has and turn his back on wealth and ease and loving comfort of friends and the praises of those he loves. But that is the part God requires of a Christian.

Oh, this story of blessed saints of God in the past shows clearly that a good Christian must suffer persecution. Faithful and good John the Baptist was imprisoned and beheaded. James, the brother of John, died by the sword of Herod (Acts 12:2). Peter and John were imprisoned again and again. They were beaten (Acts 5:40,41). The Roman tradition about their death is unreliable. Peter was never in Rome. But all the apostles must have suffered for the Lord Jesus more than we can ever know. Spirit-filled Stephen was stoned to death for his witness. The Apostle Paul was beaten many times, was stoned and left for dead; he fought the wild beasts at Ephesus; he was shipwrecked; he was in peril continually of Jews; he was betrayed by friends; he spent years in prison and at last died a martyr's death in Rome.

The history of saints of God reminds us that it costs something to be a true disciple for Jesus. We remember Savonarola and Luther and Wycliffe and Lattimer and Ridley. We remember the thousands of missionaries who died in heathen lands.     We remember those murdered by communists. We remember the sneers, the slander, the mockery, the heartbreak that a wicked world has brought on many a saint of God who did not die but who suffered persecution.

Oh, Paul the apostle earnestly sought that he might be fit to suffer for Christ. "I have suffered the loss of all things, and do count them but dung, that I may win Christ. . .That I may know him, and the power of his resurrection, and the fellowship of his sufferings" (Phil. 3:8,10). We are plainly entreated that since the Lord Jesus "suffered without the gate," then "let us go forth therefore unto him without the camp, bearing his reproach. For here have we no continuing city, but we seek one to come" (Heb. 13:12-14).

I fear that we are so accustomed to a decadent and lukewarm Christianity that we do not see the glory there is in being able and willing to suffer for Christ. But good Christians should. Paul was troubled on every side.

Yet in the midst of all the troubles of the world, what joys are those of a Christian! Romans 12:12 says the Christian may be "rejoicing in hope; patient in tribulation." So those who sow in tears reap in joy (Ps. 126:5).

There is the sweet fellowship with the Lord Jesus that one will never know unless he suffers with Jesus and for Jesus.

So Paul is troubled on every side but not distressed; he was perplexed but not in despair; he was persecuted but never, never forsaken. He was cast down but never destroyed. Oh, we must heed the sweet words of Jesus, "In the world ye shall have tribulation: but be of good cheer; I have overcome the world" (John 16:33).

---

### VERSES 12-18:

12 So then death worketh in us, but life in you.

13 We having the same spirit of faith, according as it is written, I believed, and therefore have I spoken; we also believe, and therefore speak;

14 Knowing that he which raised up the Lord Jesus shall raise up us also by Jesus, and shall present us with you.

15 For all things are for your sakes, that the abundant grace might through the thanksgiving of many redound to the glory of God.

16 For which cause we faint not; but though our outward man perish, yet the inward man is renewed day by day.

17 For our light affliction, which is but for a moment, worketh for us a far more exceeding and eternal weight of glory;

18 While we look not at the things which are seen, but at the things which are not seen: for the things which are seen are temporal; but the things which are not seen are eternal.

## Triumph Over Suffering

But if death works in the Christian, it works life in those about us. If the apostle suffers, then his converts at Corinth have abundant life. And Paul tells here of his unshakeable faith in the future glory, the future payday, the resurrection time. He knows that since the Lord Jesus was raised from the dead, we also should be raised (vs. 14). So he said also in Romans 8:11. And in that resurrection time Paul will not be alone but will find himself happily with a great company won to Christ and brought with him to Heaven, because he was willing to suffer for Christ! You see, all the suffering of Paul was for the sake of others whom he might win. Thus when Paul suffered, tens of thousands would have reason to praise God and thank Him.

And he reminds us that although other sufferings go on outwardly, there is an inward renewal day by day (vs. 16). This Bible doctrine of renewal, of recuperation, is blessed. So the 23rd Psalm can say, "He restoreth my soul." Although we are to offer our bodies a living sacrifice and we cannot be conformed to this world, yet we can be daily transformed and renewed "by the renewing of your mind, that ye may prove what is that good, and acceptable, and perfect, will of God" (Rom. 12:2).

Oh, to be a living sacrifice is not bad if there always be an inward strengthening, an inward renewing, a blessed sustenance, comfort and provision!

And looking toward the future, in verse 17 Paul can say and God says to all of us that *"our light affliction, which is but for a moment, worketh for us a far more exceeding and eternal weight of glory!"*

Oh, then, the Christian must have his eyes on another world. He must be looking at things that are not seen. He must not be looking on things that are temporal but on things that are eternal. Faith to us is "the evidence of things not seen" (Heb. 11:1).

We can afford to dwell in tents now and be like Abraham who "looked for a city which hath foundations, whose builder and maker is God" (Heb. 11:10). Since those heroes of the faith in Hebrews 11 desired a heavenly country and were not much tied on to this world, "Wherefore God is not ashamed to be called their God: for he hath prepared for them a city" (Heb. 11:16). We ought to be like Moses who left all the treasures and wealth of Egypt "as seeing him who is invisible" (Heb. 11:27). We are strangers and pilgrims; we are citizens of the heavenly country. What matters then the short days of poverty or humiliation or pain now, for the glory that shall be revealed? Oh, this affliction is light compared to the weight of glory that is coming. These dreary days and long nights are *"but for a moment,"* considering eternal joy and blessing.

May God make us willing and fit to suffer with the Lord Jesus and for Him, for that is the great heritage of those who are Christ's disciples.

# II CORINTHIANS V

FOR we know that if our earthly house of this tabernacle were dissolved, we have a building of God, an house not made with hands, eternal in the heavens.

2 For in this we groan, earnestly desiring to be clothed upon with our house which is from heaven:

3 If so be that being clothed we shall not be found naked.

4 For we that are in this tabernacle do groan, being burdened: not for that we would be unclothed, but clothed upon, that mortality might be swallowed up of life.

5 Now he that hath wrought us for the selfsame thing is God, who also hath given unto us the earnest of the Spirit.

6 Therefore we are always confident, knowing that, whilst we are at home in the body, we are absent from the Lord:

7 (For we walk by faith, not by sight:)

8 We are confident, I say, and willing rather to be absent from the body, and to be present with the Lord.

## We Will Trade This Body for an Eternal One

Here the apostle looks forward with comfort, even with longing, to the time when he will lay aside this mortal body and take up immortality. An older generation who was poorer in this world's goods, who was not so enamored of wealth and riches and culture and science of this generation, sang sweet songs about Heaven and looked forward to meeting loved ones there. That generation sang, "O sing to me of Heaven, when I am called to die." It sang, "Tell Mother I'll be there." It sang,

> O land of rest, for thee I sigh;
> When will the moment come,
> When I shall lay my armor by,
> And dwell in peace at home?

Those who had little here but had Christ and His riches, rejoiced that the time was coming when they would be poor no more, sick no more, despised no more, but happy and triumphant.

Oh, Christians will never know how to appreciate Heaven much until they get somewhat divorced from this world and its wealth and its pleasures and its favor. When we come to feel the sweet sentiment of my favorite hymn:

> **Jesus, I my cross have taken,**
> **All to leave, and follow Thee;**
> **Destitute, despised, forsaken,**
> **Thou, from hence, my all shalt be:**
> **Perish every fond ambition,**
> **All I've sought, and hoped, and known;**
> **Yet how rich is my condition,**
> **God and Heaven are still my own!**

then we will be more ready to enjoy Heaven.

Paul has been near to death (II Cor. 1:8,9). He was conscious that he was *"always bearing about in the body the dying of the Lord Jesus"* (vs. 10). So here he exults in the time he will lay aside this body, this poor abused body growing old, afflicted, and often painful. And what if we lay down our body here, our "tabernacle"; then we have "a building of God, an house not made with hands, eternal in the heavens." For that Paul longed.

Does Paul mean here that before the resurrection there will be some heavenly body prepared for us? It seems so. He expects to be clothed and *"not be found naked"* (vs. 3). He says *"not for that we would be unclothed, but clothed upon"* (vs. 4).

When the departed Samuel appeared to the Witch of Endor, did he not have some kind of a body, although he had died and was not yet resurrected? Moses and Elijah appeared to the Lord Jesus and three apostles on the Mount of Transfiguration. Did they not have some bodies —visible and definite bodies? Elisha had been changed and had been taken to Heaven without dying, but Moses died and God had buried him.

So whatever that heavenly mystery shall prove to be, those who die now are not left as wandering spirits, without form, without recognition by other loved ones, without physical senses. The Lord Jesus in Heaven has a physical body, a resurrected, glorified body. Do you think the saints in Heaven that rejoice with Him when a soul is saved do not have some form of body also, or the equivalent of a body, while they wait? Oh, Paul rejoiced that he would not be unclothed.

And we have a wonderful token, a down payment, or an "earnest" payment to guarantee the glorified body later, and that earnest is the Holy Spirit who has come to dwell within us (vs. 5; II Cor. 1:22; Eph. 1:13,14). Oh, He is not of this world but of the next world. We will have His blessed presence in eternity as now. He represents "Christ with us," and He guarantees that there will be wonderful clothing upon for us in the next world, when we lay aside this body.

Now verse 6 tells us that *"whilst we are at home in the body, we are absent from the Lord,"* but we can know by faith that we will one day be present with the Lord when we are absent from the body. And for that Paul looks forward in happiness; so should we.

Paul would be *"willing rather to be absent from the body, and to be present with the Lord"* (vs. 8). Does he mean he would prefer to die and go on to be with the Lord? I think yes. For in Philippians 1:21-24 Paul said,

*"For to me to live is Christ, and to die is gain. But if I live in the flesh, this is the fruit of my labour: yet what I shall choose I wot not. For I am in a strait betwixt two, having a desire to depart, and to be with Christ; which is far better: Nevertheless to abide in the flesh is more needful for you."*

Yes, to die would be gain for a Christian living in the will of God. Paul was in a strait, "having a desire to depart, and to be with Christ," for that is far better. But to please Christ and do His work and for the sake of Christians who need him, Paul was content to remain until God's time for his Homegoing.

---

**VERSES 9-13:**

9 Wherefore we labour, that, whe- | ther present or absent, we may be

accepted of him.

10 For we must all appear before the judgment seat of Christ; that every one may receive the things done in his body, according to that he hath done, whether it be good or bad.

11 Knowing therefore the terror of the Lord, we persuade men; but we are made manifest unto God; and I trust also are made manifest in your consciences.

12 For we commend not ourselves again unto you, but give you occasion to glory on our behalf, that ye may have somewhat to answer them which glory in appearance, and not in heart.

13 For whether we be beside ourselves, it is to God: or whether we be sober, it is for your cause.

## Facing the Judgment Seat of Christ

Of all the apostles, Paul was "in labours more abundant" (II Cor. 11:23). He went "publickly, and from house to house. , .night and day with tears" in soul winning (Acts 20:20,31). Evidently, because of this pressure in his soul, he never married because he could not take time for home and family, and worked himself nearly to death. Why? Oh, one thought was continually in his heart—that *"we may be accepted of him."* He said whether I go now to meet the Lord Jesus or whether being absent from Him now and present in the body, I come later to the judgment seat of Christ. "Oh," he said, "I want the Lord Jesus to accept me, to be pleased with me."

Paul has no thought here of losing salvation. That matter he has settled forever. He could say, "Who is he that condemneth? It is Christ that died, yea rather, that is risen again, who is even at the right hand of God, who also maketh intercession for us. Who shall separate us from the love of Christ? shall tribulation, or distress, or persecution, or famine, or nakedness, or peril, or sword?" (Rom. 8:34,35). He was persuaded that nothing could separate him from Christ. He has just said in chapter 4, verse 14, that he knows that the Spirit that raised up the Lord Jesus will raise him up and present him in the heavenly kingdom. Here Paul is not wondering about his salvation.

Oh, but he wants the Lord Jesus to be pleased with him, to praise him, to reward him. When he looks into the piercing eyes of the loving Saviour, he wants to hear, "Well done, thou good and faithful servant: thou hast been faithful over a few things, I will make thee ruler over many things: enter thou into the joy of thy lord" (Matt. 25:21).

Paul is looking forward to a great judgment time at *"the judgment seat of Christ."* This is not a judgment of lost people but of saved people. It is to be a judgment in Heaven, when Christians meet in glorified bodies there. And note that *"we must all appear"*; so it is a judgment time for every Christian.

And what will be the result of that judgment? *". . .that every one may receive the things done in his body, according to that he hath done, whether it be good or bad"* (vs. 10).

Someone has said that that judgment is only for rewards. That is not true. But one may say, "Could God come to punish me, after He has already forgiven me and taken me to Heaven?" The Scripture here does not speak of an angry Saviour, nor of His now assigning punishment for wrongs we have done. Rather, we are to meet those wrongs themselves. We will receive things done in the body.

So in Heaven, there will not be the same joy nor the same reward for all.

Let us illustrate it. If one of your loved ones has been neglected and goes unwarned to eternal torment and separation from God, at the judgment seat of Christ you will face that fact which cannot then be changed. There are certain natural and inevitable results of our lives which follow us. Let me illustrate.

In Evansville, Texas, a wicked sinner called "Old Bill" was converted at the rescue mission. Before he was converted, he was in a drunken fight and lost an eye. Then he was wonderfully saved and set out to live for God. Now he called himself, and others called him, "New Bill." Old Bill had only one eye. And New Bill still had only one eye. His sins are forgiven but the results are still with him.

So, in some sense, at the judgment seat of Christ, we will receive the things done in the body.

This judgment seat of Christ is discussed in I Corinthians 3:10-15. There we learn that works are classified like wood, hay and stubble that burn and are temporary, and soon vanish in fires of judgment; but gold, silver and precious stones represent the good deeds that have pleased God and bring eternal blessing. If a man's works be burned "he shall suffer loss: but he himself shall be saved; yet so as by fire," the Scripture says. But if a man's works abide "he shall receive a reward." Not receive salvation: all these who appear at this judgment have already received salvation, but fruitful Christians will receive a reward besides.

What kind of rewards? Perhaps to reign with Christ on earth. "If we suffer, we shall also reign with him" (II Tim. 2:12). In the parable of the pounds the servant whose one pound, left in his charge, had gained ten pounds and he had the happy reward, "Well, thou good servant: because thou hast been faithful in a very little, have thou authority over ten cities." Another was rewarded with authority over five cities. Another had no reward at all. And in answer to Peter's question, Jesus said the apostles would judge the tribes of Israel (Matt. 19:28). So surely in Heaven those who have won souls and suffered more for Jesus will rejoice more and have more eternal rewards at the judgment seat of Christ.

How seriously Paul took this matter! *"Knowing therefore the terror of the Lord, we persuade men"* (vs. 11). He does not now speak of the terror of an unsaved man meeting Christ but of a Christian with a wasted life, finding loved ones gone to Hell, opportunities forever gone, and failing to have the rewards that others have earned, when they meet Christ. That is a matter so fearful that Paul persuades men that they should earnestly set out to fit into a better world that is yet to come and receive the rewards that go to faithful and persecuted and dedicated disciples.

Do you wonder that Paul speaks of the *"terror of the*

*Lord"* in warning Christians of that judgment seat of Christ? But for a Christian with a wasted life, lost opportunities, loved ones gone to Hell, no fruit to present to the Saviour, it will be a fearsome time. In I Corinthians 3:15 we read, "If any man's work shall be burned, he shall suffer loss." This saved person shall *suffer* in Heaven, have *loss* in Heaven!

And to the servant who took a pound to invest for the Master and did not use it, there is a severe rebuke in Luke 19:23-26, and we are told that "unto every one which hath shall be given; and from him that hath not, even that he hath shall be taken away from him."

In a similar parable on the same general subject, the parable of the talents in Matthew 25, the Lord answers the faithless steward, "Thou wicked and slothful servant," and he loses the talent that he had. In this case the unprofitable servant, we suppose, represents the lost man because he was to be cast into outer darkness (Matt. 25:30).

At any rate, it is a terrible thing to face Christ after a wasted life; so Paul speaks of *"the terror of the Lord."*

Now Paul reminds them that although he has labored so fervently, he is not commending himself (vs. 12). They may explain to others if they will why Paul labors so sacrificially, and *"glory in our behalf"* (vs. 12). How do you explain a man like Paul who seems beside himself, too busy to marry, day and night laboring? It is holy madness. It is to God. And what about the man so deadly sober, so serious, often at the point of tears, often pleading, warning with fanatical desperation? That, Paul says, is for the people, the lost he would win, the saved he would warn and prepare for the judgment seat of Christ.

We remember that Felix cried out to the fervent apostle, "Paul, thou art beside thyself; much learning doth make thee mad" (Acts 26:24). The surging crowd gathered to the flaming ministry of the Lord Jesus, "And when his friends heard of it, they went out to lay hold on him: for they said, He is beside himself" (Mark 3:21). May God give more of us this madness to get out the Gospel.

## VERSES 14-20:

14 For the love of Christ constraineth us; because we thus judge, that if one died for all, then were all dead:

15 And that he died for all, that they which live should not henceforth live unto themselves, but unto him which died for them, and rose again.

16 Wherefore henceforth know we no man after the flesh: yea, though we have known Christ after the flesh, yet now henceforth know we him no more.

17 Therefore if any man be in Christ, he is a new creature: old things are passed away; behold, all things are become new.

18 And all things are of God, who hath reconciled us to himself by Jesus Christ, and hath given to us the ministry of reconciliation;

19 To wit, that God was in Christ, reconciling the world unto himself, not imputing their trespasses unto them; and hath committed unto us the word of reconciliation.

20 Now then we are ambassadors for Christ, as though God did beseech you by us: we pray you in Christ's stead, be ye reconciled to God.

## We Who Are Bought at Such Cost Should Not Live for Ourselves

Why, Paul, are you so obsessed, so beside yourself? Christ's love, His sacrifice for us, constrains me, he would say! Since Christ died for all of us, none of us have a right to live our own lives but only *"unto him which died for them, and rose again"* (vs. 15). This living Saviour now has all claim on us.

The Christian is now a *"new creature"* or literally *"a new creation"* (vs. 17). This new creature, the "new man" (Eph. 4:24), ought daily to "walk in the Spirit" as one who has "crucified the flesh with the affections and lusts," thus continually opposing them (Gal. 5:16-24). "A new creature" refers, of course, to the born-again nature, not the old nature which the Christian still has. The struggle of flesh against spirit "so that ye cannot do the things that ye would" (Gal. 5:17) goes on continually. The Christian now must know, like Paul, that ". . .with the mind I myself serve the law of God; but with the flesh the law of sin" (Rom. 7:25). The new creature is the new heart, not having any allegiance to sin but anxious to serve God.

This born-again nature, the "new creature," groans with the rest of creation, "waiting for the adoption, to wit, the redemption of our body" (Rom. 8:23) when the struggle to do right will be won forever.

But now the one great obligation of the Christian is to fulfill the *"ministry of reconciliation"* (vs. 18) which is committed to us. Since we are reconciled to God, the one thing we must do in response to Christ's love and sacrifice is to win others.

---

**VERSE 21:**

21 For he hath made him to be sin for us, who knew no sin; that we might be made the righteousness of God in him.

## Christ Our Substitute

Christ was *"made. . .sin for us."* An astonishing statement! Young's Analytical Concordance gives the Greek word *hamartia* the double meaning "sin, error, sin offering." So Christ became a sin offering but in some awesome way He became sin also, though He never sinned. In the Old Testament the Hebrew word *chattath* is translated "sin" 145 times, but the same word is translated "sin offering" 82 times!

So in the mind of God, Jesus, the Sin Offering, became the embodiment of sin. God forsook Jesus on the cross as a sinner and let Him be punished as a sinner. Our sins were actually "laid on" Jesus. "All we like sheep have gone astray; we have turned every one to his own way; and the Lord hath laid on him the iniquity of us all" (Isa. 53:6). He had the pain of sin, the shame of sin, the awful separation from God that sin brings. The bloody sweat in Gethsemane when Jesus almost died and said, "My soul is exceeding sorrowful, even unto death" (Matt. 26:38), is some indication of the grief and shame and broken heart of Jesus over the sin of the world.

I believe no girl lured into sin, repudiated by parents when her shame is made public, ever felt more grief than Jesus felt. No murderer, about to die in the electric chair or on the gallows, ever suffered remorse more bitter than the agony of Jesus when He cried out on the cross, "My God, my God, why hast thou forsaken me?" (Matt. 27:46). Jesus could not simply bear physical pain with none of the shame and humiliation of sin. He must suffer all a sinner would suffer to pay the sinner's debt. So sin entered into the consciousness of Jesus, and God left Satan to torment His soul. Oh, dear sinless, pure Jesus, to be made sin, for us, although without sinning!

Here is Isaiah 53:3-5 repeated again:

*"He is despised and rejected of men; a man of sorrows, and acquainted with grief: and we hid as it were our faces from him; he was despised, and we esteemed him not. Surely he hath borne our griefs, and carried our sorrows: yet we did esteem him stricken, smitten of God, and afflicted. But he was wounded for our transgressions, he was bruised for our iniquities: the chastisement of our peace was upon him; and with his stripes we are healed."*

He made "his soul an offering for sin," not only His body.

But now who can doubt that sin is paid for? If God counted Jesus a sinner, who was not a sinner, who will wear that seamless robe of Christ's righteousness? I will, as so will all those who trust in Him. "Who is he that condemneth? It is Christ that died, yea rather, that is risen again, who is even at the right hand of God, who also maketh intercession for us" (Rom. 8:34). Since Christ paid all my debt, suffered for all my sins, past, present and future, then God can count my debt all paid, and I am not only forgiven but justified.

"By one offering he hath perfected for ever them that are sanctified" (Heb. 10:14). Now God's righteousness is shown "that he might be just, and the justifier of him which believeth in Jesus" (Rom. 3:26).

Now the blessedness promised in Psalm 32:1,2 and Romans 4:5-8 is mine, is bought for every believer!

# II CORINTHIANS VI

WE then, as workers together with him, beseech you also that ye receive not the grace of God in vain.

2 (For he saith, I have heard thee in a time accepted, and in the day of salvation have I succoured thee: behold, now is the accepted time; behold, now is the day of salvation.)

3 Giving no offence in any thing, that the ministry be not blamed:

## God's Grace Obligates Us: Be True

The apostle has told of his concern to face the judgment seat of Christ confidently. He knows the terror of facing the Lord and to be found unfaithful (5:9-11). He is standing in Christ's stead as an ambassador. But now he reminds Christians that all have the same obligation! God's wonderful grace, saving, seeking, renewing day by day, with resurrection and glory ahead sure, makes them debtors. God wants fruit for His grace. He wants the whole-souled service of those he has bought. Paul said in Galatians 2:21, "I do not frustrate the grace of God." Neither should we. Paul said, "I am debtor both to the Greeks, and to the Barbarians; both to the wise, and to the unwise" (Rom. 1:14).

How wonderful that Christ heard us in a day of salvation and did not turn us away. Now in view of His blessings, we should bear fruit.

*"Giving no offence"* (vs. 3). The Greek word is *proskope*, "stumbling block." In the sense of causing the weak to stumble, tempting others to do wrong, getting them discouraged, a careless, or frivolous or critical attitude might hurt those we would bless. This does not contradict the Scriptures' oft insistence for plain preaching against sin. "Them that sin rebuke before all, that others also may fear" (I Tim. 5:20). ". . .reprove, rebuke, exhort with all longsuffering and doctrine" (II Tim. 4:2). "Cry aloud, spare not, lift up thy voice like a trumpet, and shew my people

their transgression, and the house of Jacob their sins" (Isa. 58:1). One must boldly warn sinners, must demand repentance but must lovingly watch that our service, our witness, be not hindered and the weak caused to stumble (see I Cor. 9:19-23).

---

**VERSES 4-7:**

4 But in all things approving ourselves as the ministers of God, in much patience, in afflictions, in necessities, in distresses,

5 In stripes, in imprisonments, in tumults, in labours, in watchings, in fastings;

6 By pureness, by knowledge, by longsuffering, by kindness, by the Holy Ghost, by love unfeigned,

7 By the word of truth, by the power of God, by the armour of righteousness on the right hand and on the left,

## The Cost of a Godly Ministry

Read those verses above again! The inspired apostle proved himself a good minister of Christ. Does God expect equal devotion from us? What requirements?

1. *"Much patience."* Another way of saying persistent faithfulness. Like Hebrews 12:1,2, ". . .run with patience the race that is set before us." If you cannot take hard times, rebuff and disappointment, and stay on the job, you are not a good minister.

2. *"In afflictions."* Can you keep at it when sick, when in pain, when persecuted?

3. *"In necessities."* Almost always poverty is a factor in a successful ministry, specially at first. If you cannot serve God faithfully, resisting the better income, the pleasanter surroundings in other work in order for yourself and family to serve God, you are not a good minister of Christ.

In my young days as an evangelist, in the summer vacation from seminary, I went to preach in a series of revival services. I left my wife, a two-year-old baby and another on the way in a tiny two-room apartment. There was no telephone nor car. I could leave only five or six dollars for an emergency, food and milk, for two weeks. One afternoon I was so burdened down with concern, I had to find a place to pray in a country schoolhouse. What if Mrs. Rice or the baby were sick? What if some accident—a fall or a fire? How would one reach a doctor, get help or medicine? With a broken heart I waited on God to settle forever, I hope, that I can safely trust God for me and mine in poverty.

4. *"In distresses."* Consider again the perils, the hardships of Paul.

*"Are they ministers of Christ? (I speak as a fool) I am more; in labours more abundant, in stripes above measure, in prisons more frequent, in deaths oft. Of the Jews five times received I forty stripes save one. Thrice was I beaten with rods, once was I stoned, thrice I suffered shipwreck, a night and a day I have been in the deep; In journeyings often, in perils of waters, in perils of robbers, in perils by mine own countrymen, in perils by the heathen, in perils in the city, in perils in the wilderness, in perils in the sea, in perils among false brethren; In weariness and painfulness, in watchings often, in hunger and thirst, in fastings often, in cold and nakedness. Besides those things that are without, that which cometh upon me daily, the care of all the churches. Who is weak, and I am not weak? who is offended, and I burn not?"*—II Cor. 11:23-29.

Remember that when a Christian does his best, he will often be misunderstood. Best friends will often forsake one for Christ's sake. Jesus said, "Think not that I am come to send peace on earth: I came not to send peace, but a sword. For I am come to set a man at variance against his father, and the daughter against her mother, and the daughter in law against her mother in law. And a man's foes shall be they of his own household" (Matt. 10:34-36).

5. *"In stripes."* A man of God may often be beaten or attacked physically. That has not been my privilege, but perhaps I was not a good enough preacher.

A mayor of Plainview, Texas, threatened me with a knife

publicly on the streets because of my message on modern dancing.

Recently a famous preacher had teenagers publicly spit in his face. Sometimes the slander, the accusations, the loss of friends of a lifetime have been more painful than stripes.

6. *"In imprisonments."* Remember James, Peter, John, Stephen. How many Russian Christians went to Siberia for Christ? I knew an ardent young man who was heartbroken by lewd movies, violent, anti-Christian movies shown in his town. He appealed to the theater owner. He must take the movies in blocks as sent him. The godly young man appealed to the city council. This group said the people wanted the lewd, the immoral, the pro-criminal movies. The young man took an ax, went up to the projector room, broke up the projector, and the spare projector. He went to prison for two years. I do not say his method was right; possibly he felt required to make up for the callous, worldly Christians, the compromising preachers who took no stand. But I have wept before God, thanking Him for such concern and envying his ministry. It may be Carry Nation's hatchet breaking up saloons, is not the best way, but sometimes Christians ought to go to prison for Christ.

7. *"In tumults."* Should not preachers preach so plainly against sin that riot crowds like those of Ephesus in Acts 19, like that at Corinth which threatened Paul in Acts 18, would gather against one? If communists and hippies and Black Panthers sometimes protest and march against a president or against a university administration, wouldn't such tumults arise over preaching if it were strong enough and reached enough people? Would not Moslems or Jews sometimes assault a powerful preacher in their area as some did Stephen?

8. *"In labours."* Can a servant of God be true and work for Him only an eight-hour day? Can one feel the awful urgency of those about to go to Hell without sometimes laboring like Paul who "by the space of three

years. . .ceased not to warn every one night and day with tears" (Acts 20:31)?

9. *"In watchings."* Staying awake in the night watches. Christians should sometimes pray "day and night" (Luke 18:7). Jesus "went out into a mountain to pray, and continued all night in prayer to God" (Luke 6:12). Again "rising up a great while before day, he went out, and departed into a solitary place, and there prayed" (Mark 1:35). Sometimes Paul must stay awake to win souls, or because he has no bed. No one is a good servant of Christ who suffers no inconvenience, no discomfort for the Gospel's sake. Nights of prayer, nights traveling or sitting in an airport or station, or sleeping on a bench, are required in a good ministry sometimes.

10. *"In fastings."* To miss regular meals seeking God's blessing and power. But sometimes in poverty, hungry with no money, no food, no one to provide. When Jesus won the woman of Samaria, He refused food at mealtime, saying, "I have meat to eat that ye know not of," and "my meat is to do the will of him that sent me, and to finish his work" (John 4:32,34). Some scholars think the "prayer and fasting" listed as a requirement for greater power in Mark 9:29 and Matthew 17:21 are glosses, but certainly fasting is often proper when holy concern takes away the normal desire for food, or when Christians thus choose to concentrate their hearts on getting an answer from God.

The disciples fasted when Jesus was taken away (Matt. 9:15). Esther and her maidens fasted before deliverance of Jews from Haman's wicked plot (Esther 4:16). Ezra and his returning Jews fasted at the river Ahava and were kept safe from bandits (Ezra 8:23). A formal fast, without hearts seeking God, a mere religious rite like that of the Pharisees, is not recommended, but surely sometimes every earnest Christian should so earnestly seek God as to put aside usual comforts, pleasures and duties to pray.

11. *"By pureness."* Timothy was exhorted to deal with women "with all purity" (I Tim. 5:2). In I Timothy 5:22

Timothy was commanded, "Keep thyself pure." He was to be "an example of the believers, in word, in conversation, in charity, in spirit, in faith, in purity" (I Tim. 4:12). In I Corinthians 7:1,2 Paul says, "It is good for a man not to touch a woman. Nevertheless, to avoid fornication, let every man have his own wife, and let every woman have her own husband." So, for the same reason it is expected that a pastor be "the husband of one wife," and so the deacon (I Tim. 3:2,12). The bishop must be "blameless" and of "good report of them which are without" (I Tim. 2:2,7).

So it is urgent with any who serve God to do it with "pureness." Surely that purity must be obvious, and one must "abstain from all appearance of evil" (I Thess. 5:22), just as one must be "providing for honest things, not only in the sight of the Lord, but also in the sight of men" (II Cor. 8:21). Heart purity, purity of action and blameless repentance are marks of "a good minister of Jesus Christ."

12. *"By knowledge."* It is no accident that people expect the preacher to be one of the best educated men in the community. God often calls men with little education, little formal learning. But D. L. Moody with only a grade school education usually spent two early hours each day with his Bible and in study. Paul wrote Timothy, "Give attendance to reading" (I Tim. 4:13).

We know a pastor, only a high school graduate, greatly blessed of God in soul winning and building a tremendous congregation who, when he saw doctors and lawyers coming to hear him, set out to master Greek and other studies in order to be a good minister of Christ. God can use anyone who learns all he can to be useful and He chooses many weak ones, but He does not want any Christian to be "willingly ignorant."

13. *"By longsuffering."* With what patience, with what unflurried peace must the man of God lead God's people, deal with their sins and failures, without much surprise or discouragement. Leadership should be settled in character,

not giving up one's peace, nor one's task, nor giving up the
wayward.

14. *"By kindness."* How thoughtful of others to "rejoice
with them that do rejoice, and weep with them that weep"
(Rom. 12:15). What doors are opened by a smile, a kind
word, a helpful deed! So, "be ye kind one to another,
tenderhearted, forgiving one another, even as God for
Christ's sake hath forgiven you" (Eph. 4:32). Christian love
"suffereth long, and is kind" (I Cor. 13:4).

15. *"By the Holy Ghost."* To be all the above, the servant
of God must have the anointing, the fullness of the Holy
Spirit, His wisdom, His power. Other requirements of the
good ministry of Christ are branches, but this and the love
unfeigned are the trunk of the tree, the source of the
character, the boldness, the faithfulness required.

The prophet said, "Not by might, nor by power, but by
my spirit, saith the Lord of hosts" (Zech. 4:6). All the
ministry of Jesus, our example, was done in the power of
the Holy Spirit, after God "anointed Jesus of Nazareth
with the Holy Ghost and with power: who went about
doing good, and healing all that were oppressed of the devil;
for God was with him" (Acts 10:38).

Paul and Barnabas went out, "sent forth by the Holy
Ghost" (Acts 13:4). Let us never forget the promise that "ye
shall receive power, after that the Holy Ghost is come upon
you: and ye shall be witnesses unto me both in Jerusalem,
and in all Judaea, and in Samaria, and unto the uttermost
part of the earth" (Acts 1:8).

16. *"By love unfeigned."* The love of Christ constrained
Paul to his abundant labors and sacrifice. His love for his
people Israel drove him continually to prayer and witness
(Rom. 10:1) and "God so loved the world, that he gave his
only begotten Son." So love is the greatest motivation in
the world, as the Holy Spirit power is the greatest power in
the world.

The command of the master who gave a great supper was
to his servant to "compel them to come in." Love compels

sometimes. As I Corinthians 13 teaches so emphatically, all gifts and services of a Christian are vain without love.

17. *"By the word of truth."* Zeal is admirable. Love is the greatest human attribute in the world. But zeal and love are frustrated without honest presentation of the Word of Truth, the message of the Scriptures. Ephesians 1:15 uses the same phrase, "the word of truth" and so does II Timothy 2:15, in each case meaning the revealed truth of Scriptures. Remember, "The law of the Lord is perfect, converting the soul" (Ps. 19:7) and "being born again. . .by the word of God" (I Pet. 1:23). But the term here could mean "truthfulness," that God's man must most rigidly watch to be honest and truthful in every contact, conversation, doctrine and illustration.

18. *"By the power of God."* Since already this passage has spoken of one proving his ministry "by the Holy Ghost," the phrase here may refer to the power of God, not in word, not in anointed witnesses, but in miracles and healings (See II Cor. 12:12; I Cor. 2:5; 12:10,28,29). We dare not dismiss the many, many cases in the New Testament where miraculous power was present in the ministry of Christ and the apostles.

Miracles were never to be the plaything of the curious, but there is no Bible statement that miracles would cease. If the teachings of Jesus in Mark 9:23; Matthew 17:23; John 14:12, the disputed passage in Mark 16:17,18 (which we accept as authentic), and James 5:12-16 are for us, then miracles as God sees fit are sometimes for us today. Finney, Moody, Torrey, Dr. Blanchard of Wheaton College, as well as this writer, give solemn, proved witness of such miraculous events. Certainly in Paul's ministry this miraculous element was present as proof of his authority and message, and it would be normal for him to mention this as essential to the "good minister of Jesus Christ."

19. *"By the armour of righteousness."* A Christian's armor is mentioned in Romans 13:12 as "the armour of

light," and in Ephesians 6:11,13 we are told to put on "the whole armour of God." In that armour is named "the breastplate of righteousness," with the same meaning as here. That emphasis "on the right hand and on the left" means, we think, extra care about dealing righteously with everybody on every basis. So the minister must have the character required in I Timothy 3:1-7. Romans 8:3,4 tells us that Christ came and condemned sin and we are to reckon ourselves to be dead to sin (Rom. 6:11) so "that the righteousness of the law might be fulfilled in us." There is no substitute for godly living.

---

**VERSES 8-13:**

8 By honour and dishonour, by evil report and good report: as deceivers, and yet true;

9 As unknown, and yet well known, as dying, and, behold, we live; as chastened, and not killed;

10 As sorrowful, yet alway rejoicing; as poor, yet making many rich; as having nothing, and yet possessing all things.

11 O ye Corinthians, our mouth is open unto you, our heart is enlarged.

12 Ye are not straitened in us, but ye are straitened in your own bowels.

13 Now for a recompence in the same, (I speak as unto my children,) be ye also enlarged.

## The World's Reaction to Good Ministers of Jesus Christ

There is a striking paradox in a good Christian life. The way to be great is to be a servant of all (Matt. 20:26-28). The way to have is to give (Luke 6:38; Prov. 11:25; II Cor. 9:8). The way to save one's life is to lose it (Mark 8:35). So the good Christian minister, warning, pleading, witnessing to many, will have honor and praise from those blessed by his ministry. But those who resist, who continue in sin, will avoid and disparage the zealous one. To some he is the "savour of life unto life," to others he is "the savour of death unto death" (II Cor. 2:16). He will be of good report of the best people, the earnest Christians, but slandered, sneered at, counted queer or a nuisance by others. What godly preacher, with power and winning many, has not been slandered?

So the good servant of Christ will be unknown, like Paul, imprisoned by the Sanhedrin, finally beheaded in a Roman prison, yet unknown to millions as the greatest of the apostles.

So the Christian may die of persecution or starve from neglect or wither from the betrayal of friends but inwardly be renewed day by day. He may be chastened, yet always protected so he cannot die till God's time.

Sorrow for good Christians? Yes, but always rejoicing too. Sowing in tears and reaping in joy. Poor (voluntarily or not) but making the drunkard sober and giving him back to his job, supporting his family. Teaching the character that makes for success in this world, but staying poor, and making many rich forever by getting them saved. Oh, the Christian who loses all for Christ may temporarily seem to have nothing. But wait! "All things are your's; And ye are Christ's; and Christ is God's" (I Cor. 3:22,23). How rich are we who have Christ, and sins forgiven, and Heaven and all things!

Oh, God's Word means not to restrict the Christian's life, to make drab the future, to limit enjoyment (vs. 12)! He wants them to develop a great standard, a great goal for Christian living with power and joy.

---

## VERSES 14-18:

14 Be ye not unequally yoked together with unbelievers: for what fellowship hath righteousness with unrighteousness? and what communion hath light with darkness?

15 And what concord hath Christ with Bē-lĭ-ăl? or what part hath he that believeth with an infidel?

16 And what agreement hath the temple of God with idols? for ye are the temple of the living God; as God hath said, I will dwell in them, and walk in them; and I will be their God, and they shall be my people.

17 Wherefore come out from among them, and be ye separate, saith the Lord, and touch not the unclean thing; and I will receive you,

18 And will be a Father unto you, and ye shall be my sons and daughters, saith the Lord Almighty.

## Be Not Unequally Yoked With Unbelievers

Note carefully the command of verse 14. Not all yokes, not all ties, not all fellowships are forbidden, but the yoke with *unbelievers* is. And note also that it is the *unequal* yoke which is forbidden.

First Corinthians 5:9,10 tells us, "I wrote unto you in an epistle not to company with fornicators: Yet not altogether with the fornicators of this world, or with the covetous, or extortioners, or with idolaters; for then must ye needs go out of the world." We cannot go out of this world, and there are some areas when our welfare and happiness require the same circumstances as the welfare and happiness of those all about us, saved and lost. My country is my country, and I must love it, support it, defend it. But many a lost man, as a citizen, pays taxes, obeys the laws, serves in the armed services, celebrates the 4th of July. I can be a good citizen along with other good citizens and the question of spiritual fellowship is not involved.

When a lost man buys groceries and a saved man buys groceries, it is not an unequal yoke that may throw them together. Lawyers may belong to the bar association or physicians may belong to the medical association. Lawyers make common cause of those who deal in the courts. Doctors make common cause of those who wish to save lives. But only in the spiritual realm must Christians not yoke up with unbelievers. That would be an unequal yoke.

Note the disparity here between righteousness and unrighteousness, between light and darkness, between Christ and Belial, between a believer and an infidel! And what agreement has the temple of God with idols? One man has Christ in his heart, is a child of God, has Heaven as his home. Another is a child of Satan, has a wicked, unregenerate heart, will not receive Christ and is headed for Hell and eternal torment. These two can have no genuine fellowship until the child of Hell becomes a child of God, until they start in the same direction.

How often this teaching is given in the Bible. Psalm 1:1

says, "Blessed is the man that walketh not in the counsel of the ungodly, nor standeth in the way of sinners, nor sitteth in the seat of the scornful." Ephesians 5:11 commands us, "Have no fellowship with the unfruitful works of darkness, but rather reprove them." In II John, verses 9 to 11, we are plainly commanded, "Whosoever transgresseth, and abideth not in the doctrine of Christ, hath not God. He that abideth in the doctrine of Christ, he hath both the Father and the Son. If there come any unto you, and bring not this doctrine, receive him not into your house, neither bid him God speed: For he that biddeth him God speed is partaker of his evil deeds." One who does not abide in the Bible teaching about Christ is not saved; he "hath not God," he is not a Christian and ought not be given Christian recognition. I ought not receive him in the pulpit as a preacher, ought not receive him as a Christian teacher in the Sunday school or Bible college or seminary. I ought not call him "brother," ought not entertain him in the prophet's chamber in my home. I might help any poor, troubled soul with food and raiment, but I ought not call him brother if he is an unconverted child of Satan.

That means I ought not have fellowship and church membership with those who do not claim to be born again. No one ought ever be received as a church member who does not profess faith in Christ as his own personal Saviour. I cannot take part in a ministerial association if by doing so I must call "brother" unconverted men, infidels or those who deny the deity of Christ and His virgin birth and bodily resurrection, deny the blood atonement and inspiration of the Bible. If membership and association means count them brothers I cannot and must not do it. I must not support, with my money, denominational institutions that feed and honor and promote such men who are not Christians and who do not believe the Bible and deny the historic Christian faith.

When Jehoshaphat, the godly king of Judah, joined in with Ahab to fight the Syrians, he returned home and was rebuked. "And Jehu the son of Hanani the seer went out to meet him, and said to king Jehoshaphat, Shouldest thou help the ungodly, and love them that hate the Lord? therefore is wrath upon thee from before the Lord" (II Chron. 19:2).

Before that, Jehoshaphat's father Asa made a league with Ben-hadad, king of Syria, and was rebuked by the Prophet Hanani in II Chronicles 16:7: "And at that time Hanani the seer came to Asa king of Judah, and said unto him, Because thou hast relied on the king of Syria, and not relied on the Lord thy God, therefore is the host of the king of Syria escaped out of thine hand." And it is remarkable that the father was rebuked by Hanani the seer and Jehoshaphat the son was rebuked by Hanani's son, Jehu.

This command against the unequal yoke will forbid the marriage of saved with the unsaved. We are told that the widow "is at liberty to be married to whom she will; *only in the Lord*" (I Cor. 7:39). And what a sad tale it is of Solomon who married heathen women and his wives turned away his heart. "For it came to pass, when Solomon was old, that his wives turned away his heart after other gods: and his heart was not perfect with the Lord his God, as was the heart of David his father. For Solomon went after Ashtoreth the goddess of the Zidonians, and after Milcom the abomination of the Ammonites" (I Kings 11:3-5).

We plead with Christians everywhere not to give money where it will support seminaries and men who break down the faith of others in the Bible, not to support a denominational program that thus makes them yoked up with unbelievers. We entreat saved young people not to have courtships and dates with the unsaved.

No, *"Come out from among them, and be ye separate, saith the Lord, and touch not the unclean. . .; and I will. . .be a Father unto you, and ye shall be my sons and daughters, saith the Lord Almighty."* Note that the word "thing" in verse 17 is in italics which means it was not in the Greek. It is not "the unclean thing," but it is unclean people, unconverted sinners, we are to avoid.

*"I will. . .be a Father unto you."* That does not mean that this is the way to be converted, to be born into God's family. But it means surely that no one can know well God as his Father and thus manifest God as his Father and himself as a son or a daughter of God unless he lives separate from the ungodly world.

# II CORINTHIANS VII

HAVING therefore these promises, dearly beloved, let us cleanse ourselves from all filthiness of the flesh and spirit, perfecting holiness in the fear of God.

## How God's Children May Live as God's Children

*"These promises."* God is actually a Father to the Christian. His body indwelt by the Holy Spirit is a temple in a literal, real sense. But the compromising and worldly Christian, although a child of God, has not the child's joy and fellowship which is offered. There is a sense in which, tragically, many Christians are not "received" (vs. 17 above), that is, are not given the intimacy, the fellowship, which other children of God enjoy. As the prosperity in everything which is promised in Psalm 1:1-3 depends on one avoiding fellowship with the "ungodly," the "sinners" and the "scornful," so here the rich daily blessings offered depend upon not yoking up with unbelievers.

So with such promise, we should *"cleanse ourselves from all filthiness of the flesh and spirit. . . ."*

We remember when Jesus washed the disciples' feet, He taught that although they were cleansed, saved, yet they walk in a dirty world and need to spiritually get cleansing daily from this same "filthiness of the flesh and spirit." And our model prayer, the Lord's Prayer, teaches us to ask daily, "Forgive us our debts" (Matt. 6:12) or "our sins" (Luke 11:4).

*"Perfecting holiness."* Holiness means set apart for God. Such holiness is a relative matter. All who are saved are sanctified, that is, set apart for God and Heaven. "For by one offering he hath perfected for ever them that are sanctified" (Heb. 10:14). One who attends much to the Word becomes more nearly set apart in daily life, for Acts 20:31 says, "Therefore watch, and remember, that by the space of three years I ceased not to warn every one night

and day with tears." So daily the Christian is to work at "perfecting holiness," that is, putting oneself continually in God's hands, leaving all for God, as is required of a disciple (Luke 14:33).

---

### VERSES 2-7:

2 Receive us; we have wronged no man, we have corrupted no man, we have defrauded no man.

3 I speak not this to condemn you: for I have said before, that ye are in our hearts to die and live with you.

4 Great is my boldness of speech toward you, great is my glorying of you: I am filled with comfort, I am exceeding joyful in all our tribulation.

5 For, when we were come into Macedonia, our flesh had no rest, but we were troubled on every side; without were fightings, within were fears.

6 Nevertheless God, that comforteth those that are cast down, comforted us by the coming of Titus;

7 And not by his coming only, but by the consolation wherewith he was comforted in you, when he told us your earnest desire, your mourning, your fervent mind toward me; so that I rejoiced the more.

## The Apostle Rejoices Over Good News About Corinth

*"Receive us"* (vs. 2). The apostle has been severe. He must be. He must rebuke the division, the uncondemned adultery, the drunkenness at the Lord's Table, the tongues heresy. He has been so distressed, so troubled, to know about it. Are they to obey him? Will they love him still? He must insist on apostolic authority. They should receive Paul as God's apostle or they would not obey his inspired instruction. He has been sharp but has injured no man. He is not condemning them when he writes so plainly.

*"Ye are in our hearts"* (vs. 3). Yes, till death and beyond. What an expression of undying love! To the Philippians also he wrote, "I have you in my heart. . ." (Phil. 1:7). The heart of Paul with no wife, no children, not a single living relative recorded, poured out his love to his converts! How much he needed their confidence, their love in return!

But now he is exultant! "Boldness," "glorying," "filled with comfort," "exceeding joyful," he says. Yes, there are tribulations, but now instead of depression and despairing of life, Paul has victory (vs. 4). Oh, he had had *"trouble on every side; without were fightings, within were fears"* (vs. 5). But something wonderful has happened to comfort him and remove his fears.

Titus has come from Corinth. He was to report on their state. Back in chapter 2, verse 13, he had already written in this letter, "I have no rest in my spirit, because I found not Titus my brother." But now Titus has come and his report is wonderful. *". . .He told us your earnest desire, your mourning, your fervent mind toward me; so that I rejoiced the more"* (vs. 7).

How sweet is verse 6: *"God, that comforteth those that are cast down. . . ."* He who comforted Paul by the coming of Titus is ready to comfort all who are cast down!

---

**VERSES 8-12:**

8 For though I made you sorry with a letter, I do not repent, though I did repent: for I perceive that the same epistle hath made you sorry, though it were but for a season.

9 Now I rejoice, not that ye were made sorry, but that ye sorrowed to repentance: for ye were made sorry after a godly manner, that ye might receive damage by us in nothing.

10 For godly sorrow worketh repentance to salvation not to be repented of: but the sorrow of the world worketh death.

11 For behold this selfsame thing, that ye sorrowed after a godly sort, what carefulness it wrought in you, yea, what clearing of yourselves, yea, what indignation, yea, what fear, yea, what vehement desire, yea, what zeal, yea, what revenge! In all things ye have approved yourselves to be clear in this matter.

12 Wherefore, though I wrote unto you, I did it not for his cause that had done the wrong, nor for his cause that suffered wrong, but that our care for you in the sight of God might appear unto you.

## Corinthian Christians Have Repented and Vindicated Themselves

*"I did repent"* (vs. 8). Paul is glad now he sent the first Corinthian letter. But there was a time he was troubled—was it right to send it? God had surely dictated it all. Paul had written, he said, "Not in words which man's wisdom teacheth, but which the Holy Ghost teacheth. . ."

(I Cor. 2:13). But those God-inspired to write Scripture were not infallibly inspired in all their thinking and doing outside that one inspired task. Inspiration as Paul writes Scripture is infallibly correct. Illumination by the Spirit as he thinks and considers is limited, not perfect. Now as he writes by inspiration again he is sure again. But inspiration in writing Scripture does not carry over in other matters to make human authors infallible in all things. Now it has proved out the first letter was from God. It has done its work at Corinth.

They have *"sorrowed to repentence." "For godly sorrow worketh repentance. . . ."* Repentance is the turning from sin—a great decision. Godly sorrow led them to turn. The sorrow of the prodigal son in Luke 15, when he came to himself, led him to decide to face his sin, confess it and return to his father. The homecoming was repentance. The sorrow was godly because it led him to return.

Yes, the Christians at Corinth had godly sorrow, *". . .what carefulness it wrought in you, yea, what clearing of yourselves, yea, what indignation, yea, what fear, yea, what vehement desire, yea, what zeal, yea, what revenge!"* (vs. 11).

Oh, how Paul had grieved over the adulterous young man he had charged them to expel from fellowship. Paul's anxiety was not primarily for the offender of the father so wronged, but the manifestation of *"our care for you in the sight of God"* (vs. 12).

---

**VERSES 13-16:**

13 Therefore we were comforted in your comfort: yea, and exceedingly the more joyed we for the joy of Titus, because his spirit was refreshed by you all.

14 For if I have boasted any thing to him of you, I am not ashamed; but as we spake all things to you in truth, even so our boasting, which I made before Titus, is found a truth.

15 And his inward affection is more abundant toward you, whilst he remembereth the obedience of you all, how with fear and trembling ye received him.

16 I rejoice therefore that I have confidence in you in all things.

### All Are Comforted—Paul, Titus, Corinthians

After repentance and righting wrongs, the wayward, divided and confused Christians at Corinth were greatly comforted and revived. And Titus, who was there, has been refreshed and no doubt has learned much from Paul's inspired dealing with the matter and the blessed results. He was *"refreshed by you all"* (vs. 13). Paul who had boasted much to Titus about his beloved children in Christ at Corinth now rejoices that he is vindicated. They are standing true, so he has not been proved unwise and unreliable, has not been rejected. He rejoices. How Titus gloats as he recounts to Paul their repentings, *"the obedience. . .with fear and trembling."*

Now the apostle has confidence in them *"in all things"* (vs. 16).

# II CORINTHIANS VIII

MOREOVER, brethren, we do you to wit of the grace of God bestowed on the churches of Macedonia;

2 How that in a great trial of affliction the abundance of their joy and their deep poverty abounded unto the riches of their liberality.

3 For to their power, I bear record, yea, and beyond their power they were willing of themselves;

4 Praying us with much intreaty that we would receive the gift, and take upon us the fellowship of the ministering to the saints.

5 And this they did, not as we hoped, but first gave their own selves to the Lord, and unto us by the will of God.

## The Liberality of Macedonian Christians

*"The churches of Macedonia"* (vs. 1) are those in Northern Greece, that at Philippi specially but doubtless also churches at Thessalonica and at Berea (See Phil. 4:15; Acts 17:1-12).

*"The grace of God bestowed on the churches"* (vs. 1). Christian giving based on the Old Testament law required a tithe. Offerings were to be brought besides the tithe. But only as the giving becomes a glad outpouring, sacrificial liberality, moved by the Spirit of God, is it adequate Christian giving. Here God had given a special grace, a revival in the heart, a gladness in giving out of poverty. Surely no Christian should give less than a tithe, and offerings besides as God leads.

Should any New Testament Christian love God less and give less than a Jew under cermonial law? Jesus endorsed the tithe (Matt. 23:23). But unconverted Pharisees tithed. Evidently the Macedonian Christians gave far more than a tithe. "Except your righteousness shall exceed the righteousness of the scribes and Pharisees, ye shall in no case enter into the kingdom of heaven" (Matt. 5:20). And unless your giving involves more devotion, more sacrifice and more joy than the Pharisee paying his required tithe, you do not have the grace of God bestowed on the churches of Macedonia.

Note the elements in their giving.

*"In a great trial of affliction."* Love for God is the great commandment, and so giving to God must never be smothered by trouble and trials.

*"The abundance of their joy."* What a privilege to give to get out the Gospel, to support those who preach, to help those in need! God could have all He needs without our dollars or pennies. The silver and gold in every mine is His, the cattle on a thousand hills (Ps. 50:10). But as He has given to us the great privilege of winning souls, not leaving it to angels, He has chosen that we may have the privilege, the joy of giving heart love, time, energy, tears and possessions to God and be partners with Him, "fellow-helpers to the truth" (III John 8). Some say "give until it hurts." Better to give till we are flooded with *"abundance of. . .joy"* like those in Macedonia.

*"Their deep poverty."* Does it seem strange that poverty is an element of this "grace of giving"? But it is. The widow who cast in two mites to the Lord's treasury gave "more than they all" (Luke 21:3). One poor enough may give so there will be no bread on the table, no money for necessities! No one gives like these Macedonian Christians if he has as much to eat as if he had not given, as many clothes, as nice a home, as good a car, as expensive a vacation. This grace of giving is measured partly by poverty; not by the amount given but by what is left. The requirement of Jesus for discipleship was not one-tenth but that "man forsaketh. . .all that he hath" (Luke 14:33). And the suggestion of Jesus to the rich young ruler that he "sell that thou hast, and give to the poor. . .and come and follow me," was not only to urge him to personal faith in Jesus but to all-out discipleship.

God does not require every man to sell all he has and give it away but He does require that our loving hearts will count all we have His and gladly subject to His control to give or keep. ". . .Ye are not your own. For ye are bought with a price: therefore glorify God in your body, and in your spirit, which are God's" (I Cor. 6:19,20).

They gave *"beyond their power."* They begged Paul to take the gift. It was for the poor saints at Jerusalem (Rom. 15:26). The money they gave was incidental because they first gave themselves to the Lord.

In Texas, years ago, Dr. J. B. Gambrell had a famous article in the *Baptist Standard* on "Who Owns the Wool?" The title tells the story: the man who owns the sheep owns the wool. The God who owns the Christian owns everything he has.

*". . .And unto us by the will of God"* (vs. 5). There is no way to serve God but as we serve men. There is no way to give money to God but to use it to help men. Paul had said, "Be ye followers of me, even as I also am of Christ" (I Cor. 11:1). Moses said, "Who is on the Lord's side? let him come unto me" (Exod. 32:26). In Numbers 21:5 the sin of the people was, they "spake against God, and against Moses." We cannot obey God except as we obey those God has put over us—father, husband, master, spiritual leader. People know God's will as God's man teaches them.

So they gave themselves to God and to Paul. But this was in *"the will of God."* We are to "try the spirits whether they are of God. . ." (I John 4:1), and not be misled by teachers or preachers not "in the will of God." It was wrong for Barnabas and others to follow Peter, recorded in Galatians 2:11-14. But here Paul has proved his apostleship, and his converts are right to follow him, "as I follow Christ," he said.

---

**VERSES 6-8:**

6 Insomuch that we desired Titus, that as he had begun, so he would also finish in you the same grace also.

7 Therefore, as ye abound in every thing, in faith, and utterance, and knowledge, and in all diligence, and in your love to us, see that ye abound in this grace also.

8 I speak not by commandment, but by occasion of the forwardness of others, and to prove the sincerity of your love.

## The Blessed Grace of Giving

*". . .the same grace also"* (vs. 6), *". . .this grace also"* (vs. 7). The marvelously sacrificial, joyful giving of the Macedonian Christians was not only good character, it was a "grace." That is a special moving of the Holy Spirit. It was a manifestation of the brotherly love exalted in I Corinthians 13, where we learn that it is greater than all knowledge, miracles, tongues, faith and hope. It was a manifestation of the "fruit of the Spirit" of Galatians 5:22,23: "But the fruit of the Spirit is love, joy, peace, longsuffering, gentleness, goodness, faith, Meekness, temperance: against such there is no law."

This gift of the grace of giving joyfully, liberally, is a manifestation of the love that makes all men know one is a disciple of Jesus (John 13:35). It means such love for others and responsibility for others as the beatitudes of the *merciful* and the *peacemakers* in Matthew 5:7,9. Giving by a rich man might be a policy, a seeking the praises of men, without any special loss or deprivation of himself. But when it comes out of deepest poverty, great joy and is all one has the power to do, that represents a wonderful devotion, a "grace" of God.

No wonder Paul urged Titus to seek to teach those at Corinth "the same grace also."

Note the companion verses. The Corinthian Christians abounded "in every thing"—in faith, utterance, knowledge, diligence and in love for Paul—wonderful virtues but an equally important or perhaps more important quality would be this grace of joyful and sacrificial giving.

---

**VERSE 9:**

9 For ye know the grace of our Lord Jesus Christ, that, though he was rich, yet for your sakes he became poor, that ye through his poverty might be rich.

## "The Grace of Our Lord Jesus Christ"

In context, the grace of Christian giving is compared to the grace of Christ who suffered the torment of the damned and the shame of the cross to save us. Oh, then, let there be no foolish limit set on what we owe our dear Lord Jesus.

Someone has said, "God wants one-seventh of our time and one-tenth of our income." That is a wholly inadequate fraction of what God wants. God wants Monday as well as Sunday. He wants your Saturdays, your vacations, your rest hours as well as the time for visitation or midweek prayer service.

Suppose a sheep tells its owner, "I will allow you one-tenth of my wool which I grew from your feed." Suppose a slave has been about to die for a crime but is bought, is saved, is fed, is clothed, is taught and loved by the master who saved his life. Now, is it sensible for the slave to say to his master, "I'll serve you one day a week"?

One dime out of a dollar, when God provides the whole dollar, is a stingy, carnal, inadequate response of a Christian. Compared as it is here with a sacrificial, loving, suffering, unchangeable grace of our Lord Jesus Christ, a tithe is not "the grace of giving" that is taught here!

Christ endorsed the tithe for the Pharisee (Matt. 23:23) as we have said but indicated it alone was inadequate. And surely a devoted, born-again Christian would be expected to love Christ better than an unconverted Jew under ceremonial law!

*"The grace of our Lord Jesus Christ"*—more than love, for love may wish for one far away and not be able to see him. Love may wish for one to have riches that one cannot give. Love is not grace like that of the Lord Jesus until one gives and suffers and pays another's debt, suffers for another's sin. Grace—yes, more than pity. Pity may have a tear for the troubled soul, for the boy ruined in the hogpen of sin in the far country, the father's substance wasted with harlots and drink. Only grace can receive the boy as a son,

make good his waste, provide his home, his ring of sonship, his white robe of righteousness, the fatted calf of rich provision, the joy of a father's kiss and love.

Mercy is a big word but grace provides mercy, comes before mercy. "Longsuffering" is a quality of God often praised in Scripture (II Cor. 6:6; Gal. 5:22; Col. 1:11; I Tim. 1:16), but grace goes farther than that, is more than lovingkindness, is more than the daily benefits. The *"grace of our Lord Jesus Christ"* gives up the riches of Heaven to take the sinner's poverty, gives up the place of equality with the Father to be forsaken on the cross so we sinners may be received in the arms and heart of God. Grace takes our stripes on His back, our tears on His cheeks, our pains in His body, our torment in His Gethsemane and on Calvary, so we may have peace without fear, salvation without falling; we may have Heaven when we deserve Hell.

This grace on Christ's part inspires the sacrificial, loving, joyful giving on our part. Here again is the divine argument of Romans 12:1, "I beseech you therefore, brethren, by the mercies of God, that ye present your bodies a living sacrifice, holy, acceptable unto God, which is your reasonable service." We are not our own; we are bought; so I Corinthians 6:20 reminds us that we are to "glorify God in your body, and in your spirit, which are God's." The inspired theme returns again in II Corinthians 9:15.

---

**VERSES 10-15:**

10 And herein I give my advice: for this is expedient for you, who have begun before, not only to do, but also to be forward a year ago.

11 Now therefore perform the doing of it; that as there was a readiness to will, so there may be a performance also out of that which ye have.

12 For if there be first a willing mind, it is accepted according to that a man hath, and not according to that he hath not.

13 For I mean not that other men be eased, and ye burdened:

14 But by an equality, that now at

this time your abundance may be a supply for their want, that their abundance also may be a supply for your want: that there may be equality: 15 As it is written, He that had gathered much had nothing over; and he that had gathered little had no lack.

## You Promised: Now Do It!

They had promised a year ago (vs. 10; 9:20) to send help to the poor saints at Jerusalem who were suffering from the famine foretold by Agabus in Acts 11:27-30. It is proper to make a vow, a promise to God. Jacob did at Bethel (Gen. 28: 20-22), that the Lord would be his God. The stones he erected at Bethel should be the house of God and to God he would surely give a tenth of his income.

Jephthah vowed that if God would give him victory over the enemies of Israel, he would sacrifice to the Lord the first person or thing that came to meet him on his return (Judg. 11:30). It was his beloved daughter, and he kept his vow (Judg. 11:39).

Hannah vowed that if God would give her a son, "I will give him unto the Lord all the days of his life" (I Sam. 1:11). So Samuel was given and was a Nazarite all his life in answer to that vow.

The Psalms often mention joyfully vows to the Lord (Ps. 22:25; 66:13; 116:14; 50:14; 61:5,8; 65:1).

The Apostle Paul had a vow for a season as a Nazarite (Acts 18:18; 21:18-26). The Scriptures exhort us to "vow, and pay unto the Lord your God" (Ps. 76:11). Long-term planning and vows to God, honestly made, keep us on a straight path, require steadfastness, and so are often good.

Many men have "surrendered to preach" but have never preached. They were not willing to leave good income to trust God to care for the family, or they were not willing to defer marriage or to go the laborious, sacrificial way of training and education. Probably not a third of those who solemnly declared they had given themselves to be foreign missionaries ever saw the foreign field. Many did not count the cost as is required of a disciple in Luke 14:28-33.

Some, no doubt, made such a surrender of the will "to go to Africa," which may have been the only graphic way they could express the honest dedication which they meant. God wants everybody to be willing to go to Africa; He does not want everyone to go there. But what one vows he should pay.

In giving, there is a special joy in planning ahead what we will give as God provides. We can give more if we plan ahead and ask God to help us and thus keep our vows.

How much shall I give? What a willing mind wants to give! The gift should be according to what one has. One's giving would ordinarily be in proportion to his income. The widow's two mites were more in God's sight than rich gifts of others because it was all she had (Mark 12:41-44). Heart love and joy in the Lord are better values than any amount of money.

When manna was sent from Heaven to Israel in the wilderness, one might gather more than another but all was from God and it was then divided equally and came out as an omer each (Exod. 16:18).

---

### VERSES 16-24:

16 But thanks be to God, which put the same earnest care into the heart of Titus for you.

17 For indeed he accepted the exhortation; but being more forward, of his own accord he went unto you.

18 And we have sent with him the brother, whose praise is in the gospel throughout all the churches;

19 And not that only, but who was also chosen of the churches to travel with us with this grace, which is administered by us to the glory of the same Lord, and declaration of your ready mind:

20 Avoiding this, that no man should blame us in this abundance which is administered by us:

21 Providing for honest things, not only in the sight of the Lord, but also in the sight of men.

22 And we have sent with them our brother, whom we have oftentimes proved diligent in many things, but now much more diligent, upon the great confidence which I have in you.

23 Whether any do enquire of Titus, he is my partner and fellowhelper concerning you: or our brethren be enquired of, they are the messengers of the churches, and the glory of Christ.

24 Wherefore shew ye to them, and before the churches, the proof of your love, and of our boasting on your behalf.

## The Messengers—Honest, Open Dealing

Paul had sent Titus to visit these at Corinth to prove their love, give Paul's instructions and report to him. But especially Titus had been sent to report to them the grace of God on the churches in Macedonia and to *"finish in you the same grace also"* (vs. 6). Titus loved them and was greatly comforted by their repentance, their anxiety to please Paul and to prove worthy (II Cor. 7:7-15). Paul had boasted of them to Titus (II Cor. 7:14) and Titus had for them *"the same earnest care"* as Paul had (vs. 16). He went *"forward, of his own accord"* to teach them the joy of giving (vs. 17).

Now Titus and an unnamed brother or more are sent to collect gifts they are preparing laying by according to the instructions of I Corinthians 16:1,2. These messengers are good men of good report and prove trustworthy. More than one will handle the money—men elected by the churches. Paul must not handle the money alone lest some should blame him (vs. 20). Christians in the Lord's work must not only be honest in God's sight but strictly careful to prove themselves honest to others, to give no reason for distrust and temptation for someone without supervision to misuse God's money.

The preacher should not count the church offering, but several men so none could be suspected nor tempted. Regular reports of the income and disbursement of funds should prove that God's work is carefully done and above reproach. Now the love of these Corinthians for Paul and for Christ will be shown by their giving and all can understand that evidence of love.

# II CORINTHIANS IX

FOR as touching the ministering to the saints, it is superfluous for me to write to you:

2 For I know the forwardness of your mind, for which I boast of you to them of Macedonia, that Ā-chāi-ă was ready a year ago; and your zeal hath provoked very many.

3 Yet have I sent the brethren, lest our boasting of you should be in vain in this behalf; that, as I said, ye may be ready:

4 Lest haply if they of Macedonia come with me, and find you unprepared, we (that we say not, ye) should be ashamed in this same confident boasting.

5 Therefore I thought it necessary to exhort the brethren, that they would go before unto you, and make up beforehand your bounty, whereof ye had notice before, that the same might be ready, as a matter of bounty, and not as of covetousness.

## Paul Will Come: Perhaps
## Macedonians Also

Instructions of the need to help Jerusalem saints was "superfluous" (vs.1). Evidently the famine was widely known. Thousands had been saved at Jerusalem (Acts 2:41; Acts 4:4; Acts 5:14). Great persecution had arisen. Stephen had been stoned, many had been arrested (Acts 7:54-8:4). Many fled for their lives. Doubtless many lost jobs and income. All this was of such magnitude, it would have been known among Christians wherever they lived in the Roman Empire.

The Corinthians had been much moved the year before by the suffering and need of the saints, and had been an example to others in planning to send gifts, and had not, we infer, done much about it. Paul had boasted of their zeal; now what if he comes and some of these liberal Macedonian Christians come with him and find the Corinthian Christians negligent?

Achaia is Southern Greece including Athens and Corinth: Macedonia is Northern Greece including Philippi, Macedonia and Berea.

Paul had sent back Titus and some others to begin

collecting funds, that a sizeable gift might be ready when he comes and he will not be ashamed of his praise of them and their zeal and promises a year ago.

It is to be a matter of bounty, gladly given, not reluctantly given to please covetous leaders.

---

## VERSES 6-9:

6 But this I say, He which soweth sparingly shall reap also sparingly; and he which soweth bountifully shall reap also bountifully.

7 Every man according as he purposeth in his heart, so let him give; not grudgingly, or of necessity: for God loveth a cheerful giver.

8 And God is able to make all grace abound toward you; that ye, always having all sufficiency in all things, may abound to every good work:

9 (As it is written, He hath dispersed abroad; he hath given to the poor: his righteousness remaineth for ever.

## Giving to God Is Sowing for Sure Reaping

Giving to God is really investing. Grain planted into the ground might seem to be a wasting of good food; but no, it is multiplying food. Here is a part of the paradox of God. One who saves his life shall lose it, and one who loses his life for Christ's sake and the Gospel's will save it (Mark 8:35). One who would be great among Christians must minister to others, and one who would be a chief must be a servant (Matt 20:26,27). The humble shall be exalted (Matt. 18:4; Matt. 23:12; I Pet. 5:6). So the one who gives more shall have more. Here is the blessed teaching that giving to God means sowing with sure return. The more we sow, the more we reap. The more we give, joyfully and trustingly, the more the returns will surely be.

In Malachi 3:10 to 12 the Jews are promised:

*"Bring ye all the tithes into the storehouse, that there may be meat in mine house, and prove me now herewith, saith the LORD of hosts, if I will not open you the windows of heaven, and pour you out a blessing, that there shall not be room enough to receive it. And I will rebuke the devourer*

*for your sakes, and he shall not destroy the fruits of your ground; neither shall your vine cast her fruit before the time in the field, saith the LORD of hosts. And all nations shall call you blessed: for ye shall be a delightsome land, saith the LORD of hosts."*

God definitely controlled the rain, the pests, so that crops were better when they brought in the tithes and offerings to the Temple at Jerusalem. When they withheld these, it was robbing God and He punished them with poor crops. When the Jews returned from captivity, God's displeasure that they did not restore the Temple speedily is shown thus:

*"Ye looked for much, and, lo, it came to little; and when ye brought it home, I did blow upon it. Why? saith the LORD of hosts. Because of mine house that is waste, and ye run every man unto his own house. Therefore the heaven over you is stayed from dew, and the earth is stayed from her fruit. And I called for a drought upon the land, and upon the mountains, and upon the corn, and upon the new wine, and upon the oil, and upon that which the ground bringeth forth, and upon men, and upon cattle, and upon all the labour of the hands."*—Hag. 1:9-11.

It is true that God now has no temple on earth but the bodies of Christians, which are the temple of God, since God the Holy Spirit now dwells in every Christian's body (I Cor. 3:16,17; I Cor. 6:19,20; Rom. 8:9,10). Now there is no designated place where God orders us to bring the tithes and offerings. God does not only here deal legalistically with the tithes of the Corinthians and with us, but God still rewards those who give to Him. He rewards more those who give more.

If God rewards the tithe, He rewards more that given above the tithe. More sowing, more reaping. When Christians are sparing and stingy in their giving, they often suffer poverty beyond what God wants them to suffer. Someone may say, "I cannot afford to tithe." In truth, no

Christian can afford to give less than the tithe and freewill offerings beyond.

How often the Bible teaches this!

Proverbs 3:9,10 says: "Honour the LORD with thy substance, and with the firstfruits of all thine increase: So shall thy barns be filled with plenty, and thy presses shall burst out with new wine."

And Proverbs 11:25 promises: "The liberal soul shall be made fat: and he that watereth shall be watered also himself."

And Jesus said it so plainly in Luke 6:38: "Give, and it shall be given unto you; good measure, pressed down, and shaken together, and running over, shall men give into your bosom. For with the same measure that ye mete withal it shall be measured to you again."

Here the promise is that as you give to others, *men* will give to you. And the return is more abundant than the giving. "Good measure, pressed down, and shaken together, and running over." More than seventy years ago and living far from the store, if my mother should borrow two cups of sugar to make some apple pies, when she repaid the sugar she sometimes took a pie to her neighbor also! Oh, God is a good and faithful God. He rewards those who seek to please Him.

"Shall men give into your bosom," says Luke 6:38. I saw how careful God is to repay good deeds in another matter. For many years when cars were not so good, tires were short-lived and frail, filling stations far apart, cars had many more flat tires. There was no gas measure on Ford cars. I have stopped many times to help change a tire, to help patch a tire and pump it up, to push a car to a filling station. It was a conviction that thus I should help those in trouble. Now, strange as it seems, I never run out of gas or have trouble on the road but immediately there is help at hand. So often it has happened. No matter how lonely the road or how late at night, I am compelled to see it. It is God's repayment of help to others.

*"God is able to make all grace abound toward you"* (vs. 8). Does not God repay grace for grace? Cannot God give abundantly to those who give abundantly? Well, since God can, may we not confidently expect that He will? He is a giving God, a righteous God who wants you to be *"always having all sufficiency in all things"* (vs. 8). And God gives that you may give the more!

---

## VERSES 10-15:

10 Now he that ministereth seed to the sower both minister bread for your food, and multiply your seed sown, and increase the fruits of your righteousness;)

11 Being enriched in every thing to all bountifulness, which causeth through us thanksgiving to God.

12 For the administration of this service not only supplieth the want of the saints, but is abundant also by many thanksgivings unto God;

13 Whiles by the experiment of this ministration they glorify God for your professed subjection unto the gospel of Christ, and for your liberal distribution unto them, and unto all men;

14 And by their prayer for you, which long after you for the exceeding grace of God in you.

15 Thanks be unto God for his unspeakable gift.

### The Blessings We Reap by Sowing Bountifully

*"Seed to the sower"* (vs. 10). Those who give will have more to give. *"Bread for your food."* God gives both and both will be enlarged—what we give and what we use for ourselves—by generous giving. The apostle thus rejoices in their giving because they will be prospered by it. God will *"increase the fruits of your righteousness"* as well as *"multiply your seed sown."*

Paul also rejoiced in the liberal giving to him by the Philippian Christians: "Not because I desire a gift: but I desire fruit that may abound to your account" (Phil. 4:17). But there is a blessing in another way. The poor saints who received the offerings which were so greatly needed in Jerusalem and perhaps elsewhere, will not only be fed, but God will be honored by their thanksgiving (vss. 12,13). And they will be led to pray more for those who give. Thus in every way, liberal giving to please God results in blessing on the giver, support to the needy, thanksgiving to God, blessed example for others, and fervent prayers for the giver.

Again the inspired apostle is lifted up to the great Example as he says, *"Thanks be unto God for his unspeakable gift"* (vs. 15). How could anybody think about Christian giving without remembering the marvelous Gift beyond all expression, when God gave His Son and when Christ Himself gave Himself, to pay the price for our sins and to save us.

Paul reverted to that in chapter 8 and verse 9. And so he does again. Who then is the proper example for a Christian in giving? No one less than the Lord Jesus Himself. And how much should we give? Oh, we should give all, without stint, without hesitation, without special regard of the consequences. Such a wonderful Saviour God has given, and there is no way that I can represent the Lord Jesus or follow His example without giving all, giving joyfully, giving beyond my power, as these Macedonian Christians did.

# II CORINTHIANS X

NOW I Paul myself beseech you by the meekness and gentleness of Christ, who in presence am base among you, but being absent am bold toward you:

2 But I beseech you, that I may not be bold when I am present with that confidence, wherewith I think to be bold against some, which think of us as if we walked according to the flesh.

3 For though we walk in the flesh, we do not war after the flesh:

4 (For the weapons of our warfare are not carnal, but mighty through God to the pulling down of strong holds;)

5 Casting down imaginations, and every high thing that exalteth itself against the knowledge of God, and bringing into captivity every thought to the obedience of Christ;

6 And having in a readiness to revenge all disobedience, when your obedience is fulfilled.

7 Do ye look on things after the outward appearance? If any man trust to himself that he is Christ's, let him of himself think this again, that, as he is Christ's, even so are we Christ's.

8 For though I should boast somewhat more of our authority, which the Lord hath given us for edification, and not for your destruction, I should not be ashamed:

## Paul Defends His Apostolic Authority

Paul was called not simply as a preacher of the Gospel, but, in some sense, one who received the Gospel directly from God, to write it down for us. The apostles were especially sent, especially authorized. When there was no New Testament, God gave Paul the substance of the New Testament in his heart. So he writes here by divine authority, writes inspired words from God.

We must not be surprised, then, at the boldness with which Paul writes here. In nine of his epistles, Paul begins with the claim of his apostleship and authority. That is true in Romans, I and II Corinthians, Galatians, Ephesians, Colossians, I and II Timothy and Titus. Among his beloved Philippians, we suppose his apostleship and authority were never questioned. Philemon is a brotherly letter to an individual, asking a favor. While in his letters to the Thessalonians Paul does not begin labeling himself as an apostle, yet he reminds them, "For our gospel came not unto you in word only, but also in power, and in the Holy Ghost, and in much assurance." And he says, "And ye became followers of us, and of the Lord" (I Thess. 1:5,6). And in the second chapter of I Thessalonians he goes to great detail to remind them, "But as we were allowed of God to be put in trust with the gospel, even so we speak; not as pleasing men, but God, which trieth out hearts" (I Thess. 2:4). And he said, "When ye received the word of God which ye heard of us, ye received it not as the word of men, but as it is in truth, the word of God" (I Thess. 2:13). In Romans 11:13 Paul says, "For I speak to you Gentiles, inasmuch as I am the apostle of the Gentiles, I magnify mine office." He had very powerfully insisted on his apostleship and unique authority in I Corinthians 9:1.

In the next chapter, II Corinthians 11, he will go into great detail, proving himself an apostle of the apostles. Paul insists that divine power is upon him. He has mighty weapons though not weapons of the flesh (vs. 4). Those weapons are powerful to pull down strongholds, to cast down imaginations, "and every high thing that exalteth itself against the knowledge of God." God will help him to bring, in the church, "into captivity every thought to the obedience of Christ" if necessary, and he has "a readiness to revenge all disobedience," he says.

Do they honor any man as belonging to Christ and serving him? Then let them honor Paul, for even so he is Christ's in proven authority and power.

But Paul would not use this authority, these heavenly weapons, for destruction, but rather they are for edification (vs. 8).

We remember how the sorcerer Elymas was struck blind for opposing Paul's Gospel (Acts 13:11) and how Ananias and Sapphira were struck dead at the word of the Apostle Peter (Acts 5:1-11). We remember the young man raised from the dead at Troas in Acts 20:9-12 and the healing of Publius' father, on the island of Melita, in Acts 28:7-15.

But Paul uses such mighty power rarely, and longs to use it only for edification and good, not for destruction or punishment.

---

9 That I may not seem as if I would terrify you by letters.

10 For his letters, say they, are weighty and powerful; but his bodily presence is weak, and his speech contemptible.

11 Let such an one think this, that, such as we are in word by letters when we are absent, such will we be also in deed when we are present.

## The Difference Between Paul's Inspired
## Scripture and His Usual Speech

We must remember that the letters which Paul wrote—I and II Corinthians and others which we have in the New Testament—were inspired of God, were infallibly perfect. Yes, they are indeed "weighty and powerful," but they were not in Paul's usual speech. We understand that Paul was not eloquent like Apollos, and, no doubt, people were right when they said about Paul, ". . .but his bodily presence is weak, and his speech contemptible." In Paul's preaching, God had chosen the weak things to confound the mighty, but in his letters we have the infallible, inerrant, verbally inspired Word of God.

Nevertheless, Paul had apostolic authority and could deal in power when necessary. So the miraculous power that God sometimes gave was powerful, as the Scripture was powerful, though his usual talents and speaking ability were not considerable.

---

12 For we dare not make ourselves of the number, or compare ourselves with some that commend themselves: but they measuring themselves by themselves, and comparing themselves among themselves, are not wise.

13 But we will not boast of things without our measure, but according

to the measure of the rule which God hath distributed to us, a measure to reach even unto you.

14 For we stretch not ourselves beyond our measure, as though we reached not unto you: for we are come as far as to you also in preaching the gospel of Christ:

15 Not boasting of things without our measure, that is, of other men's labours; but having hope, when your faith is increased, that we shall be enlarged by you according to our rule abundantly,

16 To preach the gospel in the regions beyond you, and not to boast in another man's line of things made ready to our hand.

17 But he that glorieth, let him glory in the Lord.

18 For not he that commendeth himself is approved, but whom the Lord commendeth.

## Paul Compares Himself With Other Preachers

The apostle here writes with some modesty but determined that they will take this letter as from God and on the authority of Paul. When Paul claims to be an apostle and to have authority from God, he is not stretching himself "beyond our measure." In his great missionary journeys at Corinth and elsewhere he had proved himself specially called, specially equipped and specially empowered to spread the Gospel. And he reminds these Corinthian Christians that he had not come to them to build upon another man's foundation but he came to them when they were in heathendom, the Jews among them bound to the ceremonial law. He did not build upon another man's foundation. He hopes that these people at Corinth will give him the love and respect, and support that he deserves and has earned as God's apostle and the man who led them to Christ (vs. 15).

But verse 17 says, *"But he that glorieth, let him glory in the Lord."* Paul will not be received because of his own commendation but by the commendation of the Lord who had so verified and vindicated his ministry.

But there is an authority which every God-called and God-empowered preacher has. Isaiah 54:17 says, "No weapon that is formed against thee shall prosper; and every tongue that shall rise against thee in judgment thou shalt condemn. This is the heritage of the servants of the LORD, and their righteousness is of me, saith the LORD." When the Christians were filled with the Spirit again after Pentecost, in Acts 4:31 we are told, "And they spake the word of God with boldness." And they had prayed for that: "Lord, behold their threatenings: and grant unto thy servants, that with all boldness they may speak thy word, By stretching forth thine hand to heal; and that signs and wonders may be done by the name of thy holy child Jesus."

One who has upon him the power of God can be bold in preaching the truth. And there is a sense in which God has given this saving power into the hands of men. And He had said to all the disciples in the Upper Room, "Whose soever sins ye remit, they are remitted unto them; and whose soever sins ye retain, they are retained" (John 20:23). If I have preached the Gospel truly in the power of God, I have a right to say that those who will accept it and accept the Christ I preach will have forgiveness and eternal life, and I have a right to say that those who reject the Gospel and reject the Saviour continually, will be lost forever. And men who are called and anointed of God ought to be so certain of their message and so certain of the will of God that they can speak with the boldness of Martin Luther, of Savonarola, of Spurgeon, Wesley, Moody, Sam Jones, Billy Sunday, and other prophets of God.

But we are not to suppose that because Paul was an apostle of God or because other men are filled with the Spirit in their preaching they will necessarily escape persecution, pain and trouble. John the Baptist was beheaded. Stephen was stoned to death. It is still true that "all that live godly in Christ Jesus shall suffer persecution" (II Tim. 3:12). The Lord Jesus died at the hands of wicked men, and we are reminded that "if the world hate you, ye know that it hated me before it hated you. . .The servant is not greater than his lord" (John 15:18,20). We know that John the Baptist died under Herod; Stephen was stoned; James was beheaded; Paul was imprisoned for years and then martyred in Rome. The mighty power of God which He gives to Spirit-filled men does not mean that we will not enter into the sufferings of Christ as we should.

# II CORINTHIANS XI

WOULD to God ye could bear with me a little in my folly: and indeed bear with me.

2 For I am jealous over you with godly jealousy: for I have espoused you to one husband, that I may pre-sent you as a chaste virgin to Christ.

3 But I fear, lest by any means, as the serpent beguiled Eve through his subtilty, so your minds should be corrupted from the simplicity that is in Christ.

## Paul's Jealous Care for the Churches

*"I am jealous over you with godly jealousy. . ."* (vs. 2), Paul says. Few men can understand the burden of Paul for the Christians of Corinth. A pastor has a special burden for his own flock; that is his responsibility. A teacher is responsible for his class; a father or mother for their children; so they carry a burden. We are told that God "gave some, apostles; and some, prophets; and some, evangelists; and some, pastors and teachers" for the church, the body of Christ. But remember, there were few apostles and Paul was the only apostle for the Gentiles. Paul said, "A dispensation of the gospel is committed unto me" (I Cor. 9:17; I Tim. 1:11).

So Paul was chosen of God to write thirteen or fourteen of the books of the New Testament (fourteen if he wrote Hebrews). He had a burden for the whole cause—at Corinth, at Ephesus, at Colosse, at Philippi, at Thessalonica, for the churches of Galatia, even at Rome, as well as Jerusalem. He was not simply a minister to a church or to an area but to the whole body of Christ. He says "for his body's sake, which is the church: Whereof I am made a minister, according to the dispensation of God which is given to me for you, to fulfil the word of God" (Col. 1:24,25). On the Apostle Paul, more than any other minister of God in all the New Testament times, was there a dispensation of the Gospel, a responsibility for the whole cause of Christ. And so with a godly jealousy, he wept over those of Galatia who were led astray, he corrected the heresies and worldliness at Corinth and was pressed nearly to death with the burden of it!

Paul desired to *"present you as a chaste virgin to Christ"* (vs. 2). The picture is of a wedding when the father of a chaste and lovely virgin presents her to be a bride to the king's son. That wedding is pictured in a parable in Matthew 22. Even now the minister at a wedding may say, "Who giveth this woman to be married to this man?" And the Father may say, "I do." So Paul looked forward to the judgment seat of Christ when all those he had won to Christ in Corinth would appear. Oh, that they might meet Christ without embarrassment and shame! For idolatry or spiritual wickedness would be counted as spiritual harlotry and it would be shameful when they faced Christ.

The judgment seat of Christ loomed large in Paul's inspiration. He reminded all Christians they must face it (I Cor. 3:10-15; II Cor. 5:9-11). Of it is said, "Knowing therefore the terror of the Lord, we persuade men . . ." (II Cor. 5:11). That is, it would be a terrifying thing to meet Christ with shame and disgrace even though one was saved and a child of God, if his works had to be burned as wood, hay and stubble. Paul looked forward to the judgment seat of Christ as his crowning day and day of joy. Oh, to see those he had won when they came before Christ! That, he hoped, would be a great joy. So in II Corinthians 1:14 he said, "As also ye have acknowledged us in part, that we are your rejoicing, even as ye also are our's in the day of the Lord Jesus." And in I Thessalonians 2:19 he said, "For what is our hope, or joy, or crown of rejoicing? Are not even ye in the presence of our Lord Jesus Christ at his coming?" And he called the dear Philippians "my joy and crown" (Phil. 4:1).

We have the blessed promise that "they that be wise shall shine as the brightness of the firmament; and they that turn many to righteousness as the stars for ever and ever" (Dan. 12:3). Oh, at that time not anything else will matter much but those whom we won to Christ and kept out of Hell, those we won over to love, trust, serve and live with Christ.

---

## VERSES 4-12:

4 For if he that cometh preacheth another Jesus, whom we have not preached, or if ye receive another spirit, which ye have not received, or another gospel, which ye have not accepted, ye might well bear with him.

5 For I suppose I was not a whit behind the very chiefest apostles.

6 But though I be rude in speech, yet not in knowledge; but we have been throughly made manifest among you in all things.

7 Have I committed an offence in abasing myself that ye might be exalted, because I have preached to you the gospel of God freely?

8 I robbed other churches, taking wages of them, to do you service.

9 And when I was present with you, and wanted, I was chargeable to no man: for that which was lacking to me the brethren which came from Macedonia supplied: and in all things I have kept myself from being burdensome unto you, and so will I keep myself.

10 As the truth of Christ is in me, no man shall stop me of this boasting in the regions of Ă-chāi-ă.

11 Wherefore? because I love you not? God knoweth.

12 But what I do, that I will do, that I may cut off occasion from them which desire occasion; that wherein they glory, they may be found even as we.

## Who Else Would Show Signs of Apostleship More Than Paul?

Did someone preach "another Jesus"? Had not Paul preached the only Saviour? Had they received "another spirit" more important than the Holy Spirit whose power had come on Paul's message and ministry? Remember that he had come "in demonstration of the Spirit and of power" (I Cor. 2:4). And in I Corinthians 2:10 Paul reminds them that the matter in the Scriptures he was writing was given him by the Holy Spirit.

Some brought "another gospel," but there was no saving Gospel but what Paul preached. If Paul's Jesus, Paul's Gospel, Paul's Holy Spirit were all Paul's, and another brought the true, "ye might well bear with him." The inspired sarcasm is overwhelming. Paul himself at first brought them the saving Gospel in mighty power. Whoever else came now to comment on the Gospel or teach it further would not have Paul's apostolic position, nor vindication and evidence of the power and blessing of God.

So Paul's speech was rude as they had said in II Corinthians 10:10, but he was not rude in knowledge, and others who preached the same Gospel would not properly lead anybody away from Paul's leadership. Some wickedness was behind those who were against Paul and denied his apostolic authority. In verse 13 Paul plainly says they were "*false apostles.*"

He had abased himself, working without support from them, sometime at tentmaking (Acts 18:3). He had taken help from Macedonia and other churches (I Cor. 8:4,5; Phil. 4:10-15). At Corinth, Paul at first preached every Sabbath day, and, we suppose, worked during the week to support himself. But after Silas and Timothy came from Macedonia (Acts 18:4,5,9), we suppose bringing gifts for Paul and help at that time, then he was pressed in Spirit and vigorously preached all the time he could. Paul's "boasting" is clearing himself of the charges that he might preach for money, and his selfless service rebuked the "false prophets" who criticised him and would woo the new converts at Corinth away from the truth he preached.

Is Paul writing so strictly because he does not love these people at Corinth? No! But he must save them from false teachers as he defends his apostleship.

---

**VERSES 13-15:**

13 For such are false apostles, deceitful workers, transforming themselves into the apostles of Christ.

14 And no marvel; for Satan himself is transformed into an angel of light.

15 Therefore it is no great thing if his ministers also be transformed as the ministers of righteousness; whose end shall be according to their works.

## Satan's Prophets Appear as Angels of Light

Does it seem strange that Satan should appear in the preaching business? And in the churches? And pretending to show the way to Heaven? Well, many, many warnings in the Bible show us that often Satan's ministers are in the pulpit, and those who appear to be *"the apostles of Christ"* (vs. 13) and "the ministers of righteousness" are actually "false prophets, deceitful workers."

So Paul wrote to Titus:

*"For there are many unruly and vain talkers and deceivers, specially they of the circumcision: Whose mouths must be stopped, who subvert whole houses, teaching things which they ought not, for filthy lucre's sake. One of themselves, even a prophet of their own, said, The Cretians are alway liars, evil beasts, slow bellies. This witness is true. Wherefore rebuke them sharply, that they may be sound in the faith."*—Titus 1:10-13.

In his farewell message to Timothy, Paul urged him:

*"Preach the word; be instant in season, out of season; reprove, rebuke, exhort with all longsuffering and doctrine. For the time will come when they will not endure sound doctrine; but after their own lusts shall they heap to themselves teachers, having itching ears; And they shall turn away their ears from the truth, and shall be turned unto fables."*—II Tim. 4:2-4.

And in II Timothy 3:13 he said, "But evil men and seducers shall wax worse and worse, deceiving, and being deceived."

The Lord Jesus Himself warned us, "Beware of false prophets, which come to you in sheep's clothing, but inwardly they are ravening wolves. . . .Ye shall know them by their fruits" (Matt. 7:15,16). And many of these false prophets may deceive even themselves, for Jesus continued in the same chapter:

*"Not every one that saith unto me, Lord, Lord, shall*

*enter into the kingdom of heaven; but he that doeth the will of my Father which is in heaven. Many will say to me in that day, Lord, Lord, have we not prophesied in thy name? and in thy name have cast out devils? and in thy name done many wonderful works? And then will I profess unto them, I never knew you: depart from me, ye that work iniquity.*"—Vss. 21-23.

The danger is tremendous and ever present and urgent, because the Lord God inspired the warning in II Peter 2:1-3:

*"But there were false prophets also among the people, even as there shall be false teachers among you, who privily shall bring in damnable heresies, even denying the Lord that bought them and bring upon themselves swift destruction. And many shall follow their pernicious ways; by reason of whom the way of truth shall be evil spoken of. And through covetousness shall they with feigned words make merchandise of you: whose judgment now of a long time lingereth not, and their damnation slumbereth not."*

Second John, verses 7 to 11, warn us likewise:

*"For many deceivers are entered into the world, who confess not that Jesus Christ is come in the flesh. This is a deceiver and an antichrist. Look to yourselves, that we lose not those things which we have wrought, but that we receive a full reward. Whosoever transgresseth, and abideth not in the doctrine of Christ, hath not God. He that abideth in the doctrine of Christ, he hath both the Father and the Son. If there come any unto you, and bring not this doctrine, receive him not into your house, neither bid him God speed: For he that biddeth him God speed is partaker of his evil deeds."*

Then let no minister of the Gospel think that he is faithful if he does not, like Paul, do as Bible preachers are commanded to do—rebuke any outright heresy. The sin of such false prophets is so terrible that in Galatians 1:8,9 the apostle wrote, "But though we, or an angel from heaven, preach any other gospel unto you than that which we have preached unto you, let him be accursed. As we said before, so say I now again, If any man preach any other gospel unto you than that ye have received, let him be accursed."

That does not mean that one who has a minor misunderstanding of some of the lesser doctrines or instructions is necessarily a false prophet. Many devout, godly men have been wrong, let us say, on the form of baptism, or on the organization of a church, or on the security of a believer, or perhaps on the matter of tongues or sanctification. And one who is thus in the historic Christian faith, that is, he believes that "faith of the gospel" (Phil. 1:27), we are to love and receive, if he is "weak in the faith. . .but not to doubtful disputations" (Rom. 14:1). And his errors are to be corrected.

But there are many false cults that are wrong on the essentials, such as the deity of Christ, the virgin birth, the blood atonement and the inspiration of the Scriptures. And if a preacher be faithful, he must take a plain stand against those who come with false religions such as Christian Science, Herbert Armstrongism, Jehovah's Witnesses, and other cults that are wrong about the person of Christ and His atoning death, the inspiration and accuracy of the Scriptures and the plan of salvation.

We are commanded to "try the spirits whether they are of God" (I John 4:1). Every doctrine and every teacher must be strictly held to account by the Scriptures themselves. Christians ought not ever subject themselves willingly to the influence and teachings of those who deny the great essentials of the Christian faith. We are not to bid them Godspeed nor receive them into our houses lest we be held accountable for their evil deeds, says II John 11.

---

**VERSES 16-27:**

16 I say again, Let no man think | me a fool; if otherwise, yet as a fool

receive me, that I may boast myself a little.

17 That which I speak, I speak it not after the Lord, but as it were foolishly, in this confidence of boasting.

18 Seeing that many glory after the flesh, I will glory also.

19 For ye suffer fools gladly, seeing ye yourselves are wise.

20 For ye suffer, if a man bring you into bondage, if a man devour you, if a man take of you, if a man exalt himself, if a man smite you on the face.

21 I speak as concerning reproach, as though we had been weak. Howbeit whereinsoever any is bold, (I speak foolishly,) I am bold also.

22 Are they Hebrews? so am I. Are they Israelites? so am I. Are they the seed of Abraham? so am I.

23 Are they ministers of Christ? (I speak as a fool) I am more; in labours more abundant, in stripes above measure, in prisons more frequent, in deaths oft.

24 Of the Jews five times received I forty stripes save one.

25 Thrice was I beaten with rods, once was I stoned, thrice I suffered shipwreck, a night and a day I have been in the deep;

26 In journeyings often, in perils of waters, in perils of robbers, in perils by mine own countrymen, in perils by the heathen, in perils in the city, in perils in the wilderness, in perils in the sea, in perils among false brethren;

27 In weariness and painfulness, in watchings often, in hunger and thirst, in fastings often, in cold and nakedness.

## Paul Mocks Their Boasted Wisdom

The young converts at Corinth had set themselves up as very wise (vs. 19). Those at Corinth had been "puffed up" (I Cor. 4:18; 5:2). They had gloried in themselves while continuing in sins (I Cor. 5:6). They had thought of themselves as rich and had reigned as kings (I Cor. 4:8). They counted themselves wise while Paul was despised and was made "as the filth of the world, and are the offscouring of all things. . ." (I Cor. 4:10-13). Yes, Paul was "a fool for Christ's sake" (I Cor. 4:10).

So now he takes the part as if he were a fool. In effect he says, "So you think me a fool?" (vs. 16). He speaks of himself as a fool in verses 16,17,19,21,23. So, under the guise of foolish boasting, Paul really shows their blindness and their wickedness in being misled by false teachers. False prophets would bring him into bondage to the ceremonial law. He would insist on having their money, he would praise himself, he would smite them (vs. 20). So Paul says that he will boast also, if he seems to be foolish, and he will be bold.

*"That which I speak, I speak it not after the Lord"* (vs. 17). That does not mean that the word here is not inspired, but rather that Paul's defense of himself here was not such as the Lord Jesus gave, was not following any pattern set by the Lord Jesus on earth. Jesus did not set out to prove Himself, and when the Pharisees and others asked of him, "Show us a sign," that is, in evidence of His deity and evidence that came from God, He said to them, "There shall no sign be given to it, but the sign of the prophet Jonas." As Jonah was three days in the belly of the whale and came out, so He, after three days in the heart of the earth, would be resurrected (Matt. 12:39,40; Matt. 16:4). See a similar case in I Corinthians 7:12, where Paul was inspired to say, "But to the rest speak I, not the Lord. . . ." That is, the Lord Jesus in His ministry on earth had not given this same command in the Gospels, although it was clearly inspired of God in that case, as is his statement here in verse 17. A new revelation was as certainly inspired of God as the revelation which Jesus might have mentioned in the Gospels.

We must never forget the standard which Paul was inspired to clearly announce in I  Corinthians 2:12,13:

*"Now we have received, not the spirit of the world, but the spirit which is of God; that we might know the things that are freely given to us of God. Which things also we speak, not in the words which man's wisdom teacheth, but which the Holy Ghost teacheth; comparing spiritual things with spiritual."*

Were any of these false teachers bold? Well, Paul was bold also. Were they Hebrews? So was he. He said in Philippians 3:4-6:

*"Though I might also have confidence in the flesh. If any other man thinketh that he hath whereof he might trust in the flesh, I more: Circumcised the eighth day, of the stock of Israel, of the tribe of Benjamin, an Hebrew of the Hebrews; as touching the law, a Pharisee; Concerning zeal,*

*persecuting the church; touching the righteousness which is the law, blameless."*

Were others ministers of Christ? Paul was more. By the standards that he himself had been inspired to write in II Corinthians 6:4-10, he had proved himself a good minister of Jesus Christ: "In labours more abundant, and stripes above measure, in prison more frequent, in deaths oft." Which of the false prophets would try to match that evidence: that he pleased God, that he was God's anointed, unselfish and a Spirit-filled man?

Remember the beatitude, "Blessed are they which are persecuted for righteousness' sake: for their's is the kingdom of heaven" (Matt. 5:10). The Apostle Paul had earned a glorious resurrection. We are not surprised at the triumphant paean of praise when he wrote to Timothy, "For I am now ready to be offered, and the time of my departure is at hand. I have fought a good fight, I have finished my course, I have kept the faith: Henceforth there is laid up for me a crown of righteousness" (II Tim. 4:6-8).

It would be good for all of us to read verses 23 to 27 again and again and often consider our peaceful living, our safe and comfortable lives, and compare these to the way the Apostle Paul served the Lord Jesus.

---

**VERSES 28-33:**

28 Beside those things that are without, that which cometh upon me daily, the care of all the churches. 29 Who is weak, and I am not weak? who is offended, and I burn not? 30 If I must needs glory, I will glory of the things which concern mine infirmities. 31 The God and Father of our Lord Jesus Christ, which is blessed for evermore, knoweth that I lie not. 32 In Damascus the governor under Ắr-ĕ̆-tắs the king kept the city of the Dắm-̓ắs-çēnes̓ with a garrison, desirous to apprehend me: 33 And through a window in a basket was I let down by the wall, and escaped his hands.

## The Care of All the Churches

It would be well for you to look through all the epistles of

Paul and see if you can make up his daily prayer list. To saints in Rome whom he had never seen he wrote, "Without ceasing I make mention of you always in my prayers" (Rom. 1:9)

To these Corinthian Christians he said, "I thank my God always on your behalf" (I Cor. 1:4). And he wrote to them "out of much affliction and anguish of heart" (II Cor. 2:4). And again, "Now I pray to God that ye do no evil" (II Cor. 13:7).

To the Galatians he wrote, "My little children, of whom I travail in birth again until Christ be formed in you" (Gal. 4:19).

To the saints at Ephesus he wrote, "I. . .cease not to give thanks for you, making mention of you in my prayers" (Eph. 1:16).

Paul thanked God for the Philippians: "Always in every prayer of mine for you all making request with joy" (Phil. 1:4).

He wrote the Colossians that he gave thanks to God, "praying always for you" (Col. 1:3).

For the Thessalonians also he gave "thanks to God always for you all, making mention of you in our prayers" (I Thess. 1:2).

To Timothy he wrote, "That without ceasing I have remembrance of thee in my prayers night and day" (II Tim. 1:3).

And to Philemon he wrote, "I thank my God, making mention of thee always in my prayers" (Philem. 4).

Do you see what Paul meant by "the care of all the churches"? Whenever a Christian was weak, Paul got troubled and burdened about it. If one stumbled or was offended, he burned in holy indignation against the wrong. Paul looks back and recounts with joy the time in Damascus when he barely escaped with his life. He gloried in the fact that God counted him worthy to suffer.

# II CORINTHIANS XII

## VERSES 1-6:

IT is not expedient for me doubtless to glory. I will come to visions and revelations of the Lord.

2 I knew a man in Christ above fourteen years ago, (whether in the body, I cannot tell; or whether out of the body, I cannot tell: God knoweth;) such an one caught up to the third heaven.

3 And I knew such a man, (whether in the body, or out of the body, I cannot tell: God knoweth;)

4 How that he was caught up in-to paradise, and heard unspeakable words, wnich it is not lawful for a man to utter.

5 Of such an one will I glory: yet of myself I will not glory, but in mine infirmities.

6 For though I would desire to glory, I shall not be a fool; for I will say the truth: but now I forbear, lest any man should think of me above that which he seeth me to be, or that he heareth of me.

## Paul's Heavenly Vision and Revelation

God's dealing with the apostle was amazing. When saved on the road to Damascus (Acts 9:1-7), he had seen the resurrected Jesus as one "born out of due time" (I Cor. 15:8), that is, before the normal time at the resurrection when we will all see Christ. Even then Paul had such a passion to be filled with the Spirit that he prayed and fasted three days. His prayers were answered when Ananias laid hands upon him, "that thou mightest receive thy sight and be filled with the Holy Ghost" (Acts 9:17). God had foretold to Ananias, "Go thy way: for he is a chosen vessel unto me, to bear my name before the Gentiles, and kings, and the children of Israel" (Acts 9:15). So it was intended and came to pass that Paul's ministry was far wider than any other of the apostles, and it dominates the scene in the Scriptures after Acts 12. We should expect, then, the amazing revelations and sufferings and authority given this apostle. "More abundant in labours" than all others, suffering more, reaching farther and more people with the Gospel.

*"I knew a man in Christ"* (vss. 2,3,4). Does he thus speak of himself in the third person? We think so.

*"Above fourteen years ago."* Ussher's chronology dates this letter about 60 A.D. More than "fourteen years ago" would place Paul and Barnabas on the first missionary journey, about 45 or 46 A.D., probably at Derbe or Lystra. It seems very probable that the visions mentioned were given when Paul was stoned at Lystra and drawn out of the city as dead. We would infer that his spirit was then, for a season, taken to Heaven and saw and heard things so marvelous and so beautiful that he was not allowed to tell them. We do not wonder that afterwards he always had a "desire to depart, and to be with Christ; which is far better" (Phil. 1:23). That may explain, too, his, "Knowing therefore the terror of the Lord, we persuade men" (II Cor. 5:11).

A glimpse of Heaven! Now and then some sweet dying Christian tells of the glory he or she begins to see. My stepmother's father, a few hours before departing, kept hearing and speaking of the most beautiful music! D. L. Moody said, "Heaven opens; earth is receding. This is my coronation day!" On her deathbed, my own dear mother had all who were near her to give assurance they would meet her in Heaven. Then she asked my cousin, "Georgia, will you play and sing for me?"

"What shall I sing, Aunt Sadie?" asked the tearful young woman.

"Sing, 'How firm a foundation, ye saints of the Lord, Is laid for your faith in His excellent Word!' "And my cousin played it on the little cottage organ and sang with trembling voice. My mother clapped her thin, frail hands, rejoiced and said, "I can see Jesus and my baby now!" Then she fell asleep. I knew that she was not delirious but that she really saw the Saviour and her departed little one.

So Paul saw heavenly visions, had revelations that prepared him for his apostolic authority, his sufferings and his certainties.

## VERSES 7-10:

7 And lest I should be exalted above measure through the abundance of the revelations, there was given to me a thorn in the flesh, the messenger of Satan to buffet me, lest I should be exalted above measure.

8 For this thing I besought the Lord thrice, that it might depart from me.

9 And he said unto me, My grace is sufficient for thee: for my strength is made perfect in weakness. Most gladly therefore will I rather glory in my infirmities, that the power of Christ may rest upon me.

10 Therefore I take pleasure in infirmities, in reproaches, in necessities, in persecutions, in distresses for Christ's sake: for when I am weak, then am I strong.

## Paul's Thorn in the Flesh

The more one would be like Christ, the more one must suffer, for he "learned obedience by the things which he suffered" (Heb. 5:8). There is a promise in II Timothy 2:12, "If we suffer, we shall also reign with him," and in Romans 8:17, ". . .if so be that we suffer with him, that we may be also glorified together."

*"Lest I should be exalted above measure. . ."* (vs. 7). How often God, in loving mercy, may protect us from sin by some trouble. The prodigal never "came to himself" until the famine and want came (Luke 15:17). God brought proud King Nebuchadnezzar low when he was proud until he knew the Most High rules nations and puts up rulers and puts them down (Dan. 5:21).

We are commanded,

*"Take, my brethren, the prophets, who have spoken in the name of the Lord, for an example of suffering affliction, and of patience. Behold, we count them happy which endure. Ye have heard of the patience of Job, and have seen the end of the Lord: that the Lord is very pitiful, and of tender mercy."*—Jas. 5:10,11.

What was Paul's thorn? The word thorn is the Greek word *skolops*, more like a stake or a large splinter. It was in his body. We suppose it was some physical affliction, probably poor eyesight. He had been temporarily blinded by the great light from Heaven when he was saved (Acts

9:8; Acts 20:1-6). He reminded the Galatian Christians,

*"Ye know how through infirmity of the flesh I preached the gospel unto you at the first. And my temptation which was in my flesh ye despised not, nor rejected; but received me as an angel of God, even as Christ Jesus. Where is then the blessedness ye spake of? for I bear you record, that, if it had been possible, ye would have plucked out your own eyes, and have given them to me."*—Gal. 4:13-15.

That indicates that his "temptation in the flesh" was with his eyes. And in Galatians 6:11 he said, "Ye see how large a letter I have written unto you with mine own hand." Or perhaps the Greek would be better understood: "with how large letters. . .with mine own hand."

Of course, we do not know what was the thorn in the flesh and that is good that we don't. For whatever thorn any of us may have, whatever weakness, whatever infirmity, whatever temptation in the flesh, thank God, His grace is sufficient, and we may know that God had it written down for our instruction, comfort and encouragement.

It is instructive that God did not remove Paul's thorn in the flesh. Doubtless, God healed many people in answer to Paul's prayers (Acts 20:10; Acts 28:8,9). And Paul himself was raised up when thought to be dead at Lystra and was healed of the poisonous serpent's bite on the island of Melita (Acts 28:4-6). But in II Timothy 4:20 he said, "Trophimus have I left at Miletum sick." To Timothy he wrote, "Use a little wine for thy stomach's sake and thine often infirmities" (I Tim. 5:23). (Doubtless the wine was new wine, that is, fruit juices needed for the vitamin and other helpful effects.) But healing is not always the will of God for Christian people.

Is not healing in the atonement? Yes, in a certain ultimate sense it is. But so also is the glorified body which we will get at the resurrection, but it is not now available.

All healing now is temporary, incomplete. Those who are healed, later get sick and die.

Paul had earnestly besought the Lord for three periods that the thorn might be removed, but God did not see fit to remove it. Rather, he taught Paul, *"My grace is sufficient for thee: for my strength is made perfect in weakness"* (vs. 9). It is far better to have a big God and a little Paul. It is far better to have a Paul utterly dependent on the dear Lord for His help day by day than one confident in his natural strength. So resignedly Paul said, *"Most gladly therefore will I rather glory in my infirmities, that the power of Christ may rest upon me"* (vs. 9).

I would suppose that when Paul was pleading for the thorn to be removed, he was really wanting power upon himself to win souls, to preach without limit, to go day and night. Surely he meant it for good. But when Paul sees that the answer to his prayer is better another way, he changes the prayer, as we must often do when we wait upon God and find that He has a better way than what we had asked for. So Paul says, *"Therefore I take pleasure in infirmities, in reproaches, in necessities, in persecutions, in distresses for Christ's sake: for when I am weak, then am I strong"* (vs. 10). "God hath chosen the weak things of the world to confound the things which are mighty" (I Cor. 1:27). God chose a rod in the hand of Moses to deliver the nation Israel from Egypt. He chose a stone and a sling in the hands of David to kill Goliath and to deliver Israel from the Philistines. He chose five loaves and two fishes, the boy's lunch, to feed five thousand. Oh, He can use whatever we have. It pleases God to use the weak. So He kept Paul weak so God could get the glory.

You remember that Nadab and Abihu, when strictly commanded to put no fire on the altar, sinned against God in building a fire and God killed them both (Lev. 10:2). We can be the bullock, but God must provide the fire. We can be an instrument, but God must furnish the power and get the glory.

Once in a great time of trouble and testing, I found great joy in Paul's thorn in the flesh and in the promise of verse 9 that, *"My grace is sufficient for thee: for my strength is made perfect in weakness."* And so I knew God could use me, His weak servant, just starting out to preach the Gospel.

---

### VERSES 11-19:

11 I am become a fool in glorying; ye have compelled me: for I ought to have been commended of you: for in nothing am I behind the very chiefest apostles, though I be nothing.

12 Truly the signs of an apostle were wrought among you in all patience, in signs, and wonders, and mighty deeds.

13 For what is it wherein ye were inferior to other churches, except it be that I myself was not burdensome to you? forgive me this wrong.

14 Behold, the third time I am ready to come to you; and I will not be burdensome to you: for I seek not your's, but you: for the children ought not to lay up for the parents, but the parents for the children.

15 And I will very gladly spend and be spent for you; though the more abundantly I love you, the less I be loved.

16 But be it so, I did not burden you: nevertheless, being crafty, I caught you with guile.

17 Did I make a gain of you by any of them whom I sent unto you?

18 I desired Titus, and with him I sent a brother. Did Titus make a gain of you? walked we not in the same spirit? walked we not in the same steps?

19 Again, think ye that we excuse ourselves unto you? we speak before God in Christ: but we do all things, dearly beloved, for your edifying.

## The Fatherly Heart of the Apostle Toward His Converts

*"I am become a fool in glorying. . ."* (vs. 11). This is part of the same defense in the preceding chapter, and in this passage Paul has five times called himself a fool, and twice he said he speaks foolishly. By this he simply means that it ought to have been needless for him to defend himself; he ought not to have been compelled to boast of all his sufferings, of his unselfish labor. But he is compelled to do so, to maintain the authority and place as an apostle which God had given him, and to fulfill his responsibility. He is saying that the people at Corinth, instead of doubting his

authority or his message, instead of comparing him with other men, ought to have been praising him and following him gladly, since his work was so obviously of God. He was the anointed and empowered apostle, sent to turn them from heathendom and from darkness to light.

But new converts were often foolish, unsteady, and quickly turned aside from the path, so it was necessary for him to remind them of the price he had paid and the marvelous blessing of God upon his ministry.

Yes, *"the signs of an apostle were wrought among"* them (vs. 12), and how foolish and how unstable all of them were not to have recognized it and not to have put down anybody at once who would question Paul's righteousness and leadership.

Paul loved them so much. It is a great church, coming behind no church in many of the great gifts and blessings (I Cor. 1:4-7). But in one matter they were inferior to other churches—they had not supported the preaching of the Gospel as they should. And so Paul unselfishly allowed them to go along, while he was supported by others. And now that he has brought the matter up, he will not require them to support him when he comes the third time. Rather, he is glad to spend himself and be spent, even though in their careless, childish ways these young Christians do not give him the devotion and honor that is properly due him.

He had plainly taught the Christians at Galatia, "Let him that is taught in the word communicate unto him that teacheth in all good things" (Gal. 6:6). These at Corinth had been taught, had been won, had been blessed for more than eighteen months, and they had not carried their part. Paul had not pressed upon them their duty toward him, and he would not do so the next time.

And when he sent Titus and another brother, had he asked them to raise money to take care of Titus' expenses? He had not. Titus had followed the example of Paul, unselfishly serving without remuneration (vs. 18).

20 For I fear, lest, when I come, I shall not find you such as I would, and that I shall be found unto you such as ye would not: lest there be debates, envyings, wraths, strifes, backbitings, whisperings, swellings, tumults:
21 And lest, when I come again, my God will humble me among you, and that I shall bewail many which have sinned already, and have not repented of the uncleanness and fornication and lasciviousness which they have committed.

## Will Their Disputing and Worldliness Break Out Among Them Again?

Young converts at Corinth were still "carnal," not spiritual (I Cor. 3:1-4). Paul knew, and let every God-called pastor, teacher, and evangelist know also, that it takes "precept upon precept; line upon line, line upon line; here a little, and there a little" (Isa. 28:10), persistent teaching and preaching to grow good Christians. We are sometimes amazed at how slowly the twelve apostles seemed to grow, how poorly they seemed to understand the persistent teachings of the Lord Jesus. Little was their faith, after long experience of the blessings with Christ and seeing the miracles that He did.

Then let us remember that Christians grow slowly, and they need constant tending, teaching, loving, warning and reminding.

And how sad the apostle would be if, coming the third time to Corinth, he was humbled and felt shamed if he should find many had fallen into sin and had not repented of the uncleanness of fornication, which he had rebuked before but which may not have been really blotted out in the lives of some of the people.

# II CORINTHIANS XIII

## VERSES 1-10:

THIS is the third time I am coming to you. In the mouth of two or three witnesses shall every word be established.

2 I told you before, and foretell you, as if I were present, the second time; and being absent now I write to them which heretofore have sinned, and to all other, that, if I come again, I will not spare:

3 Since ye seek a proof of Christ speaking in me, which to you-ward is not weak, but is mighty in you.

4 For though he was crucified through weakness, yet he liveth by the power of God. For we also are weak in him, but we shall live with him by the power of God toward you.

5 Examine yourselves, whether ye be in the faith; prove your own selves. Know ye not your own selves, how that Jesus Christ is in you, except ye be reprobates?

6 But I trust that ye shall know that we are not reprobates.

7 Now I pray to God that ye do no evil; not that we should appear approved, but that ye should do that which is honest, though we be as reprobates.

8 For we can do nothing against the truth, but for the truth.

9 For we are glad, when we are weak, and ye are strong: and this also we wish, even your perfection.

10 Therefore I write these things being absent, lest being present I should use sharpness, according to the power which the Lord hath given me to edification, and not to destruction.

## Farewell Warnings

There had been genuine repentance on the part of the man who had sinned with his father's wife and, we suppose, on the part of many others. There was much evidence of genuine effort to clean up the church and please the apostle. He acknowledges the fine report from Titus of their anxiety to please, their sincerity of heart, their love for Paul. But Paul remembers that many, many other lives have been touched by their sins. They withdrew their fellowship from the young man especially guilty; he repented and is now restored to fellowship. But in such a case, there will always be kinsfolk, and close friends, worldly minded people who hold grudges who would bring division and strife, who would insist that others were to blame, that others were equally guilty.

Sin is an infectious thing. After a cancer is removed, the surgeon must try to find if little colonies of cancer cells have spread to other parts of the body. So the apostle knows there must be a persistent effort to clean up the church membership and correct worldly practices and false doctrines.

Would you suppose that all those people who were guilty of the tongues heresy would be corrected and cured in one exhortation and explanation, as given in I Corinthians, chapter 14? They would not. Because Paul had rebuked them for going to law one with another, would there be no bitterness, no threats, no bad after-feelings of the sins of the past? Likely there would be. Since they had been rebuked for careless taking of the Lord's Supper, even drunkenness at the table, would one solid rebuke by the apostle correct a sin that had led many to die and many others to be sick? It is true that there seems evidence that the principal leaders and the bulk of the church had accepted Paul's word on all these matters, but Paul well knows that the infection must be stamped out.

Oh, in every human heart there is already the infection of sin. People do not have to copy somebody else's sin to go wrong, so wicked, so deceitful is the human heart.

So the apostle here reminds the people again of his apostleship, the authority that he expects plainly to exercise when he comes among them.

And now, let every pastor, every evangelist, everyone who seeks to lead and bless God's people remember that there must be loving, Spirit-filled but positive denunciation of sin. God had required in Isaiah 58, "Cry aloud, spare not, lift up thy voice like a trumpet, and shew my people their transgression, and the house of Jacob their sins" (Isa. 58:1). Paul had commanded Timothy, "Them that sin rebuke before all, that others also may fear" (I Tim. 5:20). And in his farewell message to Timothy he had said:

*"Preach the word; be instant in season, out of season; reprove, rebuke, exhort with all longsuffering and doctrine.*

*For the time will come when they will not endure sound doctrine; but after their own lusts shall they heap to themselves teachers, having itching ears; And they shall turn away their ears from the truth, and shall be turned unto fables.''*—II Tim. 4:2-4.

And Titus, working under Paul's direction, had been instructed:

*''For there are many unruly and vain talkers and deceivers, specially they of the circumcision: Whose mouths must be stopped, who subvert whole houses, teaching things which they ought not, for filthy lucre's sake. One of themselves, even a prophet of their own, said, The Cretians are alway liars, evil beasts, slow bellies. This witness is true. Wherefore rebuke them sharply, that they may be sound in the faith.''*—Titus 1:10-13.

Oh, even devout Christians sometimes would need the correction of plain Bible preaching or strong rebuke, even as Paul had rebuked the Apostle Peter for his compromise in leading Barnabas and others astray by their ''dissimulation,'' recorded in Galatians 2:11-14. Even in the red-hot fires of evangelism and power following Pentecost, Peter saw the necessity of a strong rebuke to Ananias and Sapphira, and had God strike them dead. Simon the sorcerer in Samaria ''believed also'' under the preaching of Philip, was baptized, and we ought to believe that he probably was sincerely converted. But the old life and all the conditions and habits of the old superstition and spiritism were strong in his mind, and when he offered to buy the power to give people the Holy Ghost, he was strongly rebuked by Peter. ''Thy money perish with thee, because thou hast thought that the gift of God may be purchased with money. Thou hast neither part nor lot in this matter: for thy heart is nct right in the sight of God.'' He had no part in the business of laying hands on others that they might receive the power of the Holy Spirit, and even if he was converted, as we believe he was, his heart was not right.

I am saying that everywhere, after one is soundly converted, the old ways must be plowed up, must be rebuked, must be mortified.

*"Examine yourselves, whether ye be in the faith"* (vs. 5). There is a certain group of essential doctrines called in the New Testament "the faith." "And so were the churches established in *the faith"* (Acts 16:5).

⋆ "Him that is weak in *the faith* receive ye. . ." (Rom. 14:1). "Stand fast in *the faith"* (I Cor. 16:13). ". . .the household of *faith"* (Gal. 6:10). ". . .the unity of *the faith"* (Eph. 4:13). ". . .great boldness in *the faith"* (I Tim. 3:13). Some "have erred from *the faith"* (I Tim. 6:10,21). ". . .reprobate concerning *the faith"* (II Tim. 3:8). "I have kept *the faith"* (II Tim. 4:7). And there are many other Scriptures.

"The faith" represents certain fundamental essential doctrines of the Christian religion and the Christian faith. In Philippians 1:27 it is called "the faith of the gospel." That means those doctrines which are themselves a part of the Gospel as given in I Corinthians 15:3,4, ". . .how that Christ died for our sins according to the scriptures; And that he was buried, and that he rose again the third day according to the scriptures." So, man's sinful, lost condition, the atoning death of Christ, His resurrection from the dead, and therefore His deity and virgin birth, and the infallible accuracy of the Scriptures, are essentials of "the faith."

In II John, verses 9 to 11, this faith, this essential foundation of the Christian religion, is called "the doctrine of Christ." That is what the Bible teaches about Christ, who He is, His atoning death, His resurrection, His offer of salvation, His second coming, etc.

In Jude 3 we are commanded to "earnestly contend for the faith." We are not necessarily to contend about little details, but no one ought ever consent to disbelief in these great essentials according to II John, verses 9 to 11. One who does not abide in this Bible doctrine about Christ Himself, this "the faith," "hath not God," is not saved.

Now here is the command: *"Examine yourselves, whether ye be in the faith; prove your own selves. Know ye not your own selves, how that Jesus Christ is in you, except ye be reprobates?"* (vs. 5). That is, Christ is in them, they are born again, unless they pretend to claim Christ without accepting the faith. One who does not believe that Jesus Christ was born of a virgin, does not believe He rose from the dead, does not believe that Jesus is really God—that one cannot have saving faith in Christ. So Paul earnestly urges them, "Prove your own selves. Make sure you are saved!"

Does that warning seem unnecessary? It was necessary for Martin Luther, the pious monk who was trying so hard to earn salvation. Tradition says that, climbing the "Holy Stairs" at Rome on his knees, he remembered a portion of the Scripture, "The just shall live by faith," or have life through faith! Light dawned upon his heart and he trusted the Saviour.

John Wesley needed this exhortation for he, an earnest Oxford don, a most religious young man, born and reared in an Anglican rectory, and even going as a missionary to America, found, alas, that he had not been converted and had not known personal saving faith in Christ. I say people need to make sure.

And all need to make sure, too, that you are accepting those great fundamental essentials which comprise "the faith of the gospel," "the doctrine of Christ," without which one cannot be saved.

These Corinthians could know for sure how Paul contended for the faith and was not a reprobate.

## VERSES 11-14:

11 Finally, brethren, farewell. Be perfect, be of good comfort, be of one mind, live in peace; and the God of love and peace shall be with you.

12 Greet one another with an holy kiss.

13 All the saints salute you.

14 The grace of the Lord Jesus Christ, and the love of God, and the communion of the Holy Ghost, be with you all. Amen.

## The Benediction

*"Be perfect,"* that is, be complete (vs. 11). It is true that no one in this life can be perfect. But in the sense of the Scriptures, one can be wholly committed to Christ again and again. And besides, when God would set a standard, He sets a perfect standard. In the Sermon on the Mount, Jesus commanded, "Be ye therefore perfect, even as your Father which is in heaven is perfect" (Matt. 5:48). And everyone should have the holy ambition:

*"That I may know him, and the power of his resurrection, and the fellowship of his sufferings, being made conformable unto his death; If by any means I might attain unto the resurrection of the dead. Not as though I had already attained, either were already perfect: but I follow after, if that I may apprehend that for which also I am apprehended of Christ Jesus. Brethren, I count not myself to have apprehended: but this one thing I do, forgetting those things which are behind, and reaching forth unto those things which are before, I press toward the mark for the prize of the high calling of God in Christ Jesus."*—Phil. 3:10-14.

No, Paul, who had struggled so hard to live a perfect and resurrected life, had not "already attained, either were already perfect," but how he struggled after that holy living and that perfect image of Christ which he longed to be and would be at his resurrection.

*"Be of good comfort"* (vs. 11). Christians should be happy. *"Be of one mind, live in peace"* (vs. 11). Oh, that they would cure their divisions and that they would

maintain the unity of the Spirit! And if they do, *"the God of love and peace shall be with you."*

*"An holy kiss"* (vs. 12). Five times in the Scriptures such a command is given—here and in I Corinthians 16:20; Romans 16:16; I Thessalonians 5:26; and I Peter 5:14. Doubtless, the custom was then, as it is now in India, Japan, Korea, China, and the Eastern countries, for men to kiss each other upon one cheek and then the other. It should be a *holy* kiss. And remember that this is no excuse for careless nor inexpedient intimacies of men with women.

*"All the saints salute you,"* said Paul in verse 15. Probably Paul was at Philippi and the Christians there sent greetings, and likely others with whom Paul had been in contact.

Note in Romans how carefully and lovingly Paul remembers all the Christians he knew who were then in Rome. We can be certain that Paul was especially careful to express his love, to greet people cheerfully, to make them feel at home in his presence. Courtesy and good manners are part of the same thing which is commanded elsewhere. We are to "weep with them that weep" (Rom. 12:15). That is a part of compassion. That is feeling with people or suffering with people.

When people come together in a local congregation there ought to be greetings and shaking hands and happy fellowship. I think it far more important to shake hands with a friend, to ask a newcomer to sit beside you or share a hymnbook, than to have a funeral calm and formal dignity. The idea, "If you must whisper, whisper a prayer," and other formal teachings do not tend toward the informality or the loving fellowship which was common in New Testament congregations.

And the final benediction is a prayer. Perhaps we do well sometimes to dismiss our congregation with such a benediction. But far more important it is that we make it as an expression of our heart's love and genuine prayer for God's blessings on them.

# 7 Great Commentaries—All by Dr. John R. Rice

*Church of God at Corinth* (Commentary on I and II Corinthians) by Dr. Rice. Surprisingly up-to-date, practical, down-to-earth teaching on local church problems. 29 chapters, 271 pages,

*Filled With the Spirit* (Commentary on Acts)—A verse-by-verse teaching on the Holy Spirit: New Testament churches, their message and method; speaking with tongues; dispensational truth; and soul winning. 28 chapters, 55 pages,

*King of the Jews*—A verse-by-verse commentary on Matthew reflecting the scholarly diligence and discipline of an editor. Profound yet simple. A best seller. 28 chapters, 555 pages,

*Son of Man* (Commentary on Luke)—Profundity clothed in simplicity in this volume of verse-by-verse Bible teaching. 24 chapters, 563 pages,

*Son of God* (Commentary on John)—Same attractive features as other commentaries, PLUS being profusely illustrated with pictures throughout. 21 chapters, 416 pages,

*"In the Beginning. . ."* (Commentary on Genesis), Excellent help on Creation, the Flood, "Gap" Theory, Evolution, etc. Another great verse-by-verse commentary. 559 pages,

*"Behold, He Cometh!"* Verse-by-verse commentary on the Book of Revelation. Allegedly mysterious Scripture made plain and practical. Complete text of Scripture included with lucid comments. 22 chapters, 348 pages